**ORACLE**® *Oracle Press*™

Quick Start Guide to Oracle Fusion Development: Oracle JDeveloper and Oracle ADF

Grant Ronald

 Mc Graw Hill

New York   Chicago   San Francisco
Lisbon   London   Madrid   Mexico City   Milan
New Delhi   San Juan   Seoul   Singapore   Sydney   Toronto

Sponsoring Editor
Lisa McClain

Associate Acquisitions Editor
Meghan Riley

Editorial Supervisor
Janet Walden

Project Manager
Vasundhara Sawhney, Glyph
International

Technical Editors
Laura Akel, Patrice Daux, Jeremy
Duggan, Susan Duncan, Jeff Gallus,
Pam Gamer, Simon Haslam,
Kate Heap, Chris Lewis, Chris
Lowes, Glenn Maslen, Duncan
Mills, Chris Muir, Lynn Munsinger,
Frank Nimphius, Steve Noton, Katia
Obradovic-Sarkic, Philip Prosser,
Blaise Ribet, Dana Singleterry, and
Gary Williams

Copy Editor
William McManus

Proofreader
Claire Splan

Indexer
Claire Splan

Production Supervisor
Jean Bodeaux

Composition
Glyph International

Illustration
Glyph International

Art Director, Cover
Jeff Weeks

Cover Designer
Pattie Lee

For those who never found it easy.

About the Author

Grant Ronald is an Oracle ACE and senior group product manager working in the Application Development Tools division at Oracle responsible for JDeveloper, Oracle ADF, and Oracle Forms, where he has a focus on opening up the Java platform to Oracle's traditional developer base. Grant joined Oracle in 1997, working in Oracle Support, where he headed up the EMEA support group for Oracle Forms, Reports, and Discoverer. In 2000, Grant joined the Product Management team, where he was responsible for product evangelism and strategy. Prior to Oracle, Grant worked in various development roles at EDS Defence. Grant has a BSc in computing science and has been working in the IT industry since 1989.

About the Technical Editors

Laura Akel is a principle product manager for Oracle's Application Development Framework and is specifically responsible for providing product direction for both ADF Faces and MDS Customization. She joined Oracle through the acquisition of PeopleSoft, where she began her career in enterprise application development and development tools in 1995. Laura has been responsible for both managing the development of application development tools and providing product direction in the role of product management for the past 15 years.

Patrice Daux has been working for Oracle for the past 20 years. He started as an IT project developer before joining Oracle as an instructor, teaching Oracle Database tools and techniques. After a few years, he moved to Curriculum Development, working on the Oracle Designer tool. He then joined the JDeveloper team, working as a curriculum developer, writing training material around JDeveloper and Java technology.

Jeremy Duggan is a senior consultant (UK-based) for JemKa Consulting Limited. In 24 years as an Oracle development professional, he has held the positions of senior consultant, project manager, business analyst, and developer. He is also Chair of Development Special Interest Group of the UK Oracle User Group.

Susan Duncan is a principal product manager in the Application Development Tools division at Oracle, specializing in Application Lifecycle Management, Team Development, and Application Development Framework. She joined Oracle UK Consulting in 1997 and worked on various projects worldwide promoting standards and designing and implementing Oracle Designer and Forms Server applications. In addition, Susan worked on developing Oracle Designer training courses, and in 2001 joined Product Management, focusing on Oracle Designer and UML in JDeveloper. From 2002 Susan was closely involved in the development of JDeveloper's support for web services and SOA, and more recently has focused her attention and skills on database modeling, XML, and ALM, including the development of Oracle Team Productivity Center.

Jeff Gallus lives in the Chicago area, where he has worked at Oracle Corporation for 19 years. For his first eight years with Oracle, Jeff was a CASE tools instructor and then moved to be a curriculum developer for the Oracle Designer product. Eight years ago he moved into the JDeveloper group. Before working at Oracle, Jeff worked in Boston for four years for a CASE tools company named Cortex.

Pam Gamer has over 20 years of experience using Oracle development tools and has been with Oracle for nearly 15 years. She started in Oracle Support, specializing in Forms, and then moved to Curriculum Development. She has been responsible for development and maintenance of courses and OTN content pertaining to Forms and JDeveloper, and has spoken at various internal and external venues around the globe, including Oracle OpenWorld. Pam is based in Colorado Springs, Colorado.

Simon Haslam is the founder of Veriton Limited in the UK and a technical consultant specializing in Oracle Fusion Middleware. He has been working with Oracle products since 1994 and is an Oracle ACE Director for Middleware and SOA.

Kate Heap graduated in Modern Languages and spent the first 15 years of her working life as a teacher of French, German, and Italian. After moving into IT in 1985, she became a systems analyst in the insurance industry, subsequently spending two years as a business analyst at Lloyds of London. She joined Oracle 16 years ago as an instructor for Oracle Designer, having used similar CASE tools extensively in her analysis work. After two years teaching Designer courses, she started producing the courses as a member of the Curriculum Development team. In 2000 she moved to the Application Development Tools team as a curriculum developer, primarily writing courses for Oracle JDeveloper.

Chris Lewis is a software engineer in the Application Development Tools group. He joined Oracle in 1992 and worked as a consultant on a number of projects before switching to technical support for all of Oracle's product development tools. As the toolset grew, he specialized in supporting Oracle Forms, and in 1999 he moved into the Oracle Forms development group, where he managed a team of developers. Chris joined the ADF Controller team in 2006.

Glenn Maslen is senior curriculum manager for development tools at Oracle. He has worked with Oracle for over 15 years, first as an instructor and then as a course developer for a variety of subjects, including the database, Oracle Forms, and multimedia tools. Glenn currently works with Oracle University and Product Management to provide international training for its development tools, including JDeveloper and ADF, using a variety of delivery methods.

Duncan Mills is senior director of product management for Oracle's Application Development Tools, including Oracle JDeveloper, Oracle Enterprise Pack for Eclipse, NetBeans, Oracle Forms, and the ADF Framework. Duncan is currently responsible for product direction, evangelism, and courseware development around the development tools products. He has been working with Oracle in a variety of application development and DBA roles since 1988. For the past 18 years he has been working at Oracle in both Support and Product Development, spending the last eight years in Product Management. Duncan is the co-author of the Oracle Press books *Oracle JDeveloper 10g for Forms and PL/SQL Developers: A Guide to Web Development with Oracle ADF* and *Oracle JDeveloper 11g Handbook: A Guide to Oracle Fusion Web Development*.

Chris Muir is an Oracle ACE Director and a senior Oracle systems developer and trainer for SAGE Computing Services in Perth, Australia. With over ten years of working in traditional Oracle development, he has more recently earned battle scars working with, training with, and promoting JDeveloper, ADF, Web Services, and Fusion Middleware. He is a founding member of the ADF Enterprise Methodology Group, an online forum for discussing best practices and methodologies around ADF development.

Lynn Munsinger is a senior principal product manager for the Java Tools development group at Oracle, specializing in JDeveloper and ADF. Her career at Oracle began in 1998, and she has been responsible for the support, education, and technical evangelism of Oracle's application development tools ever since. Lynn is the primary developer of the Fusion Order Demo sample application for Fusion Middleware, and is a frequent presenter at user group and industry conferences. Her most recent contribution to the world of ADF is as co-author of an in-depth book titled *Oracle Fusion Developer Guide: Building Rich Internet Applications with Oracle ADF Business Components and Oracle ADF Faces*, available from McGraw-Hill/Oracle Press.

Frank Nimphius is a senior principal product manager for application development tools at Oracle Corporation. In his current role, Frank contributes to the development of Oracle JDeveloper and the Oracle Application Development Framework, with a special focus on JavaServer Faces, ADF Faces, and application security. Frank is also co-author of the McGraw-Hill/Oracle Press book *Oracle Fusion Developer Guide: Building Rich Internet Applications with Oracle ADF Business Components and Oracle ADF Faces*.

Stephen Noton graduated from Cardiff University with an honors degree in pure math and computing in 1988, after which he held a number of positions building up his programming and Oracle database experience. Most notable among them was his participation in the development effort for an Oracle-based UK address database for the UK's national mapping agency. Stephen joined Oracle in 1995, initially working in technical support covering a wide range of Oracle products but then specializing in 3GL Oracle precompilers and Oracle JDBC drivers. He joined Product Development in 2000, initially working on Oracle Forms before moving on to his current position working in the ADF Metadata Services development team.

Katarina Obradovic-Sarkic is a senior product manager in the Oracle Application Development Tools Product Management team and is currently responsible for ADF Data Visualization Components in JDeveloper. Katarina joined Oracle in 1998 as a Java developer. She moved to Product Management in 2002 to work on Oracle Business Intelligence Beans, and in 2006 joined the JDeveloper/ADF PM team. She represented Oracle ADF Data Visualization components and BI Beans at several OracleWorld and IOUG conferences. Katarina holds a master's degree in computer science from Northwestern University, Chicago, and a BSc in computer science from Southampton University, England.

Phil Prosser is an SOA/JEE architect with Oracle Corporation. His role involves working with major public sector UK customers to understand their SOA and application requirements. Phil architects enterprise solutions to address their requirements. Phil has been working in the IT industry for over 20 years. Phil has practical experience of designing and building major enterprise applications using a range of middleware technologies. These technologies include JEE, Tuxedo, SOA Suite, WebLogic Integration, EntireX, DCOM, and a range of development technologies. Phil has specialized in the designing and building of highly available and scalable enterprise systems.

Blaise Ribet is a principal product manager for JDeveloper and ADF, working at Oracle headquarters in California. As an inbound product manager, she manages requirements and defines features for ADF Business Components, ADF databinding, and ADF Controller; runs the team that ensures UI consistency across the JDeveloper platform; and gives advice and help to internal and external developers who are building ADF applications.

Dana Singleterry is a principal product manager in the Oracle Development Tools group, specializing in JDeveloper, ADF, ADF Faces, and Web Services. He has been working at Oracle since 2004, initially in consulting, and then as a product manager in the Application Server group. He is the author of many Oracle How-Tos and actively contributes to the development of JDeveloper and ADF. Dana is a frequent presenter at user group and industry conferences both nationally and internationally, including various Oracle user groups and Oracle OpenWorld.

Gary Williams has been with Oracle for 16 years. He started as an instructor teaching software design principles and practice using Oracle's CASE toolset Designer 2000. Before his life with Oracle, he worked as an IT systems analyst in the petrochemical industry. After teaching for five years, he moved into the Curriculum Development organization, where he develops curriculum for Java and JDeveloper. Throughout his career, Gary has worked with a number of software technology stacks including J2EE as well as all of the ADF technologies.

Contents at a Glance

PART IV
Common Coding Patterns

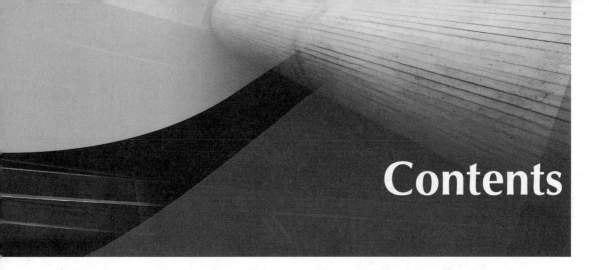

Contents

PART I
Introductions and Overviews

PART II
Building Business Services

PART III
Building the User Interface

Foreword

The software industry is an exciting field to be working in, but in many ways it leads a contradictory existence. On the one hand, innovation drives us; the bright young things and vendors continually push the boundaries, coming up with new ideas and standards. On the other hand, rapid churn does not sit well with the needs of the CTOs and CFOs of this world for whom long-term planning is the focus, and stability and supportability are the watchwords.

So the reality is that most of the IT world, Oracle customers included, exists in a state of punctuated equilibrium, ponderously hanging on to their existing technology for as long as humanly possible, with only small pockets of cutting-edge adoption and innovation, before finally switching to the next safe technology. There is nothing wrong with this model, and indeed it's really the only sensible course for most organizations to take. However, from time to time a sea change will occur, and a broad new horizon will open up to the developing majority. I, for one, fervently believe that with the advent of the industry-leading Oracle Fusion Middleware 11g and the Oracle Application Development Framework (ADF) we have arrived at just such a time.

These products from Oracle are immensely exciting and offer the developer huge amounts of power and flexibility for building rich user interfaces and the services needed to back them. For the beginner, however, this incredible set of capabilities comes at a price; there is a lot of technology to cover and understand, making it all seem rather overwhelming at first. Fortunately, with this book, help is at hand. Grant effectively demystifies the topic and opens the door to the world of Oracle ADF for any developer from any background.

Through all the years that I have known the author, Grant Ronald, both as a friend and as a colleague, he has always been on a mission—a mission to simplify and explain "why." For the last six years or so we've been working together at Oracle on JDeveloper and ADF. Throughout all of that time, Grant has been a veritable Jiminy Cricket, representing the views of our users to the development team, questioning design decisions, and most important of all, working out how best to explain the framework and tools to new audiences. His immense experience in this task shines through in the book, providing, as it does, an accessible and refreshing approach to the material. Having written a book about Oracle ADF myself, I am full of admiration for what Grant has chosen not to say. He has managed to keep the material tight and well targeted, making it truly deserving of the "quick start" designation.

The future is here—just turn the page and read on.

Duncan Mills
Senior Director of Product Management
Oracle

Acknowledgments

No book, or author, is an island. While my own blood, sweat, and tears run through every page, metaphorically speaking of course, this book could never have been achieved without the support and help from some very dear friends and colleagues.

To the team at McGraw-Hill who saw the potential in the book and were willing to take on the project, thank you for having faith in my idea. I'd also like to thank the fantastic team of unseen copy editors, reviewers, and designers who did a great job of transforming my words into a printed book.

To the technical reviewers who ensured I was clear, consistent, and, most importantly, correct, I owe you all a heartfelt thanks and at least one beer on me. In alphabetical order, I'd like to thank Laura Akel, Patrice Daux, Jeremy Duggan, Susan Duncan, Jeff Gallus, Pam Gamer, Simon Haslam, Kate Heap, Chris Lewis, Chris Lowes, Duncan Mills, Chris Muir, Lynn Munsinger, Frank Nimphius, Steve Noton, Katia Obradovic-Sarkic, Philip Prosser, Blaise Ribet, Dana Singleterry, and Gary Williams. I'd also like to thank Glenn Maslen for overseeing the review process. Thank you all.

I'd like to thank my manager, Duncan Mills, for supporting me on this project. Duncan, your technical guidance, advice on book writing, and support while I also tried to juggle my day-to-day commitments to the Oracle team have been invaluable. Thank you.

I must also thank Steve Muench, the godfather of ADF Business Components, who, at all hours of the day, was always happy to answer "just one more quick question," which invariably was never that quick.

My final thanks are reserved for my family, who supported me and gave me inspiration. To my Mum and Dad, who always asked, "how's the book?" thank you for your support; I love you both very much. I know you never really understood what my job was; well, this it!

And finally, to my wonderful wife Justine. Despite all the nights and weekends that we missed out on while I was working on the book, you always encouraged, listened to, and supported me. You are truly an inspiration and I love you with all of my heart. Thank you for being you.

Introduction

I'm sure it would make a much more interesting introduction to the book if I were to tell you I was lying in the bath one day and had a eureka moment that what the world needs is a quick start guide to Fusion development. Instead, the inspiration was a little more mundane, but no less important.

Over my many years of using JDeveloper and Oracle ADF, I have encountered two common issues time and time again. First, while there are thousands of pages of developer guides and online help, the new development audience often can't see the wood for the trees. To get started on building an application, or to exploit a specific feature, a huge investment of time often is required to plow through the documentation, trying to separate the basic details of how to get something working from the coverage of advanced and more obscure features.

The second issue I've encountered is that when I meet new developers, they typically say their first perception of the technology was that "it is just too difficult." I often make the point that it is more of a case of the technology being different from what they are used to rather than being just too difficult. While many have relished the Oracle ADF adventure, others looked up from base camp to see an Everest and decided they wanted to pack up and go home.

It is only when I get a chance to sit down one-on-one with these doubters and say "let me show you" that they actually see how far they can get with only a little knowledge. At times, I swear I've seen a light go on deep inside them and then a sudden "ah, I get it now" look of enlightenment.

And that is where the inspiration for this book came from. I want more people to have that moment where they see a clear path through the forest and are able to understand and harness the power of Oracle Fusion technology. This book doesn't try to teach you every nuance of every feature, but instead focuses on the essential features and knowledge required to build a Fusion application using JDeveloper and Oracle ADF in as short a time as possible.

How to Use This Book

This book follows a typical development scenario, starting with a database schema, and then building a business service based on database tables, adding validation, lists, and lookups, and finally moving to the user interface development. The book is therefore best read from start to finish rather than using it as a reference guide that you dip in and out of. However, you may well find yourself bookmarking specific pages to remind yourself how to implement a specific feature or trick.

One decision that was made early in the book-writing process was not to include pages and pages of very specific and detailed step-by-step instructions of how to build a sample application. The problem with these types of instructions is that you often mechanically follow the steps without really thinking about what you are doing. Instead, each chapter shows you how to create and build a feature within a suggested development scenario and encourages you to build that into your application without holding your hand through every keypress. Throughout the chapters, you will build on top of previously discovered features so that by the time you reach the last chapter, you will have a rich and functional Fusion application. The key is that you are free to explore and experiment as you progress through the chapters.

Note that you can download a completed sample application from https://qsfusionsample .samplecode.oracle.com/. (OTN logon is required.)

All that remains is for me to thank you, the reader, for buying the book. I sincerely hope it helps guide you on your first steps along the Fusion development path.

PART
I

Introductions and Overviews

CHAPTER
1

An Introduction to Oracle Fusion and the Fusion Technologies

raditionally, most people familiar with Oracle, whether as a developer, implementer, or consumer of Oracle's "off the shelf" packaged business applications or just as an interested industry observer, have considered the name Oracle to be synonymous with the term "database." And to be fair, Oracle has built a hugely successful business and supporting ecosystem on the back of the database. However, businesses and technologies evolve, and while the database remains a principle element in the Oracle development armory, Oracle now offers many more development choices than it did in the past. No longer is a typical Oracle development résumé simply based upon understanding some core database terms and a bit of PL/SQL.

This is no more evident than in the past five years with the introduction of a new term into the Oracle development vocabulary: Fusion. What is Fusion? What are the associated skills and technologies? And is there really a quick start to Fusion development? In this first chapter, we'll look at what is meant by the term Fusion, and what constitutes Fusion development.

What Is Fusion?

Of course, "Fusion" isn't really a tangible thing. You won't be able to go into your local computer shop or phone up your Oracle account manager and order half a dozen Fusions. Fusion itself is not a product or a specific technology but is a name that was originally "Project Fusion" and has now evolved to a wider marketing term to brand a set of Oracle business applications and technologies.

But, as my high school history teacher used to say, to truly understand where you are going, you need to understand the road on which you traveled. So, let's take a step back to see how we came to arrive at Project Fusion.

The History of Fusion

As noted earlier, for many of you reading this book, your first and probably most familiar view of Oracle is as a database company. And Oracle can be incredibly proud of the success and position as the number one database vendor on the planet. Much of the rapid expansion of Oracle as a company is directly attributable to the success of the database. As Oracle grew its database business, it also complemented that business with development tools, such as Oracle Forms and Oracle Reports, and its own set of business applications (Oracle E-Business Suite), including HR (Human Resources), Financials, and CRM (Customer Relationship Management), to name only a few.

This growth allowed Oracle to become hugely successful, but, never one to rest on its laurels, Oracle started looking further afield and in 2004 kicked off a series of major acquisitions starting with PeopleSoft, which was then quickly followed by Siebel Systems in 2005. As well as bringing new employees and customers to Oracle, both companies also had significantly popular offerings in the business application space, including HR and CRM. There then followed a host of other acquisitions, including Hyperion Solutions, BEA Systems, and Sun, who brought to the Oracle camp leading-edge technology solutions such as business intelligence, application server, and middleware products.

So, at the end of a very significant spending spree, Oracle had acquired a portfolio of new technologies, tools, and business applications. And this presented a major new challenge for Oracle: how to plan for Oracle's next generation of business applications given this veritable mixture of applications and technologies. As challenges go, this was a pretty significant one. Oracle couldn't simply "glue" together the best bits of each of the business applications and expect that to be its next-generation offering. These applications were built with different technologies and computing languages, and with different tools using different development approaches.

Mixed with this considerable challenge came the opportunity to make a fresh start. As a new generation of business applications, Oracle had the chance to make some real fundamental changes to how these applications were built. Oracle could embrace new technologies and architectures that were not available when the original applications were conceived, and could standardize on a set of technologies right across the board. And so a project was initiated to modernize and redevelop the business applications on a standard technology stack, which itself was based on the best of the technology acquisitions. This was Project Fusion.

The Fusion Brand

So, *Project Fusion* became the term to cover the development of Oracle's next-generation business applications onto a unified, standard stack: a development effort of thousands of Oracle developers building both the applications and the supporting technology infrastructure. The specific use of "project" was soon dropped, allowing "Fusion" to be applied generically to any part of this development effort or its building blocks. While there are no hard and fast rules to the use of the Fusion brand, there are three broad technology pillars with which the "Fusion" tag is commonly associated.

Oracle Fusion Applications

Oracle's next-generation business applications are grouped under the name *Oracle Fusion Applications*. These are the Fusion Applications developed by Oracle, such as CRM, Financials, Procurement, and Supply Chain Management. These applications are delivered as modules, and customers typically purchase one or more of these modules to address their business needs.

Furthermore, any applications developed by customers using the same principles and technologies could equally be called Fusion Applications. For the most part, this book focuses on generic Fusion application development rather than being restricted to a particular module of Oracle Fusion Applications.

Oracle Fusion Middleware

Oracle Fusion Applications are primarily web-based applications. As such, they need an application server and infrastructure to serve them up to the customers who use them. *Oracle Fusion Middleware* is the term used to describe the platform on which Fusion Applications run. It provides features such as runtime engines, security, and management consoles. Oracle Fusion Middleware is a product that, in addition to running Fusion Applications, can also support custom-built applications developed using different technologies within the platform, such as Oracle Forms, portals, and web services.

Oracle Fusion Architecture

This is a more loosely used term, but still as important. Fusion Applications are built to blueprints outlining the best practices and technologies for building Fusion Applications on Fusion Middleware. These blueprints include principles such as service-oriented architecture (SOA), Java Platform, Enterprise Edition (Java EE), and a number of other concepts discussed throughout this book.

NOTE
While the term Oracle Fusion Architecture does not refer to a specific document or architecture diagram, at the time of writing, Oracle has been working on a set of guidelines called the Oracle Fusion Reference Architecture. This is a formally documented set of references as to how Oracle builds Fusion Applications.

The Fusion Technologies

When Oracle launched the Fusion initiative, there were a number of high-level business drivers that influenced the technology choices. These included

- Ability to exploit the resources offered from a standards-based environment
- Agility to business change and ease of integration
- Clear, intuitive, and rich user interface deliverable through multiple end user devices such as browsers or mobile devices

The good news was that Oracle didn't have to go out and invent a bunch of new technologies and concepts to meet these requirements. There already existed a range of well-established and proven technologies as well as some newer emerging technologies that would address these needs and give the Fusion Applications their cutting edge: Java, SOA, and Web 2.0.

Java

Given the driver that the Fusion initiative be based on standards, the Java programming language was a natural choice. Java has been around since 1995 and is a mature and popular programming language with a well-established developer community. It is already widely used in the software industry and is a popular programming language in colleges and universities—thus ensuring a deep pool of new development talent.

As a programmer, you write Java classes that get compiled into a format called bytecode. A platform-specific runtime engine called a Java Virtual Machine (JVM) then interprets this bytecode. Thus, the same Java class (or Java program) will run the same way on different hardware platforms.

How Much Java Do I Need to Know?

One of the most common questions from new Fusion developers, specifically those coming from a traditional Oracle development background, is, "How much Java do I need to know?" Given that Fusion Applications are based on the Java platform and the Java programming language, it would be folly to suggest that you should embark on building a production Fusion Application with no Java language experience. However, as this book will explain, the features of the Fusion toolset and architecture mitigate the requirement that all of your developers have to be experts in Java. At the entry level, knowledge of basic Java programming structures, data types, and concepts will allow new developers to be productive. More experienced Java developers will find it easier to extend and customize the architecture, and typically a team should have at least one experienced Java developer who can make such architectural decisions.

Java Standard and Enterprise Editions

Whereas Java is the programming language, the packaging of the language, the runtime, and supporting libraries is defined by two terms.

Java Standard Edition   The combination of the Java language, the JVM, and a set of libraries for performing common functions such as enabling file access or presenting a desktop GUI is collectively known as Java Platform, Standard Edition (Java SE). Each of the standards for the Java SE platform is agreed upon by a community of developers—and it is a community in the truest sense, given that anyone can sign up to become a part of the Java Community Process (JCP). For example, there is a standard API that defines how a client can programmatically access a database from Java (Java Database Connectivity—JDBC). This API is implemented as part of the Java runtime.

Java Enterprise Edition   Java Platform, Enterprise Edition (Java EE) includes the features of Java SE but expands on that edition to include specifications to address the challenges of enterprise-level, distributed, multitier, server-based applications. For example, Java EE includes specifications that address data persistence, distributed messaging, and web user interfaces. Any application server that wants to be Java EE compliant has to implement each of these specifications, and as you might expect, Oracle Fusion Middleware implements the Java EE specification.

So, basing Fusion Applications on Java EE guarantees a baseline of compliant features that the platform will provide and portability of these applications between Java EE–compliant platforms.

SOA

SOA is an architecture in which business processes are implemented as reusable, loosely coupled services that can be easily orchestrated together to provide a more complex business process. Key to the concept of SOA is that the implementation of a service can be easily discovered, reused, governed, monitored, and exposed, the latter of which may involve exposing it through a user interface (UI) or in a "UI-less" mode like a web service.

As an example, in a service-based architecture, the business process of setting the compensation plan for an employee might be implemented as a service that involves setting targets, commission levels, and base salary, all governed by a number of business rules. That service might be exposed through a manager's dashboard for setting his sales team's quarterly targets. It might also be utilized by an HR department when transferring, hiring, or promoting employees. The idea is that each business process, in this case the need to compensate an employee, is implemented in a standard way that can easily be discovered, shared, and reused.

Oracle Fusion Applications are based on SOA, and while it is not essential for you to understand more than the high-level concept of SOA to read this book, it is useful to remember that the business application developed through the course of this book could also be regarded as a service.

Web 2.0

Completing the Fusion technology checklist is a ubiquitous term, Web 2.0. The goal for Oracle Fusion Applications was to provide an incredibly rich, productive, and interactive user experience. Furthermore, a more social and collaborative approach to applications was required, leveraging features like online chat, forums, and RSS (Really Simple Syndication) feeds. And this is the very essence of Web 2.0.

While the technologies behind Web 2.0 are themselves not prescribed, Fusion adopts the umbrella technologies of AJAX (Asynchronous JavaScript and XML). The core of an AJAX user experience is that, instead of being delivered rather dull and boring static HTML pages, dynamic pages of rich interactive content are delivered to a browser through a mix of HTML and JavaScript. HTML provides the base markup while JavaScript calls can initiate asynchronous XML messages back to the server as the user moves around the screen, giving the user rich and instantaneous feedback on their actions. Manipulation of the browser's internal representation of the page, called the Document Object Model (DOM), allows partial refreshing of the pages rather than having to reload the entire page. All of this functionality gives the browser a rich and almost "desktop application" feel.

Summary

Now that you are familiar with the history of and the technologies behind the Fusion development effort, you should understand that:

- Fusion is a branding for Oracle's next-generation business applications, technologies, and middleware.
- Oracle Fusion Applications are based on Java, SOA, and Web 2.0.
- Any applications based on the Fusion technology stack can also be classed as Oracle Fusion Applications.

Armed with the background and technologies behind Fusion, the next step is to understand how tools and frameworks can be used to harness these technologies.

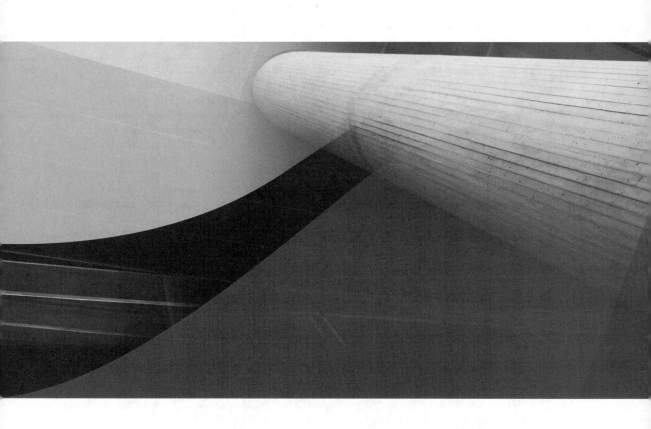

CHAPTER
2

An Introduction to Oracle JDeveloper and Oracle ADF

As outlined in the previous chapter, Oracle chose Java EE, SOA, and Web 2.0 as the technology pillars for the Fusion initiative. Each of these pillars includes a veritable alphabet soup of technologies and standards: JPA, EJB, JDBC, BPEL, DOM, SOAP, WSDL, XML, and HTML, to name only a few. And herein lies the fundamental problem: to use these technologies, developers feel they have to pretty much know them inside out, which, arguably, is beyond the abilities of all but the most elite developers.

To many developers who are used to a declarative or fourth-generation programming language (4GL) approach to development, including Oracle E-Business Suite developers, the Fusion initiative might seem like a step back into the Dark Ages. Rather than focusing development effort on writing code to solve a business problem, the developer was now going to be confronted with a Pandora's box of technologies that had to be understood, integrated, and maintained. Even using external solutions from third parties only added to the integration headache by introducing a mishmash of code and licenses.

So, how is Oracle able to harness the power of these technologies in a way that abstracts away the complexities of the technologies, enabling developers to focus on the application-specific challenges? The answer: Oracle JDeveloper and Oracle Application Development Framework (ADF).

Oracle JDeveloper

Whether you are writing a computer program, fixing a leaking radiator, or changing the spark plugs in your car, having the right tool makes the job so much easier. Oracle JDeveloper is Oracle's tool for Fusion development. JDeveloper provides an integrated development environment (IDE) that aids the developer in the full life cycle of building Fusion applications right across the various technology pillars.

J Is for Java

As you might have expected, the *J* in JDeveloper stands for Java. Typically, Java development involves the creation and management of hundreds of files, and JDeveloper provides an environment that aids the developer in writing, building, and running Java programs. In addition to code-editing features like formatting and refactoring, JDeveloper provides other, more advanced features such as code insight, syntax checking, code templates, file comparison, pop-up documentation, debuggers, code profilers, and a host of other features to support the Java coder.

But JDeveloper Is Not Only for Java

On the other hand, JDeveloper and Fusion development is not all about Java. You might be just as likely to build a Web 2.0 user interface or hook together some web service calls; your development environment is still JDeveloper.

For Web 2.0, JDeveloper provides page designers, simplified property inspectors, and palettes of UI components to take the building of UI pages into the realms of drag-and-drop and WYSIWYG. Development of SOA services is driven through wizards and visual designers, so you don't have to manually write configuration files one line at a time. In each of these cases, JDeveloper provides tooling that aids in the generation and manipulation of the source files of that technology in a much more productive way than having to roll up your sleeves and hand edit the source directly (although you can if you feel comfortable doing so).

However, the real power of JDeveloper comes when exploiting the power of a framework that protects the developer from the complexities of all the underlying technologies and provides common building blocks and features to both simplify and accelerate development.

Oracle ADF

As outlined in the preceding section, the complexities of the technologies underpinning Fusion presented a considerable challenge to developer productivity; thus, a framework of common services and features was required. Oracle ADF was built specifically to address this requirement by bringing together a number of subframeworks and standards to provide an end-to-end, metadata-driven framework for building online transactional processing (OLTP) business applications. While Oracle ADF and JDeveloper are two separate products that can be used independently, their full power is realized by using them together. Oracle ADF provides the building blocks and runtime features that are easily created and managed through JDeveloper.

But before embarking on a more detailed description of Oracle ADF, it's worth establishing, what is a framework?

The Role of a Framework

For many developers, it may be a new term in their vocabulary, even though they might have been using a framework without knowing it. Essentially, the role of a framework is to provide a flexible abstraction of common, but generic, features over a more complex underlying layer.

Consider this example; if you are planning a new kitchen for your house, you might decide that you are going to handcraft each cabinet and countertop to your precise requirements. That's fine if you are a skilled carpenter with the tools, knowledge, and time necessary to accomplish the task. Alternatively, with the framework approach, you could go to a kitchen supply company that sells cabinet carcasses and countertops that you cut to size and then customize with your own door fronts, handles, and surface materials. You are still building your kitchen to your specific requirements, but with a lot less blood, sweat, and tears by using a generic framework for cabinets and countertops that you fit to your needs.

Now consider a typical Oracle example of building an application based on some database tables. Anyone building this kind of application will be solving the same old problems of having to connect to the database, retrieve and cache records, manage database transactions, implement validation, and display results on the end user's screen. Doesn't it make sense to have all those features prebuilt for you, so that you just have to "cut them to size" to fit your particular need? That's the beauty of a framework: it provides the lower-level features and common building blocks that every application needs, but in a way that can be customized for a specific application. This allows the developer to focus on solving the business problems, and leave the technology problems to the very clever people who build the framework.

Model-View-Controller

Oracle ADF is based around the architectural principle of Model-View-Controller (MVC). What that means is that the framework separates the implementation of the business services (Model) from the implementation of the user interface (View), with the Controller managing application flow.

Having distinct and separate layers has a number of advantages, such as promoting reuse and testing independence.

Model

The role of the Model is to implement the business service or data model. In most cases (and the primary use case for this book) a business service will involve the querying and manipulation of data from a relational database. This requires the Model layer to provide a number of functions.

Object-Relational Mapping   Given that a Fusion application is built in an object-oriented Java environment and that the data is sitting in a relational database, a mapping must occur between these two different worlds. Often called O/R mapping, the Model is responsible for mapping a Customer Java object that lives in the application to the underlying Customer table in the relational database.

Default Operations   With a business service based on a database table, the chances are you will want to perform actions on that data, such as query, delete, insert, next record, previous record, commit, and rollback actions. It is therefore reasonable to expect that the Model will provide common functions to manipulate the data represented in the business service.

Validation   For a business service, you probably want to validate the data to ensure that it meets specific business and data requirements. For example, you need to enforce business rules such as not allowing a customer record to be created without first specifying the customer name, or not allowing a customer's credit limit to be more than $4000.

View

The role of the View is to expose the business service to the end user, typically through a browser. Some of the high-level features of the View layer are described next.

UI Component Set   The principal goal of the View is to provide a set of rich UI components. These components range from the familiar buttons, check boxes, and text fields, to richer components like tree hierarchies and data tables, and also layout components to help position content on the page.

Adaptive Rendering   A UI component should be able to render itself correctly regardless of the target device. For example, it should render correctly whether it's on one of several different browsers or on a mobile device like a cell phone.

Programming Model   The View should be responsible for providing infrastructure for allowing UI-specific code to be associated with a page.

Look and Feel   The capability to define corporate templates and application skins is a core feature of the View. For example, you can build an application for different customers that enables each customer to choose their own look and feel.

Controller

The final building block of MVC is the Controller. The Controller is responsible for event handling and determining page navigation. Some broad requirements of the Controller are described next.

Task Flow For an application that contains many pages, you would want to be able to define *"if I am on this page, then when this action happens, I want to navigate to this new page."* The Controller allows you to define this application page flow. However, you may also want to implement a case such as *"if I am on this page, then when this action happens, I want to perform some particular task first, and then navigate to the new page."* This extended use case, called task flow, goes beyond page flow to include the calling of business actions.

Reuse Given that a typical application could involve hundreds of pages, the Controller should allow subsets of application flow to be built and then reused within the main application flow whenever needed. For example, a login task flow might involve a specific flow of pages that can be reused throughout the application.

Metadata-Driven Framework

A common misconception of Oracle ADF is that the functionality is implemented by thousands of lines of Java code automatically generated as a result of stepping through the wizards in JDeveloper. This is definitely not the case. It is true that Oracle ADF itself is implemented in Java; however, the way the framework is configured for a specific application's use case is largely driven by metadata. That means that an application-specific framework use case, such as defining that the application should navigate from page A to page B, is driven by metadata defined in XML, not Java code. At runtime, the generic framework classes read the XML to implement the specific navigation from page A to page B.

Driving the Framework

Of course, you might think that XML is just as difficult to maintain as machine-generated Java code; and this is where JDeveloper exploits the full power of Oracle ADF. JDeveloper allows the manipulation of the metadata in a much more intuitive and simplified way. In the case of page navigation, the developer is presented with a page flow visual editor that shows the pages of the applications and how they flow together. As a developer, you are working with a visual representation that closely matches the job at hand. The fact that changing the visual page flow is actually changing an XML file is, generally speaking, something you don't see or need to see.

NOTE
While JDeveloper presents the editing of the framework metadata through visual diagrams, dialog boxes, and property inspectors, there is nothing to stop you from directly editing the source files as well. Whether you're editing the XML file directly or through one of the more declarative means, the same underlying file is being updated.

Metadata Advantages

There are a number of advantages to this metadata-driven approach to the framework beyond the fact that you do not have to maintain masses of generated Java code. First, it helps you to keep a clean separation between the code you write to address an application-specific business problem and the implementation of a framework feature. The metadata implements the directives for driving the framework features, while your application-specific code can reside in its own separate Java classes.

The second advantage is found at runtime. Because the metadata is read at runtime, and is not compiled at design time, you could conceivably swap in and out different metadata for different deployments without having to recompile all your Java code. Why would you want to do that? Well, you might have one set of framework validation rules that is used for some customer deployments but a different set of validation rules that is used for other customers. If these validation rules were in code, this swapping in and out would be more difficult to achieve.

NOTE
The management of metadata to allow the customization and personalization of an application is handled by a framework feature called Metadata Services (MDS). Although MDS is beyond the scope of this book, it is worth pointing out that this feature exists and is a core element of the Fusion stack for applying customizations to Fusion applications.

The Building Blocks of Oracle ADF

Now that you understand the role of a framework and the high-level architecture of Oracle ADF, the next step is to look at the specific building blocks of Oracle ADF.

If you have had the opportunity to use JDeveloper already, you may have noticed the splash screen "Productivity with choice." This mantra refers directly to Oracle ADF. Oracle ADF offers a number of different solutions for each of the layers in the MVC architecture. As you can see in Figure 2-1, the View layer offers a choice of technologies for a desktop UI or a browser-based UI. So, how do you choose which technology to use? The choice of technology stripe through Oracle ADF could be a chapter in itself, but given that the purpose of this book is a quick start guide to Fusion, we'll focus on the technology stripe used to build the Oracle Fusion Applications. This technology stripe is highlighted in Figure 2-1.

ADF Business Components

ADF Business Components (ADFbc) is the framework used in Oracle Fusion Applications for building database-centric business services. It provides a highly declarative way of developing Java objects on top of relational database tables. In addition to providing the core feature of the Model layer, described earlier, it provides value-added features such as the ability to declare calculated attributes, lists of values, query by example, and predefined filter criteria.

So, if you want to build an application based on the Customers and Orders tables in the database, ADF Business Components allows you to rapidly build a business service based on that data model. It will automatically implement database constraints for any master/detail relationships, and provide methods for manipulating the data model such as commit, rollback, and delete.

ADF Model

The ADF Model (ADFm) is the "glue" between the business services and the View layer. With an architecture like MVC, there has to be a way of binding a UI widget to an underlying piece of data. In an ideal world, the assembly of a web page shouldn't really require the UI developer to understand whether a Customer record is coming from a database table or a web service, and so it's the responsibility of ADFm to abstract the implementation of the business service from the View layer. You can think of ADF Model as a façade that exposes the attributes and actions of a business service to the View layer in a consistent way.

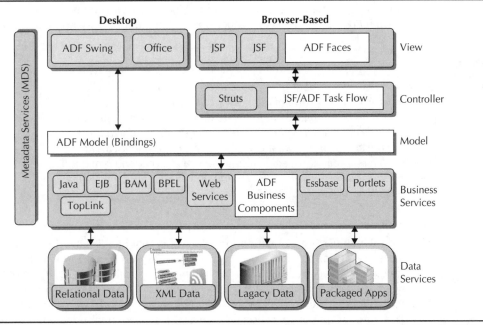

FIGURE 2-1. *The Oracle ADF technologies and Fusion technology stripe through Oracle ADF*

ADF Model is currently under proposal to become a Java standard and is subject to Java Specification Request 227 (JSR-227).

ADF Faces

ADF Faces (full title: Oracle ADF Faces Rich Client) is the ADF View (ADFv) technology for building a rich browser-based interface. ADF Faces is a set of components and features written to the Java Server Faces (JSF) standard for component-based web UIs.

In the early days of web applications, development of the front end was very much a code-focused effort. Developers had to write code, called servlets, that would dynamically generate the HTML displayed by the browser. The next evolution in web frameworks was the introduction of tag libraries, the idea being that the developer had a library of tags for rendering content, like data tables, and each tag referenced a servlet that would in turn generate the dynamic markup for that component. However, the developer building the UI still had the same problem in that designing the layout of a page with tags or servlets bore little resemblance to how the page would actually look at runtime.

With JSF, the web UI developer is able to work with WYSIWYG UI components. JSF defines a standard for a componentized framework, and vendors build their own library of UI components based on that standard. Each component exposes properties such as background color, font, height, and width. Components can also have defined behavior; for example, a button can be clicked or a text field can gain focus. At runtime, it is the responsibility of the component to generate the correct markup to be displayed in the end-user device.

There are two major benefits of this componentized view of UI widgets. First, the UI developer is working with a set of components that represent how they will be seen by the end user at runtime. Second, the UI developer isn't burdened by having to understand how that component will render itself; that is the responsibility of the developer who built the component.

NOTE
For the purposes of this book, you can expect that components generate HTML and JavaScript as the markup that will be displayed by a browser. However, one of the powerful features of JSF is that a component can be configured to generate different markup depending on the device on which it will be rendered; for example, if you are accessing the application from a cell phone, the component would generate different markup specific to that device. A component might even generate different markup depending on whether the browser is Internet Explorer or Firefox.

ADF Controller

The JSF standard includes a specification for a controller that handles the flow of application pages. However, for Fusion Applications, it was evident that this specification had its limitations and thus a solution was required that went beyond the JSF specification. ADF Controller (ADFc) was developed as a new feature in Oracle ADF 11*g* and is an extension of the standard JSF controller that includes features to allow application flow to be modularized and easily reused. It also extends the concept of application flow beyond just pages to also include features like calling code as part of the flow.

Summary

In this chapter you have learned that:

- Oracle JDeveloper is the development environment for building Fusion applications across different technology pillars.
- Frameworks provide common features and building blocks that aid application development.
- Oracle ADF is based on an MVC architecture.
- The main building blocks of Oracle ADF for Fusion development are ADF Business Components, ADF Model, ADF Controller, and ADF Faces.

So, armed with a solid understanding of the Fusion message, tools, and the technologies behind Oracle ADF, the next step is to get hands on with JDeveloper and get comfortable with the key features you need for building a Fusion application.

CHAPTER
3

Finding Your Way Around an Application in JDeveloper

efore you plunge into the depths of building a Fusion application, it is worth your while to take a quick tour around JDeveloper to become comfortable with the most important windows and menu options and to discover some ways of organizing your application.

If you have not already installed JDeveloper, the good news is that the procedure is quick, easy, and free. JDeveloper is available for free download from www.oracle.com/technology/products/jdev, and the Studio Edition contains everything you need for this book, including the JDeveloper IDE, Oracle ADF runtime, JDK, and application server.

When you start JDeveloper, you should find the look and feel of the interface to be reasonably familiar even if you are new to JDeveloper but have used other IDEs in the past. As Figure 3-1 shows, along the top is a menu bar from which you can launch actions such as creating (**File**) and editing (**Edit**) content and perform numerous other actions (you can investigate the various menus at your convenience). Below that is a toolbar for some of the most common actions, such as save and run. Immediately under the toolbar, the rest of the IDE is devoted to windows for displaying various elements of the application, including the source files, properties, system messages, and the like.

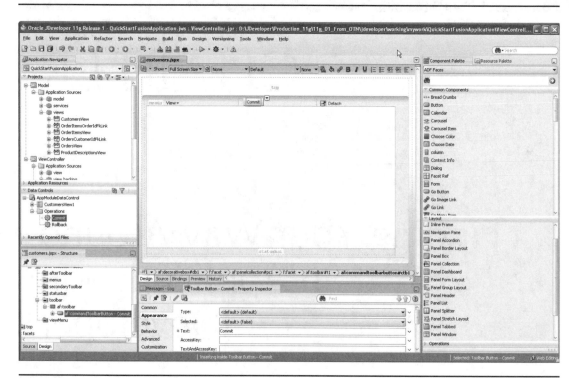

FIGURE 3-1. *The JDeveloper IDE*

Organizing the IDE

The first step is to get comfortable with the various windows and how to manage them. JDeveloper splits the IDE into a number of windows, each of which contains its own content and can be managed and positioned independently of the other windows.

Working with Windows

The following are some of the most common actions you will perform on windows.

Default Window Positions

Upon starting JDeveloper, you might find that your windows are laid out differently from the layout shown in Figure 3-1. One trick, which is also useful if your window layout becomes a bit messy, is to reset the windows to their default position. This can be done by selecting **Window | Reset Windows to Factory Setting**, which will reset JDeveloper to show the default windows in their default positions.

Opening and Closing Windows

Opening and closing windows is reasonably intuitive. Each window has a tab that displays the window name or associated filename. When the window has focus and you hover over the tab, an × appears on the right side of the tab. Clicking the × closes the window.

To open a window, select **View** from the menu bar and then choose the window you want to open. You will also see that the **View** menu includes hot keys that you can use to open windows. For example, pressing CTRL-SHIFT-A will open the Application Navigator window.

Resizing Windows

As you probably expect, clicking the edge of the window and then dragging will resize that window. You can also maximize a window by double-clicking the tab. This expands the window to fill the IDE; double-clicking the tab again reverses the action.

Positioning Windows

Each of the windows can be dragged and repositioned to fit your specific needs. To move a window, click and drag the window tab. As you move the window, JDeveloper gives a visual indication of where the window will appear when you drop it. You can either drop a window inside another window, in which case the windows share the same space and you would use the window tab to bring one in front of the other, or drop it to the side of a window. Alternatively, pressing the CTRL key as you drag a window will float the window on top of the other windows.

Introducing the JDeveloper Windows

As you become more confident building Fusion applications in JDeveloper, you will start to use more and more of the features and windows available within the IDE. However, given this book is all about getting a quick start, the more commonly used windows and their purpose are introduced in this section.

Application Navigator

The Application Navigator is, as the name suggests, the window in which you manage and navigate the application source. The Java files, web pages, ADF artifacts, and anything else you choose to build as part of your application can be accessed from here. The Application Navigator includes an Application menu, to the right of the application name, which offers options such as renaming, searching, and comparing files.

Within the Application Navigator are a number of panels for managing the application content, of which the most commonly used are the Projects and Data Controls panels.

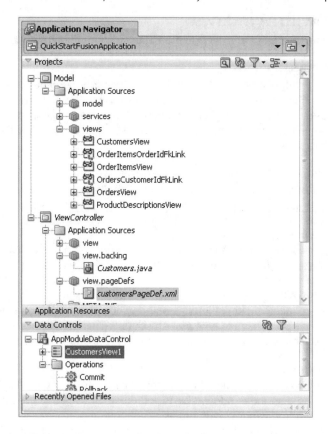

Projects Panel   The Projects panel is the principal panel in which you will create, view, and edit application source files. Right-click a node in the Projects panel and select **Open** or double-click the selected item or file to open that source in an appropriate editor.

Data Controls Panel   The Data Controls panel shows the data model for the current application. You will use this panel primarily when building the application UI, because this panel shows the various data attributes and actions exposed by the business service through ADF Model. You can drag these data collections, attributes, or actions directly onto an ADF Faces page to bind them to UI items such as fields or buttons.

Structure Window

The Structure window displays a hierarchical representation of the currently selected object. In the case of a Java file, this window shows information such as methods and class member variables, while an ADF Faces page would display the nested tree of layout and visual components. As you click a node in the Structure window, any other editors that are open on the source object are automatically synchronized. This is particularly useful when developing UI pages that may contain many nested layout containers, because it offers a more precise way of selecting and dropping content on a page at exactly the right place.

The right-click context menu is also available for editing and creating content directly in the Structure window.

Component Palette

The Component Palette offers a list of elements that can be dropped onto UI pages and other visual editors. Your primary use of the Component Palette when building a Fusion application will be to present the list of visual components that can be dragged and dropped onto an ADF Faces page or a page flow diagram.

Property Inspector

The Property Inspector automatically displays a list of properties and values for the currently selected component. In many cases, you will use the Property Inspector to examine and edit properties of ADF Faces components on pages, but it can equally be used for managing properties associated with other artifacts.

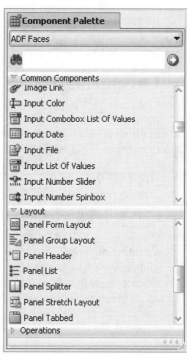

Main Editor Window

Although not explicitly named, the main editor window, which appears by default in the center of the IDE, is the principal window for editing content regardless of whether that content is a Java class, ADF Faces page, or an ADF Business Components artifact. Depending on the file type being edited, the content will appear in an appropriate editor. For example, a Java class is opened in the code editor, while an ADF Faces file is automatically displayed in the visual page editor.

Editor Tabs   A powerful feature of JDeveloper is that you have the freedom to edit application content in different ways. If you are relatively new to JDeveloper and Oracle ADF, you will probably be more comfortable with the declarative and visual editors. However, if you look at the tabs running along the bottom of the main editor window, you will notice that you have different options for how you can edit and view the selected source file. As you become more comfortable with the technology, you may find yourself, for example, clicking the *Source* tab and editing the source directly. Regardless of whether you choose to edit the source directly or through a more declarative means, you are still editing the same source file.

Organizing a Fusion Application

So, with a basic understanding of the IDE features, how do you start building an application? It was A. A. Milne, the author of Winnie the Pooh, who was credited as saying: "Organizing is what you do before you do something, so that when you do it, it is not all mixed up." So, with that thought in mind, let's look at how you can organize a Fusion application.

Organizing Your Source Files

One of the first things you will notice when building a Fusion application is that you will generate quite a number of files. The good news, however, is that JDeveloper helps you to manage and partition these application files into logical containers—just like a filing cabinet that has different drawers and different folders within those drawers.

Applications

The top-level container for your application is called, not surprisingly, an application. You can think of the application as the filing cabinet that holds all the content for a particular development initiative.

Creating an Application   To create a new application, select **File | New** and, in the New Gallery dialog that opens, select **General** and then **Application**. The first thing you'll notice in the *Items* pane is that there is more than one type of application. Given that you are creating a Fusion application, select **Fusion Web Application (ADF)** and click OK. You can then enter the name of the application and click Finish.

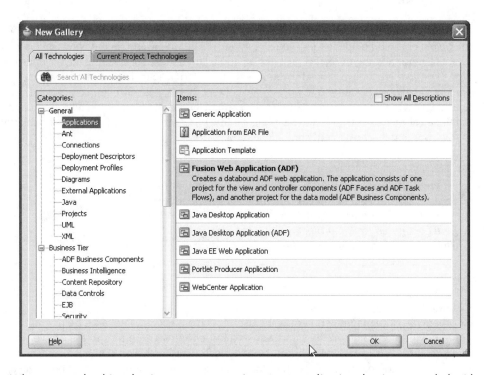

When you make this selection, you are creating a new application that is pre-seeded with all of the appropriate technologies and libraries for building a Fusion application.

TIP
*The type of application you selected is based on an Application Template. Application Templates provide a convenient way of setting a default outline for an application. As well as defining the outline of the application structure, the technologies you associate with each project will be used by JDeveloper to restrict the menu choices presented to you when working in that project. To understand more about these Application Templates, select **Application** | **Manage Templates**, which enables you to explore the different Application Templates.*

Projects

Within the application, you can have one or many projects. A project is analogous to a drawer in a filing cabinet and is just a way of further partitioning application content. For the Fusion application you have just created, JDeveloper automatically creates two projects: Model, for the business services code, and ViewController, for the UI and page flow files. The Fusion Web Application (ADF) template encourages the good practice of keeping a clean separation between the business services and the UI, exactly as Oracle ADF's MVC architecture does. Keeping a clean separation makes, among other things, packaging and reusing application content easier.

Creating a Project   If you need to create further projects—for example, you might create a project to contain common helper code—you simply select **File | New** and, in the New Gallery dialog, select **General** and then **Projects**. Just like an application, there are different flavors of project. Each type of project is simply a project that is preconfigured for a specific type of content, and, as noted earlier, JDeveloper guides you to only create content that makes sense in that project. For example, JDeveloper will try to steer you away from creating UI content in your Model project. Going back to the filing cabinet analogy, it's like the filing cabinet preventing you from filing your bank statement in a drawer that is set up to only hold tax returns.

 TIP
*If you select a project in the Application Navigator and then right-click and select **Project Properties**, JDeveloper opens a dialog showing the various technologies, libraries, and properties that are configured for the project. As you get more comfortable with JDeveloper, you can change these project settings to meet your specific needs.*

Packages

Another way of managing content is the use of a Java package. Packages help you manage content within a project in the same way as a folder helps group files in the drawer of your filing cabinet. This is particularly useful when creating artifacts like ADF Business Components, which can be compartmentalized into different functional packages. Furthermore, packages are important to avoid conflicts when it comes to integration or deployment to a production system where potentially files with the same name already exist.

Creating a Package   You can explicitly create a package by selecting **File | New** and, in the New Gallery dialog, selecting **General** and then **Java Package**. Alternatively, when creating a Java class, or artifacts like ADF Business Components, you can enter a new package name, and that package will be created for you. Package names usually follow a naming hierarchy separated by a period. So, a package name might follow a convention like `companyname.application .name`.

Summary

You should now feel comfortable exploring the JDeveloper windows and the structure of a Fusion application. Specifically, you learned:

- How to manage the windows within JDeveloper.
- Which are the most commonly utilized windows and what they are used for.
- How your source files can be managed via applications, projects, and packages.

As you become more comfortable finding your way around JDeveloper, the next step is to build your first Fusion application, starting with the business services layer, as described in the next chapter.

PART

II

Building Business Services

CHAPTER
4

Building ADF Business Components

his chapter will take you through the concepts, building blocks, and steps to create a first-cut business service based on ADF Business Components. As a Fusion developer, you have the challenge of building a business service based on a number of tables in an Oracle database.

NOTE
The examples used in this book are based on the OE (Order Entry)
Sample schema available with the Oracle database.

The Goals for ADF Business Components

As outlined in Chapter 2, there are a number of goals for a business services framework like ADF Business Components. At the most fundamental level, a business service is required to query information from an underlying database and cache that data while various operations are performed on it. It then has to validate the data changes and complete the transaction by committing the data back to the database. This use case can be broken down into the following high-level tasks:

- Defining application objects that map to database tables
- Managing data and business logic validation
- Creating application-specific views of the data
- Coordinating master/detail behavior of the business model based on foreign key relationships
- Providing default operations such as commit, delete, and update on the data model

ADF Business Components provides these core features within the framework in a generic way, allowing these generic services to be adapted for the application-specific case. However, before embarking on creating a business service based on ADF Business Components, let's first look behind the scenes at the various ADF Business Components building blocks.

How ADF Business Components Works

The core features and functionality of the ADF Business Components framework are implemented in Java. For the most part, the Java classes responsible for the previously noted features, and more, are hidden from the Fusion developer. Instead, the developer generates and maintains metadata through property pages and declarative editors, and it is this metadata that drives the generic Java framework classes when the application runs.

Building a Default Business Service

JDeveloper offers a number of different ways to build ADF Business Components, including visually through modelers or by stepping through wizards. Regardless of the actual method you choose, JDeveloper does the same job for you behind the scenes. When building ADF Business Components, JDeveloper queries the database and reads information about the tables on which the business service is to be based. For example, it discovers what columns are in the table, what data types, their precision, whether the field can be null, and whether it is a foreign key. This information is then encoded into XML files as part of the application project.

If you want to change any of this information, such as the order in which the data is retrieved or whether an attribute is updateable, you can do this by setting properties exposed in the ADF Business Components editors. It is these editors that give the developer a productive and declarative way of maintaining the metadata underpinning ADF Business Components.

Upon running the business services, either through an application or the built-in ADF Business Components tester, the framework reads the application's XML files to create application-specific instances of the more generic framework classes.

Extending the Framework

Of course, one of the key features of ADF Business Components is that the framework classes can themselves be exposed to the developer so that application-specific code can be added to the more generic framework classes. For example, if you decide that the default framework feature for committing a transaction needs some application-specific code added to it, you can get JDeveloper to expose that framework class. This takes the form of JDeveloper creating a subclass of the framework class, into which you can add your own code.

The Building Blocks of ADF Business Components

ADF Business Components is itself based on three main building blocks, as shown in Figure 4-1: the entity object, the view object, and the application module. You might be thinking, "What, more layers?" and you would be right; however, each layer of ADF Business Components has a well-defined role, and being separate and distinct makes it much more flexible and powerful.

The entity object maps directly to a database table and acts as an application cache for records from that table. The view object defines an application-specific view of records queried into the underlying entity objects. The final building block is a container called an application module, which is a collection of instances of view objects that defines the data model and transaction for a particular business task.

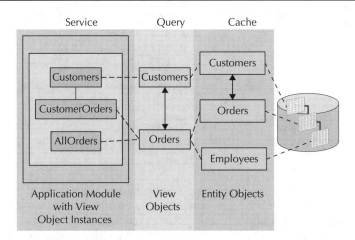

FIGURE 4-1. *ADF Business Components consists of entity objects, view objects, and application modules.*

Introduction to Entity Objects

When you build an application based on a database table, your application needs somewhere to hold the records brought back from the database. It is the responsibility of the entity object to provide this functionality.

As well as providing a data cache, the entity object performs the O/R mapping between the application and the database. For example, a Customers entity object would map to the underlying Customers table in the database. Furthermore, because the entity object is the object in which application data is held and manipulated, it is also the place where business and data validation logic is implemented.

For each of the columns in the underlying table, the entity object will typically contain an attribute that maps to that column and reflects its characteristics, like data type, precision, and whether it allows null values. Of course, an entity object doesn't require an attribute to be mapped to every column in the underlying database table. If your application never needs to manipulate, access, or display a particular column from the database, then you can remove the corresponding attribute from the entity object.

An entity object can be based on a database table, view, or synonym; however, in this book the primary use case will be an entity object based on a database table, and so you can think of an entity object as being like a local copy of the table inside the application.

Behind the Scenes of an Entity Object

The entity object is displayed in the Application Navigator as a single ADF Business Components artifact. Double-click the entity object to edit it in the appropriate editor. You can also expand the node in the Application Navigator to view the entity object implementation files.

The core implementation of an entity object is through a single XML file; for example, Customers.xml in the case of an entity object called Customers. This alone is enough for the framework to provide rich business service functionality based on the Customers table. If you look at the source of the XML file that implements the entity object, you should be able to recognize the information read from the database that is used to implement specific entity object behavior. For example, the CustomerId attribute maps to the CUSTOMER_ID database column, which is a primary key and should be not null.

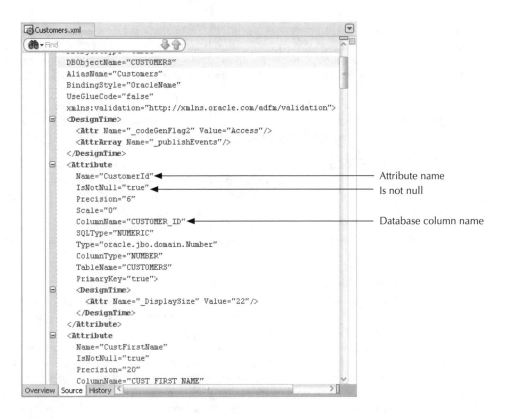

NOTE
As a developer, you will probably never have to look at or directly edit the XML source; however, it is useful to know that this is how ADF Business Components implements your business service functionality.

Optional Java File   You can also optionally generate a Java class; by default, this would be called CustomersImpl.java for the Customers entity object, which exposes the methods the framework uses for things like setting attribute values and creating new records. This is covered in more detail in Chapter 5 but is mentioned here to show that you can go beyond the declarative features of the framework to extend the default functionality, as you require.

Associations

You may have noticed that Figure 4-1 shows arrowed lines between the first two entity objects. These lines represent associations that define a relationship between entity objects, usually based on the foreign key constraints defined in the underlying tables. Associations allow the framework to be aware that there is a relationship between, for example, Customers and Orders.

Introduction to View Objects

The main role of the view object is to give an application-specific view of records queried into the underlying entity objects.

For example, a Customers entity object maps to the Customers table, and this table contains all customer records. However, if your application is applicable only for U.S. customers, you will want to define that the business service should only retrieve the records of U.S. customers. Furthermore, the application does not make use of some data and so will not expose date of birth and marital status.

The view object is responsible for providing this "shaping" of data for the application by defining an SQL statement that selects and orders only the necessary data into the underlying entity objects. A view object can be based on none, one, or many entity objects.

Read-Only View Objects

A view object that is not based on an entity object is called a read-only view object. A read-only view object can be a static list of values defined at design time or a read-only list selected directly from a database.

Read-only view objects might be used for a view of data that is never likely to change, such as a list of all countries selected from a database table, or a static list of salutations (Mr., Mrs., Miss, and so forth).

Entity-Based View Object

The most typical example of a view object is one that is based on a single entity object. So, for a Customers entity object, you would typically have a CustomersView view object that selects all, or some, of the columns into the underlying entity object.

You can also define multiple view objects based on the same entity object. For example, for stock control, you want a view of all products and their suppliers. But elsewhere in your application, in order to push the sale of certain products, you might require a view of all products that are reaching their end-of-life date. In both cases you have the same underlying source of product data in the entity object, but different application-specific views. Because both views are based on the same entity object, if a product is withdrawn by a supplier, then it will not appear in the view of end-of-life products since both view objects are pointing at the same source of data cached in the entity object.

View Object Based on Multiple Entity Objects

With a view object based on many entity objects, you join together information from different database tables into an application-specific shape. This is particularly useful when you want to bring back information defined by a foreign key lookup. For example, the Orders entity object has an attribute SalesRepId. Given that your customers don't know their sales representative by his employee number, this isn't very meaningful in the context of the application. However, with a view object, you can define that some information comes from the Orders entity object and that the employee name comes from the Employees entity object as referenced by the SalesRepId.

In all three cases previously described, a view object allows you to define an application-specific view of your data.

NOTE
A view object can also have attributes that are not based on entity attributes, but instead are based on expressions. These are called transient attributes and can be useful for features like calculated values. For example, a new view object attribute called TotalSalary, which isn't based on an entity attribute, is the sum of the attributes Salary and Commission. This is covered in more detail in Chapter 6.

Behind the Scenes of a View Object

Just like the entity object, the view object is displayed in the Application Navigator as a single ADF Business Components artifact, symbolized by the reading spectacles icon. Double-clicking the view object opens it in its associated editor.

The view object is essentially a `Select` statement defined in an XML file, with the view object editor providing a simple and intuitive way of editing information about the view object to build up this `Select` statement. As well as defining the attributes that make up the view object, you can also define information such as a `Where` and `Order By` clause and even edit the `Select` statement directly if you feel comfortable writing SQL.

Optional Java File As with an entity object, you can extend the functionality of the view object by exposing and augmenting the underlying framework classes. You might choose to do this if you wish to implement functionality such as programmatically manipulating the `Where` clause or creating a custom method that performs some application function on a view of data. This is also covered in more detail in Chapter 6.

View Links

Referring back to Figure 4-1, notice that an arrowed line also appears between the view objects. This represents a view link. View links, as the name suggests, link view objects together to implement behavior such as master/detail relationships. For example, suppose you have a view of customers and a view of Orders, but are really only interested in seeing the orders for a selected customer. When the orders view object is linked to the Customers view object with a view link, the framework automatically restricts the view of orders based on the customer.

TIP
While the view object isn't necessarily driven by the user interface, it can be a useful way of conceptualizing which view objects you need and what information they need to encapsulate.

Introduction to Application Modules

Having defined application-specific data views through view objects, the final step is to arrange instances of those view objects into a data model for a particular use case. This container of view object instances is called an application module. A typical application will contain one or more application modules, with the application module defining the transaction boundary for committing and rolling back changes made to the views of data contained within it.

Application modules can themselves contain other application modules, called nested application modules. This might be useful where a particular use case, as implemented by an application module, is also required within the transaction of a larger use case.

The application module can be thought of as a service façade or service interface to a consuming client, like a web page, that defines the public actions and data views for a particular application process or use case.

Behind the Scenes of an Application Module

The application module is displayed in the Application Navigator as a single ADF Business Components artifact. Double-click it to open the application module editor, where you can see the view objects within the project and can shuttle them over to define your application module.

As with the previously described ADF Business Components artifacts, the definition of an application module is through XML; however, the application

module editor provides a simple and declarative way of defining the view object instances and methods that make up an application module.

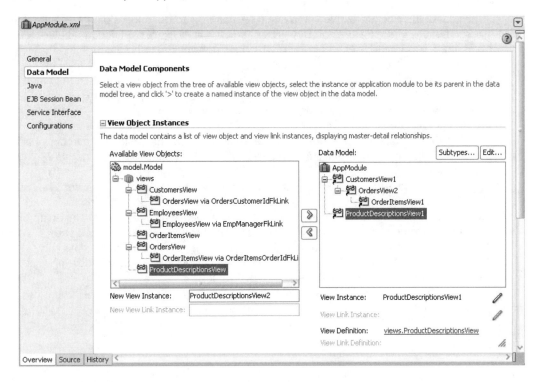

Optional Java File
The framework class that implements the application module functionality already provides methods for committing and rolling back the transaction. However, if you wish to augment that functionality, you can generate the application module implementation class and add your own code to this class.

You can also define application module–level methods that you want to expose to the consuming client. This is covered in more detail in Chapter 7.

First-Cut Business Service Development
Now that you are armed with an understanding of the building blocks of ADF Business Components, the next step is to put that knowledge into action and build ADF Business Components based on database tables. There are a number of different ways to build ADF Business Components; however, JDeveloper provides an incredibly powerful wizard that creates entity objects, associations, view objects, view links, and an application module, based on a number of database tables, all in one go. This is a great way of getting a first cut of your business services.

Application Schema for This Book

The goal of this book is to give you a quick start on how to build a Fusion application, and as such, many of the features of JDeveloper and Oracle ADF are explained in the context of building a Fusion application. However, the book doesn't aim to hold your hand through every keypress or demonstrate every feature within that sample application. Instead, the aim is to explain the concepts, how they can be built in JDeveloper, and then how they can be used in a typical Fusion application. You can then explore, build, and experiment at your convenience—after all, hands-on is the best way to learn.

Where an application example is used, it is based on the Oracle OE (Order Entry) schema that is available with the Oracle database. This schema includes a number of tables for implementing an order entry system based around customers, orders, order items, and products.

The scenario is that the application is being built to manage customer orders. The application should allow the creation, viewing, and editing of customers and their order information. Each customer can have zero or more orders, and each order is made up of one or more order items. The application has a number of pages for viewing and displaying data that is presented in a number of different ways, including data entry forms, tables, and graphs. The application also includes business rules to validating data, and features such as search facilities and lists of values.

A completed application that demonstrates the features discussed in this book is available to download from https://qsfusionsample.samplecode.oracle.com/.

Create Business Components from Tables

Creating new ADF Business Components from database tables is reasonably quick and intuitive. Assuming you've already created an empty application based on the Fusion Web Application template, as described in Chapter 3, select the Model project and then select **File** | **New**. In the New Gallery dialog, select **ADF Business Components** and then **Business Components from Tables**. This launches the Create Business Components from Tables wizard, which steps you through creating entity objects, updatable view objects, read-only view objects, and an application module.

Connecting to the Database

If you haven't yet created a connection to your database, the Initialize Business Components Project dialog prompts you to create a connection to the database. Click the green plus sign, then enter a name for the connection in the *Connection Name* field. Enter values for the *Username*,

Password, *Host Name*, and *SID*, and then click Test Connection to confirm the connection to the database.

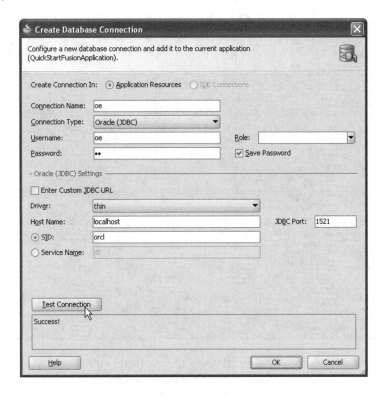

TIP
*You can alternatively create a database connection by selecting **File** |
New and, in the New Gallery dialog, selecting **Connections** and then
Database Connection. When you create a database connection, you
can choose to create the connection as part of the application or
associate the connection with the IDE. An IDE database connection
adds the connection to the Resource Palette window and provides
that connection for use within the IDE. You can then right-click a
database connection in the Resource Palette to browse the database
or add that connection to the current project.*

Selecting Tables for ADF Business Components
Now that you have established a connection to the database, the Create Business Components from Tables wizard prompts you to select the tables for which you want to build entity objects.

Click Query to view the tables in the database. You may also want to click Filter Types and choose to view synonyms as well as tables.

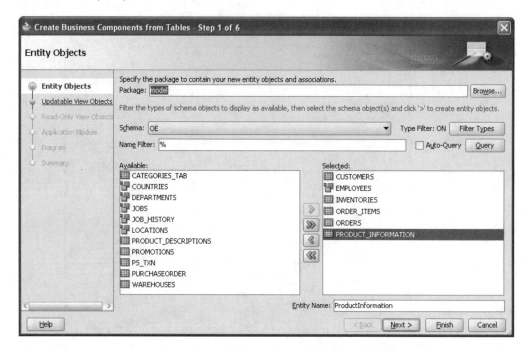

Shuttle over the Customers, Employees, Inventories, Order_Items, Orders, and Product_ Information tables. By default, the entities will be named as per the tables but using CamelCase, but you can change the entity object name on this page. You can also choose a package name to help manage your entity objects. Click Next.

For updateable view objects, shuttle over all the entity objects from the list and enter a different package name for the view objects. In this step you are creating a view object for every entity object. The next step is for read-only view objects, which we are not creating in this case, so you will move to the next step.

Click Next to move to Step 4 of 6, where you can select the *Application Module* check box and enter a package name. This will create an application module based on all of the view objects. You can now click Finish or, optionally, click Next and select *Business Components Diagram* to generate a diagram of the ADF Business Components you have just created.

JDeveloper will now generate the entity objects, associations, view links, view objects, and an application module for implementing a business service based on the chosen database tables.

Testing ADF Business Components

Congratulations! You've just created your first business service using ADF Business Components. Now you will see how you can actually test that business service to see what it does.

JDeveloper provides an indispensable feature called the ADF Business Component browser: it's like a default UI on top of your business service that allows you to test your business service without having to build a UI. Right-click the application module in the Application Navigator and select **Run**. The ADF Business Component browser connects to the database, shows the application module you just created, and shows the view object instances and view links within that application module.

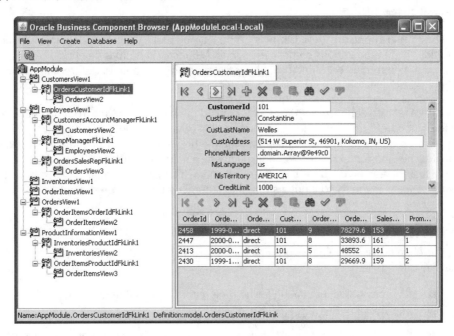

TIP
Once you get further into Fusion application development, you will find the ADF Business Component browser an invaluable aid in debugging your application. Even if you have already built a UI on top of your business service, it is worth checking any business service changes in this tool to help isolate the testing.

Testing Your Business Service

The first thing you will probably notice when looking at the browser for the business service you just created is that your application module has a lot of view object instances in it. The Create Business Components from Tables wizard obviously doesn't know what precise business use case you are trying to build, so it pretty much includes every combination of view object and how it can relate to other view objects. Later in the book, you will see how you can refine the application module to only contain the view object instances that you need.

For the moment, notice that some of the view object instances are top-level nodes while others are subnodes. This is a master/detail relationship, where the top node is the master and the subnode is the detail. This master/detail relationship can be nested down any number of levels.

Browsing Data for a View Object   To browse data for a particular view object instance, double-click the instance name. This opens the instance as a form and retrieves records. If you double-click the link between a master and detail, the data is displayed as a master form with the detail as a table.

You can now use the browser toolbar and menu to navigate through records. Here you can test that the framework is correctly connecting to your database, retrieving, caching, and navigating records.

Testing Operations on View Objects You learned earlier that ADF Business Components provides default operations on business services. Functions such as deleting a record, adding a record or committing or rolling back the translation are available to test from the browser toolbar. There is also a feature to search for specific records.

Testing Default Validation When you created the business service from database tables, information from the underlying tables, including data types and constraints, was read and implemented by the framework. You can use the browser to test this behavior. For example, try to create a new customer record without specifying a value for CustomerId, or use a duplicate value. Note that the framework traps the exception and display an appropriate error. Alternatively, test what happens if you try to input a string into a numeric field like CreditLimit.

Summary

In this chapter, you have built your first business service based on ADF Business Components and have learned that:

- An entity object is a cache for holding records from an underlying database table.
- A view object allows you to select application-specific data into entity objects.
- You can also have read-only view objects that are based on static lists of data.
- View objects can be used to reference information from different entity objects.
- The application module is a transactional container for view object instances.
- The Create Business Components from Tables wizard allows you to quickly build a business service based on tables.
- The ADF Business Component browser allows you to test your business service without the need to develop a UI.

You should now feel more comfortable with the building blocks of ADF Business Components and how you can quickly create and test a business service. The next step is to fine-tune your entity objects and understand more about their features and properties.

CHAPTER
5

The Role of
the Entity Object

ow that you have a working business service, you should feel more comfortable starting to experiment with the features of the entity objects you've just created to see how they work. This chapter looks at some of the different ways you can create, visualize, and edit entity objects and investigates and explains some of the most common features and how to use them.

Understanding Entity Objects

When learning about new technologies, you may find it helpful to map these new ideas to more familiar concepts. Therefore, as a broad generalization, you can think of each entity object as mimicking a database table inside your application. Or, to be more precise, each instance of the entity object represents a database row.

In nearly all cases, you can expect a one-to-one mapping between a database table and an entity object, with each column in the table represented by an entity object attribute. When you create an entity object, each of these attributes is created with a Java-friendly name derived from the column name. For example, the database column CUSTOMER_ID is mapped to the entity object attribute CustomerId. Each entity object attribute also maps a Java type to the underlying SQL data type, including length and precision, and automatically implements column constraints such as not null.

The entity object acts as a cache for data queried from the database and provides functionality to operate on this data. So, for example, setting attribute values, validating data, creating new records, and deleting records are all functions of the entity object.

Managing Your Entity Objects

In Chapter 4 you saw how you could create a business service, including entity objects, all with only a few mouse clicks using the Create Business Components from Tables wizard. This is a great way to get a first cut of your business service, but chances are you are going to want to start fine-tuning those entity objects. Whether it's defining that an attribute is updatable or specifying that an attribute should get its default value from a database sequence, JDeveloper provides a way of defining that framework behavior. Let's take a closer look at how you can work with entity objects.

Creating Entity Objects

There are a number of different ways to create entity objects. You might create multiple entity objects in one pass using the Create Business Components from Tables wizard, or you might create them one at a time, through either a wizard or a diagram. It is really up to you to choose which way suits the job at hand, and this is something you will explore through this chapter. Regardless of which method you use, you still create the same entity object.

At this point, you've created a business service based on a bunch of database tables, but you now realize you need to access information about departments as well. How do you add this to your existing business service?

It's simple. To create an entity object based on departments, select your Model project and the package in which you want to create the entity objects. Select **File** | **New** and, in the New Gallery dialog, select **ADF Business Components** and then **Entity Object**. This launches the Create Entity Object wizard that takes you through the steps to create a single entity object. Select the *Database Schema* "OE" and for *Schema Object* enter "DEPARTMENTS." Click Finish to create a default entity object based on all columns, or click Next to navigate through the wizard.

TIP

If you find you have created an entity object in the wrong package and want to move it, right-click the entity object and select **Refactor** | **Move**. *It's a good idea to periodically refactor the artifacts in your projects to keep things neat and organized.*

Visualizing Entity Objects

Once you have created a few entity objects, wouldn't it be great to get some sort of overview of how they all relate to each other? JDeveloper provides a great feature for visualizing and editing your ADF Business Components: the ADF Business Components diagram.

To create such a diagram, either select the Model project and select **File** | **New** or right-click the Model project and select **New**. In the New Gallery dialog, select **ADF Business Components** and then **Business Components Diagram**. Enter a name for the diagram and then click OK.

JDeveloper creates a blank Business Components diagram onto which you can drag and drop all the entity objects and associations from the Application Navigator. Figure 5-1 shows the resulting visualization of the entity objects and associations after some minor repositioning. This immediately

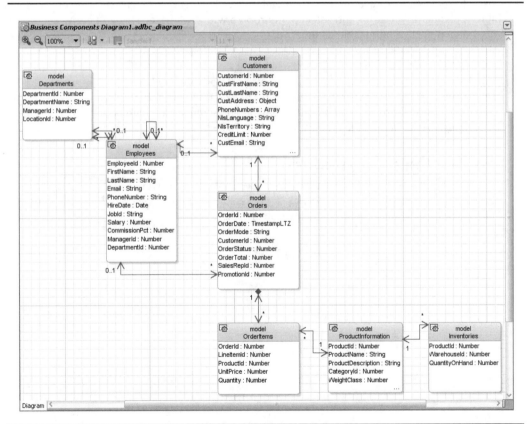

FIGURE 5-1. *Visualizing your ADF Business Components*

gives you an indication of how these entity objects relate to one another. For example, the diagram depicts a one-to-many relationship between Customers and Orders, and an association between Customers and Employees.

TIP
Right-click on the diagram to explore some of the options for laying out the shapes on the diagram, or select a shape and right-click to discover how you can change some of the visual properties of the shape.

As well as providing a useful way of visualizing the business service you are building, the diagram tool enables you to create ADF Business Components directly in the diagram by dragging elements from the Component Palette, or even by dragging tables from the Database Navigator.

Synchronizing Entity Objects with Database Changes

Having previously created an entity object, you might find that your DBA has made some changes to the underlying table, and so the table and the entity object are now out of synch. If you ever need to resynchronize your entity object with the underlying table, right-click the entity object in the Application Navigator and select **Synchronize with Database**. This will allow you to update the entity object with the table changes.

NOTE
This feature does not support synchronizing all possible database changes, such as dropped database columns or data type changes. For these cases you have to manually delete the entity object attribute or change the attribute data type.

Entity Object Attributes

You should now feel familiar with how to create entity objects, so let's drill down and look at the attributes of an entity object. Double-click the Customers entity object in the Application Navigator or diagram to open the entity object editor.

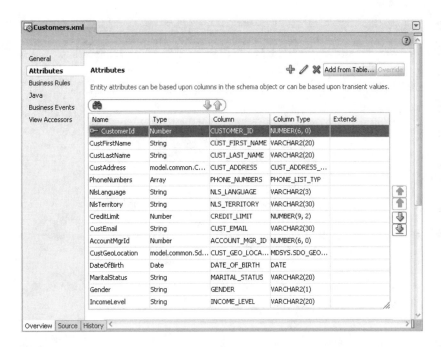

This displays a summary of the attributes for the selected entity object, including attribute name, type, and underlying database column. From here you can start managing the features of your entity object. For example, you might decide that you have an attribute for an underlying database column that you will never use in your application. Does it really make sense to query and cache this column if your application never uses it? In this case you might choose to delete it.

NOTE
If you choose to delete an entity object attribute, JDeveloper will check whether this attribute was used elsewhere (for example, in a view object) and, if so, alert you to the fact.

Double-click the CustomerId attribute to display the Edit Attribute dialog, shown in Figure 5-2. This is where you can explore and fine-tune the functionality for the selected attribute. Let's take a look at some of the more interesting and commonly used properties of an entity object attribute.

NOTE
You can also change the attribute properties using the Property Inspector.

Attribute Types

The SQL world of your database is different from the Java world of your application, and so where you might have been dealing with VARCHAR2 you are now dealing with a Java String. When creating an entity object, JDeveloper reads the data type of the database table column and

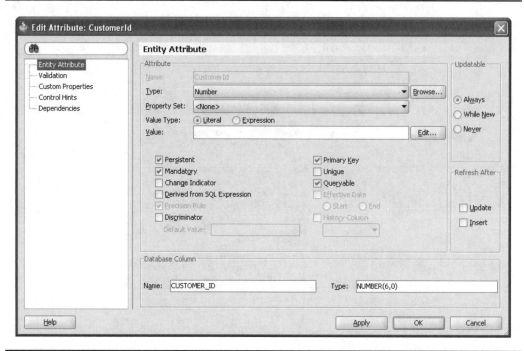

FIGURE 5-2. *Edit Attribute dialog*

maps it to an appropriate Java type. For the most part you can just accept that JDeveloper and the framework does the right thing, and you shouldn't need to change these types. Looking at the Customers entity object, you can see some of the following mapping of types:

Attribute	SQL Data Column	Java Type
CustomerId	NUMBER(6,0)	oracle.jbo.domain.Number
CustFirstName	VARCHAR2(20)	java.lang.String
CreditLimit	NUMBER(9,2)	oracle.jbo.domain.Number
DateOfBirth	DATE	oracle.jbo.domain.Date
PhoneNumbers	PHONE_LIST_TYP	oracle.jbo.domain.Array
CustAddress	CUST_ADDRESS_TYP	model.common.CustAddressTyp

Some of the types, like VARCHAR2, map directly to standard Java classes. Others, like NUMBER, map to framework classes called domains, while more specific types, like CUST_ADDRESS_TYP, map to domains that are created within your project.

Domains So, what are domains? Domains are simply specialized Java classes that wrap the basic Java types and provide additional checks on the data assigned to that type. Oracle ADF provides a number of these classes within the oracle.jbo.domain package. For custom-defined database types like CUST_ADDRESS_TYP, JDeveloper automatically creates a domain for that type within the project, and if you look in the Application Navigator you will see domains created for these complex types in the Model project. You can double-click the domain to open the domain editor.

While JDeveloper automatically creates these domains for you as required, you can also create your own custom domains by selecting **File | New** and, in the New Gallery dialog, select **ADF Business Components** and then **Domain**. One of the benefits of domains is that they can contain their own validation logic. So, for example, you might decide to represent an e-mail address by setting up a domain that contains your own logic on how that domain validates any attribute of that type.

Attribute Value

The value for the entity object attribute comes from the database, but you can define a default value for this attribute. Open the entity object editor and double-click CreditLimit to open the Edit Attribute dialog, shown in Figure 5-3. Set *Value Type* to "Literal" and for *Value* enter "100." This defines that when a new customer is created, the value of CreditLimit will default to the literal value 100. You can test this behavior in the ADF Business Component Browser.

NOTE
This value can also be based on an expression that includes a call to a Java method. This is covered later in this chapter.

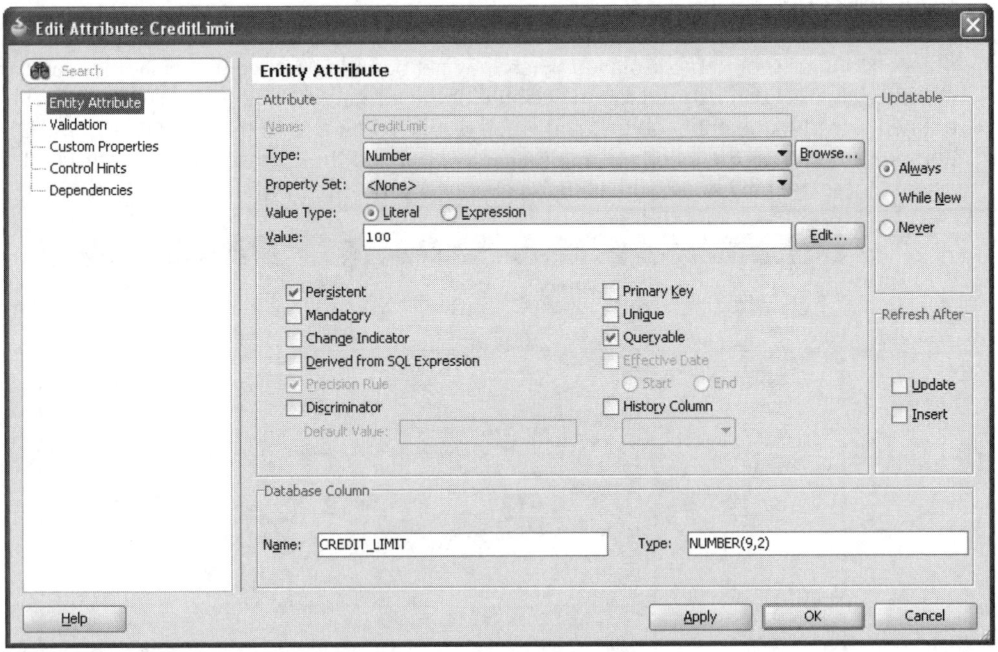

FIGURE 5-3. *CreditLimit attribute properties*

Attribute Properties

Each attribute has a number of properties that control how that attribute behaves. Figure 5-3 shows the attribute properties for CreditLimit.

Some of the more commonly used attribute properties are described next.

Persistent   This property indicates that the attribute is mapped to a column in the database. You can also have attributes that are not based on database columns, which are called transient attributes. Transient attributes can be useful for representing derived or calculated data.

Mandatory   This property indicates that the attribute is required. This is automatically set for attributes based on database columns that have a not null constraint. However, even if the underlying column doesn't have a not null constraint, you might decide that for your application the attribute is mandatory. For example, you might decide that date of birth must be entered for a customer even though it is not mandatory in the underlying database.

Primary Key   An entity object must have one attribute defined as a primary key, and this attribute is automatically set for an attribute based on a database column defined as a primary key. If your underlying table does not have a primary key defined, JDeveloper will create one based on ROWID.

Updatable   You can define when an entity object attribute can be updated: Always, While New, or Never. For example, you might want to define that an order date is only updatable when creating a new record, and cannot be changed once that record has been created.

Controls Hints

A useful feature of ADF Business Components is that you can define hints about how the entity object attributes should be displayed when they get bound to a page. For example, you can define what label will be used for an attribute or the format of a date field. These control hints are defined as part of the entity object, and when displayed on a page the properties of the UI component, such as the label, are automatically bound to the corresponding control hint. Of course, these are only hints, and as such you can override them when designing your UI.

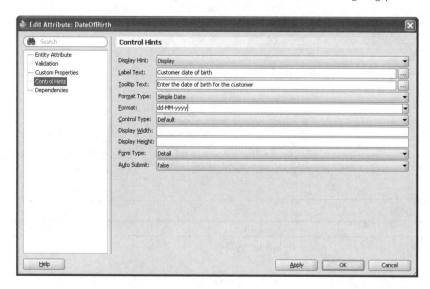

NOTE
Some control hints are not supported when rendered through ADF
Faces. Refer to the JDeveloper documentation for the current list.

Open the entity object editor for Customers, double-click an attribute, and in the Edit Attributes dialog select *Control Hints*. The following list describes the most commonly used hints.

Display Hint   This hint defines whether the appropriate attribute should be displayed. This might be useful if your business service has an attribute that you don't want to expose through the UI, such as a foreign key value that doesn't provide any detail to the end user.

Label Text   This hint allows you to define a string that will be used for the label when rendering this attribute in a UI.

Tooltip Text   A tooltip is a short text string primarily used for help text. For an ADF Faces page, this string is rendered as a help "balloon" when you click inside or, in some cases, hover over a UI component.

Format Type   This property allows you to define how the data should be formatted for date and numeric attributes. Valid values from the drop-down list are SimpleDate, Currency, and Number. For SimpleDate and Number, you can then define a format mask, but for Currency, the browser locale setting automatically controls the format mask.

Format   For a format type of SimpleDate, you can define a date format mask. For example, the 27th of March 2010 with a format of dd-MMM-yyyy would be displayed as 27-Mar-2010 in a browser running with an English-language setting.

NOTE
A common mistake is to try to use an SQL date format. These format
patterns, and the patterns for Number format type, are defined by the
Java specification, and you can get a full list from the appropriate Java
documentation.

TIP
At this point you might want to define some control hints for your
entity object attributes and test them through the ADF Business
Component Browser.

Internationalizing Your Control Hints

As you start defining strings to represent labels and hint text, you might wonder what happens if you want to deploy your application in different languages. Are these strings hard-coded into the entity object? The answer is no. When you define control hints, you should see a file in the Application Navigator called ModelBundle.properties. This file contains the actual strings, and the entity object references those strings.

To create a separate set of translations, create a new properties file by selecting **File | New** and, in the New Gallery dialog, selecting **General** and then **File**. The filename for the translated strings should include a language identifier. So, for German the file would be ModelBundle_de.properties, since "de" is the language identifier for German. You can then copy and paste the strings from the ModelBundle.properties file into the German version of the file and translate accordingly.

You can populate and manage your resource bundles by editing them directly or by selecting **Application | Edit Resource Bundle** and selecting the appropriate resource file.

To test your translations and language-specific control hints such as date format mask, select **Tools | Preferences** and, from the Preferences dialog, select **Business Components** and then **Tester**. This allows you to select the languages you wish to test from within the ADF Business Component Browser.

Now run your application module using the ADF Business Component Browser, and from the menu select **Locale** and choose the language you wish to test. This allows you to test your translated strings for your language-specific properties file as well as test the currency format for data such as the credit limit for a customer.

Property Sets

When defining control hints for a more sizable application, you may well find yourself applying the same control hints to multiple attributes. For example, you might require all date attributes to have the same date format mask and the same help text.

Property sets are a convenient way of grouping together properties like control hints and applying that group to a specific attribute. So, rather than setting *Tooltip Text*, *Format Type*, and *Format* for each date attribute, you can define a property set that includes *Tooltip Text*, *Format Type*, and *Format*, and then apply that property set to all of the attributes.

To create a property set, select **File | New** and, in the New Gallery dialog, select **ADF Business Components** and then **Property Set**. Enter a name for *Property Set Name* and click OK. In the property set editor, click the green plus button to add the following properties, some of which can be translatable:

Property	Value
FMT_FORMAT	`dd-MMM-yyyy`
FMT_FORMATTER	`oracle.jbo.format.DefaultDateFormatter`
TOOLTIP	Enter a date in the format dd-MMM-yyyy

Having defined a property set, you can apply it to an attribute by selecting the attribute and setting *Property Set* to the name of the property set you have just created.

Other Entity Object Features

As you can see already, the entity object provides a rich set of features for mapping your database data into your application. This section introduces other entity object features that are explored in more depth later in the book.

Business Rules

ADF Business Components provides declarative validation features for implementing your business rules. Some of this validation is automatically implemented based on the database column constraints, but you can also define custom validation rules, such as a rule that compares attribute values to ensure that an attribute value appears in a list of values or that an attribute value exists as a key in another entity object.

These validation rules can be defined not only on an attribute, but also at the entity object level. This is covered in detail in Chapter 9.

View Accessors

View accessors provide a convenient way of accessing the data associated with a view object from within an entity object. Why is this useful? Well, suppose you have an entity object validation rule that validates that a salary must be within a specific range for the person's job. However, the salary ranges aren't part of the entity object; they are part of a separate view object. The view accessor allows the source entity object to directly access the view object and read the salary range for that specified job. So you can think of the view accessor as a parameterized connection to a view object.

View accessors are covered when discussing validation in Chapter 8 and Chapter 9.

Associations

It may be stating the obvious, but one of the core characteristics of an application built on a relational database is that its data is related; for example, a foreign key constraint is used to designate that a customer has zero, one, or many orders. In ADF Business Components, you can also define a connection between entity objects, called an association. An association represents a relationship between a source and a destination entity object and allows the framework to access the related entity object at either end of the association. For example, the Customers entity object has an association to the Employees entity object. This allows the framework to easily build join queries where, for example, you want to view the name of a customer's account manager, the details of which are attributes of the Employees entity object.

You can think of an association as being like a wire on a circuit board connecting two components. The wire joins the components so that each one knows about the other and they can work together.

Creating and Editing Associations

Associations can be reverse engineered from database foreign key constraints when creating entity objects, or can be manually created. The Create Business Components from Tables wizard used in Chapter 4 created default associations based on the foreign key constraints in the selected tables. For example, for the entity objects Customers and Employees, an association was created with the name CustomersAccountManagerFkAssoc. The default name in this case is the foreign key name in CamelCase with the suffix "Assoc."

If you have a well-formed database that makes proper use of foreign key constraints, then you can pretty much just accept the default settings and behavior of associations as created by the Create Business Components from Tables wizard.

If your database is missing foreign key constraints, or you would like to create associations that logically exist in your data model but not in the database, then select **File** | **New** and, in the New Gallery dialog, select **ADF Business Components** and then **Association**. To edit an association, double-click the association in the Application Navigator. Whether you're creating a new association or editing an existing one, the following settings may be of interest.

Cardinality

This setting defines the number of instances on either side of an association—for example, one-to-many. When it comes to programmatically working with entity objects and associations, the cardinality defines whether you are accessing a single row or multiple rows. Although you might at first assume differently, this does not constitute a runtime validation.

Source and Destination Attribute

These settings define the attributes that link the source and destination entity objects. Looking at the OrdersCustomerIdFkAssoc, the source entity object, Customers, is associated to the destination entity object, Orders, by the CustomerId attribute. Given the cardinality of 1 to *, this means that for a specific CustomerId, there is a relationship to many Orders.

Accessors

Associations also give you the option of exposing accessors in the optional Java class that backs an entity object. These accessors allow you to programmatically "walk" between entity objects. For example, while writing code to perform a complex validation on the credit limit for a customer, the accessor allows you to programmatically access the instance of the Employees entity object for that customer.

Depending on the cardinality of the association, the accessors could use a framework class representing a single row of data or a collection of rows.

Composition Association

When creating an association between two entity objects, you can choose between two styles of relationship:

- **Reference** The association references a destination entity object
- **Contains** The destination entity can be thought of as a logical subpart of the source

A typical example of a reference association is an account manager for a customer. Both the account manager and the customer can exist independently of each other. So, removing an account manager would not require that account manager's customers to be deleted.

On the other hand, an order item can be thought of as logically being part of an order, and so it makes no sense to have an order item exist independently from an order. This is called a composition association.

For an association, you can define that the framework will implement this composite association behavior and, for example, cascade delete order items when an order is deleted.

Entity Object Classes

Now that you've started to discover and play with the features of entity objects, you might be wondering how the wizards, drag and drop, and setting of properties magically result in the runtime behavior you desire. The simple truth is that the information you have created is used at runtime to instantiate instances of Java classes that drive the framework behavior.

In many cases you probably will never need to have much more than a passing acquaintance with these framework classes. In other cases they will be your first step out of the declarative world into a place where you can start writing your own code.

The Framework Classes

As you learn more and more about Oracle ADF, you will start to become familiar with the various classes that make up the framework, but at the outset the Oracle ADF Java documentation can seem daunting. Which classes or methods are important? Which ones should you extend to add your own functionality?

For an entity object, there are three principal Java classes you will encounter.

EntityDefImpl

The functionality you've built in the entity objects so far is purely defined in XML. When you run your application, this XML information is used to instantiate a class `oracle.jbo.server` `.EntityDefImpl`, which is the definition of your entity object. There will be one instance of this class per unique entity object definition, and the methods available on this class generally relate to modifying the definition of the entity object.

You can think of an instance of this class as a template for the entity object at runtime. At this stage in your learning you'll probably never need to alter the way this works.

EntityCache

As you would expect, an entity object has to cache rows of data coming back from the database. An instance of `oracle.jbo.server.EntityCache` is responsible for providing this cache. You can think of `EntityCache` as a drawer of a filing cabinet where each entity object definition has its own drawer. Again, at this stage you will probably never need to override or directly call methods on this class.

EntityImpl

The `EntityImpl` class is the entity object framework class you will come into contact with most often. Each instantiation of `oracle.jbo.server.EntityImpl` equates to a single row of data, and, continuing the analogy of a filing cabinet drawer, it is like a single sheet of paper held in the filing cabinet drawer. When you create a new row of data, the framework instantiates a new instance of `EntityImpl`. Typical methods available on this class include creating a single row, performing a DML operation on a row, and setting attribute values of a row.

Customizing Entity Object Framework Classes

Now that you've been introduced to the main entity object classes, how and, more importantly, why would you want to change them? The simple answer is that at some point you will probably want to change or augment the default behavior of the framework. You might want to do some additional action when an attribute value is being set, or you may want to perform some logging when a record is deleted. ADF Business Components provides a convenient way to expose a subclass for the entity object classes.

Exposing a Subclass of EntityImpl

As you have just found out, `EntityImpl` is the class that represents a single row of data in the entity object cache. It provides a whole range of methods for acting on attribute values and the row of data.

Open the editor for the Customers entity object and select the *Java* tab. Click the edit pencil icon to display the Select Java Options dialog. Select *Generate Entity Object Class: CustomersImpl*. This will create a Java class `CustomersImpl`, which is a subclass of `EntityImpl`. At this point, you will choose not to generate any of the other entity object classes. Select *Accessors, Create Method, Data Manipulation Methods*, and *Remove Method* and click OK.

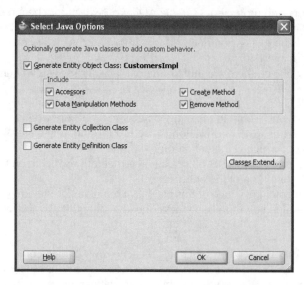

So what did you just do? Well, you asked JDeveloper to create a class that can do all the things `EntityImpl` can do—in Java-speak, a *subclass*—but specifically for the Customers entity object. You have also explicitly requested that the class, called `CustomersImpl`, expose methods that are used when accessing attribute values, creating a row of data, removing a row of data, and performing DML operations on a row of data. You now have the opportunity to augment any of the methods if you so choose.

Go to the Application Navigator and, under the Customers entity object, you should now see the newly created class. Double-click CustomersImpl.java and take a look at what JDeveloper has created, described next.

Accessors   Either by using the Java editor or the Structure window, you should see pairs of set and get methods for each attribute in the entity object. For example:

```
public String getCustLastName() {
    return (String)getAttributeInternal(CUSTLASTNAME);
}
public void setCustLastName(String value) {
    setAttributeInternal(CUSTLASTNAME, value);
}
```

The framework calls these methods whenever the value of an attribute is set or retrieved from the cache. So, if you want to force an attribute value to be displayed in uppercase, you could set the return value from the method getCustLastName() to uppercase using something like

```
public String getCustLastName() {
        String lastName = (String)getAttributeInternal(CUSTLASTNAME);
        if (lastName != null) {
            return lastName.toUpperCase();
        } else {
            return lastName;
        }
    }
```

TIP
It is good practice to test for null to prevent runtime exceptions.

create() Method   In the Select Java Options dialog, you chose to expose the following method:

```
protected void create(AttributeList attributeList) {
        super.create(attributeList);
    }
```

This is the method the framework will use when a new customer row is created, allowing you to augment the default behavior, such as setting default values.

remove() Method   You also chose to expose the following method:

```
public void remove() {
        super.remove();
    }
```

This allows you to add your own code to the framework method called when a customer row is removed. For example, you can add validation logic to prevent the removal of a record if a certain condition is met.

Data Manipulation Method   The previously discussed methods are used to manage the data and rows within your entity object cache. At some point that data will be committed to the database, in which case the following method is called:

```
protected void doDML(int operation, TransactionEvent e) {
        super.doDML(operation, e);
    }
```

This method allows you to write code at the point at which cached rows are inserted, updated, or deleted from the database. This might be an ideal point for adding extra logic before data changes are passed to the database. The operation parameter allows the method to distinguish between DML_UPDATE, DML_INSERT, and DML_DELETE.

TIP

For each of these methods, go in and add some `System.out`
.println() statements and then run the application module in the
ADF Business Component Browser. This will output a message to the
JDeveloper Log window indicating where the framework is reading
and writing values and updating rows.

Reading a Sequence in EntityImpl

Of course, one of the common uses of the `EntityImpl` class is to add code to perform a specific action on an entity object instance. For example, the code could read a database sequence and assign the value to the CustomerId. Adding the following method to the `CustomersImpl` class provides the functionality to read the next value from a database sequence:

```
protected Number nextVal(String sequenceName) {
    SequenceImpl s = new SequenceImpl(sequenceName, getDBTransaction());
    return s.getSequenceNumber();
}
```

NOTE

If JDeveloper does not prompt you, you will need to explicitly import
`oracle.jbo.server.SequenceImpl`.

The code creates an object of type `SequenceImpl`, which represents a database sequence, the name of which is passed into the method. The call to `getDBTransaction` is a call to a method on the `EntityImpl` that, not surprisingly, returns information about the database transaction for this entity object. The method then returns the next value in that sequence.

NOTE

If one does not already exist, you may have to create an appropriate
database sequence. You can do this in JDeveloper from the Database
Navigator window by going to the database connection for your
application and right-clicking Sequences and selecting **New**
Sequence.

Calling the Sequence from the Entity Object

So, how do you call this method when a new customer is being created? It's quite simple. You can call it from the `create()` method to set the value of CustomerId:

```
protected void create(AttributeList attributeList) {
    super.create(attributeList);
    setCustomerId(nextVal("Customer_Seq"));
}
```

However, there is another way you can do this rather than adding code to the `create()` method. Earlier in the chapter you learned about default values and how they can be set for an entity object attribute. Wouldn't it be useful if you could define that this method should be called to resolve the default value for CustomerId?

The good news is, you can. Going back to the Edit Attribute dialog for CustomerId, set *Value Type* to "Expression" and enter "adf.object.nextVal("Customer_seq");" for *Value*. This is a special notation using a scripting language called Groovy, more of which is covered later in the book.

At this point, all you need to know is that the notation `adf.object` allows you to access methods on the `CustomersEntityImpl` instance. Thus, when a default value is required for CustomerId, the framework will automatically call this method.

Summary

You now have a deeper understanding of the features of entity objects and associations and have learned that:

■   You can quickly create and visualize entity objects.

■   An entity object can be synchronized with database changes.

■   Oracle ADF provides mappings between database types and Java types.

■   Domains are specialized classes that simplify type mapping.

■   An entity object attribute can be set to be updatable: Always, Never, or While New.

■   An entity object can define hints for labels, help, and data formatting.

■   Associations define relationships between entity objects.

■   Oracle ADF uses framework classes to implement the entity object functionality.

■   These framework classes can be subclassed and exposed so you can add your own code.

■   You can define a database sequence for an entity object attribute.

With your new-found understanding of entity objects, you should feel at ease exploring the various features and testing through the ADF Business Component Browser. The next chapter will extend this knowledge into view objects.

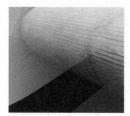

CHAPTER

6

View Objects: A Window to Your Data

S o far, you've pretty much relied on your database model to drive your business services development, which is a reasonable approach given that a sizable proportion of your application will typically be manipulating that data. However, what makes for a good database design doesn't necessarily reflect the way your application will expose data to your end user or the developer consuming your business service. This is where view objects are used to shape your underlying data sources into application-specific views.

This chapter shows how to create, manage, and edit view objects, including how you can create view objects from different underlying data sources, build master/detail relationships, and define default and calculated values for view object attributes.

Understanding View Objects

If you picture entity objects as database tables inside your application, then a view object is like a database view on those tables. And just like a database view, a view object definition is more or less just a `select` statement that shapes, filters, joins, and orders application data.

For each view object, the framework automatically creates a runtime instance of a view object cache. This view object cache doesn't hold any rows of data as such, but is instead a collection of pointers to rows in the underlying entity object. It is this view object cache that is bound to a UI item, like a table, so that you see the queried records and attributes as defined by your view object.

For example, if you had a view object for U.S. customers and a view object for high-earning global customers, there would be two view object caches containing different view rows. As shown in Figure 6-1, each view object row is pointing to a physically cached row in the same Customers entity object. Sometimes the view object caches contain pointers to the same entity object row. This means that if a row is updated through one view, then the change is automatically seen in the other view.

Extending the filing cabinet analogy used to explain entity objects, it's like having two folders marked "US Customers" and "High Earning Global Customers," each folder containing a separate sheet of paper per record. On each sheet of paper is information detailing in which filing cabinet drawer the actual data is held.

As well as defining an application-specific view of data, view objects are linked together by view links to define relationships between those views. For example, you may decide your application will never expose a list of all orders, but rather will expose only the orders for a specific customer. Thus, the combination of view objects, linked together by view links, becomes the building blocks of your application data model. And this is an important fact to bear in mind when building your view objects: it is this data model of view object instances that will be exposed through an application module to the UI developer when constructing the UI pages.

TIP

When designing your view objects, you might find it useful to think about your UI design: What information do you want to display on your UI pages? How do you want those pages to flow? Thinking "UI first" can be a useful notion when building view objects.

US Customers

101	Constantine	Welles	+1 317 123 4104
102	Harrison	Pacino	+1 317 123 4111
103	Manisha	Taylor	+1 812 123 4115
104	Harrison	Sutherland	+1 317 123 4126'
105	Matthias	MacGraw	+1 812 123 4129

High Spending Global Customers

344	Marlon	Godard	JAPAN
326	Hal	Olin	GERMANY
103	Manisha	Taylor	AMERICA

US Customers view object

Select CUSTOMER_ID, CUST_FIRST_NAME,
CUST_LAST_NAME, PHONE_NUMBERS from CUSTOMERS
where NLS_TERRITORY = 'AMERICA' order by CUSTOMER_ID

High Spending Global view object

Select CUSTOMER_ID, CUST_FIRST_NAME,
CUST_LAST_NAME, NLS_TERRITORY FROM CUSTOMERS
where INCOME_LEVEL = 'H: 150,000 – 169,999' order by CUST_LAST_NAME

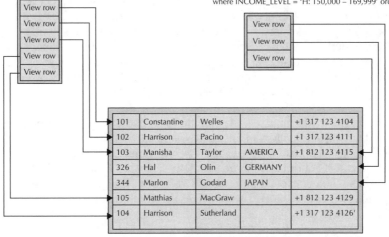

FIGURE 6-1. *View object rows point to entity object rows.*

Managing Your View Objects

In Chapter 4 the Create Business Components from Tables wizard created default view objects for each of the entity objects, with each of these view objects selecting all the attributes from the corresponding entity object. This provides a good starting point, but in reality you will want to start shaping these view objects to your application needs.

Creating View Objects

First off, it's worth looking at how to create view objects. Just like entity objects, there are a number of different ways to create a view object. Regardless of the method you choose, you will still end up with the same view object.

In Chapter 5 you created a Departments entity object. If you want to expose this through a view object, you could select **File** | **New** and, from the New Gallery dialog, select **ADF Business Components** and then **View Object**. This launches the Create View Object wizard that takes you through the steps of selecting the underlying entity object(s) and attributes to create a view object.

Alternatively, you can right-click the Departments entity object in the Application Navigator and select **New Default View Object**. This opens the Create Default View Object dialog, into which you can enter for *Package* "views" and for *Name* "DepartmentsView." This will create a view object based on all of the attributes of the Departments entity object.

Double-click the newly created DepartmentsView view object in the Application Navigator to open the view object editor. Select the *Entity Objects* tab to confirm that this view object is based on the Departments entity object. You can also select the *Attributes* tab to confirm that each of the entity object attributes is mapped in this view object.

Read-Only View Objects

With a view object based on an entity object, the entity object is providing a cache into which data is stored for update. However, what happens if you have static data that never changes, like a list of countries or list of valid values for a field? Do you need the overhead of an entity object?

ADF Business Components allows you to define a view object based only on a `select` statement with no underlying entity object. Even so, the current thinking is that for database data that never changes, there is actually very little to be gained from, and in fact some drawbacks to, using a view object with no underlying entity object. If you do require a view object that represents read-only data, create the entity object and the view object, and set the view object to be read-only.

So, for this application you might decide that the list of departments is never going to change and so is read-only in the application. In this case, you need to ensure that the DepartmentsView view object does not try to update the Departments entity object.

Open the view object editor for DepartmentsView, select the *Entity Objects* tab, and select the Departments entity object. Now deselect *Updatable* to prevent the DepartmentsView view object from updating the entity object. This indicates that for this view object, the underlying entity object is not updatable.

Read-Only View Object Based on a Static List   One use case where a view object with no underlying entity object can be useful is for a list of static data used in validation or a list of values. Consider the CustomersView attribute MaritalStatus. The possible values for this field are static and can only ever be "single," "married," "widowed," "divorced," or "separated." For this case you can create a view object based on a list of static data and then use this view object as the list of valid values.

Select **File | New** and, from the New Gallery dialog, select **ADF Business Components** and then **View Object**. Enter a *Name* of "MaritalStatusView" and select *Rows Populated at design time (Static List)*. Click Next. Click New to enter a new attribute. Enter *Name* "MarriedStatus" of type String and select *Key Attribute*. You can then add the possible values for the attribute and click Finish.

This gives you a new read-only view object whose only data is five static strings. Later, in Chapter 9, this view object will be used to define the list of valid values for the MaritalStatus attribute.

NOTE
The strings you just entered as static values are stored in a translatable resource bundle, so you can easily translate them.

Managing View Object Attributes

Most of the view objects created so far have a one-to-one mapping of a view object attribute to an entity object attribute. Let's take a closer look at these attributes. Open CustomersView in the view object editor and select the *Attributes* tab.

Figure 6-2 shows the view object editor, which should look familiar, as it is very similar to the entity object editor. It shows a list of attributes for the view object, each of which has the same name and type as its underlying entity object attribute.

Assuming that CustomersView is your application-specific view of a customer, you can decide which attributes are required in your application. For example, you may decide that for this application, when dealing with a customer, you don't plan on exposing the customer's address, CustAddress, or geographic reference data, CustGeoLocation. You can therefore remove these from your view of customers.

NOTE
By choosing to remove these attributes from the view object and not from the entity object, you are deciding that this data might still be used elsewhere in the application—just not in CustomersView.

Simply select each attribute and click the red cross button to remove the attributes from the view object.

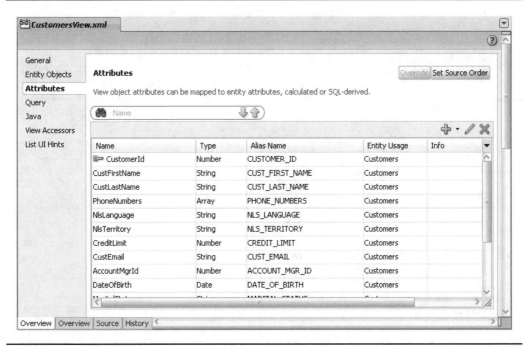

FIGURE 6-2. *View object editor for CustomersView*

Types of View Object Attributes

For the most part, the view object attributes are based on entity object attributes, and that will generally be the case throughout this book. However, it is useful to know that view object attributes can also be based on an SQL expression or a calculation derived from other view object attributes. Later in this chapter you will see how to define a view object attribute whose value is based on a calculation.

Attribute Settings

Just like an entity object attribute, each view object attribute has a number of settings to control its behavior. From the view object editor for CustomersView, double-click an attribute to open the Edit Attribute dialog. Many of these properties, such as *Updatable*, perform the same function as in the entity object.

Control Hints

You discovered in the previous chapter that entity objects could define hints such as a label and date format for an attribute. The same functionality is also available in the view object. If you define control hints in the view object, they will override any control hints defined in the entity object. Double-click a view object attribute and select *Control Hints* to set control hints for this view object.

The View Object Query

When you define a view object through the various dialogs and editors in JDeveloper, what you are actually doing is instructing JDeveloper to construct a query that will be used to select data into your application. To demonstrate this, open the view object editor for CustomersView and select the *Query* tab.

Here you can see the `select` statement that JDeveloper has created; note the absence of CustAddress and CustGeoLocation, which were removed from the view object earlier.

TIP
*As you go through this chapter, it is useful to go back to the query and
see how it changes as you edit your view object. This helps give you
an insight into how JDeveloper is implementing the features you are
building into the view object.*

Setting an order by Clause

When testing your business service in the ADF Business Component Browser, you might have
noticed that the customer data wasn't being retrieved in any discernable order. For this application,
you would like to order your customers by their customer Id.

Given that you know the view object is shaping the view of your application data, and the
fact that there is a `select` statement behind the scenes, it should not be surprising to learn that
the view object allows you to set an `order by` clause.

In the view object editor for CustomersView, select the *Query* tab and click the edit pencil
icon to display the Edit Query dialog, as shown in Figure 6-3.

Set *Order By* to "CUSTOMER_ID," noting that as you type, the `select` statement is
automatically updated. Test this change in the ADF Business Component Browser to ensure that
your customer information is being displayed in the correct order.

You can also set an appropriate order for some of the other view objects.

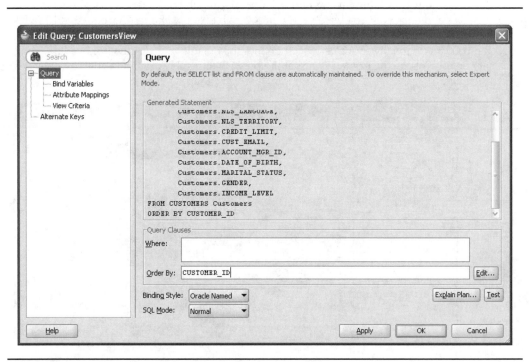

FIGURE 6-3. *Editing the query clause for CustomersView*

Setting a where Clause

Having defined a sort order for your customer data, what happens if you want to filter that data? For example, if this application is used only in your U.S. office, then maybe it makes sense to only show U.S. customers. Figure 6-3 shows that you can also define a `where` clause. Assuming NlsTerritory is the attribute on which you test whether a customer is a U.S. customer, set *Where* to "NLS_TERRITORY='AMERICA'" and test it in the ADF Business Component Browser. This will bring back only customers who are based in the United States, ordered by their ID.

Bind Variables

You should now start to see how the view object could be used to shape your data into an application-specific view. However, what if you require a little more flexibility in how you shape this data? For example, in the preceding section, a `where` clause was used to filter customers. What if your application is being deployed globally and some users will be dealing with the Italian customer base? Do you create a view object for U.S. customers and one for Italian customers?

Well, you could, but that would be overkill. Instead, you can use bind variables to introduce parameters into the view object `select` statement. Separate instances of this parameterized view object can then be added to the application module, with the bind variable specified for each instance. Alternatively, a single instance of the view object could be added to the application module and the value of the bind variables could be set at runtime based on some programmatic factor, such as detecting the country of the logged-in user or selecting a value in a search form.

Creating a Bind Variable for a where Clause   From the Edit Query dialog, select *Bind Variables* and click New to create a new bind variable. Set *Name* to "Territory_bind" and accept the other default values.

You can optionally set *Value*, which defines the default value for the bind variable, and also set control hints on the *Control Hints* tab if you wish to display the bind variable to the end user. Click OK.

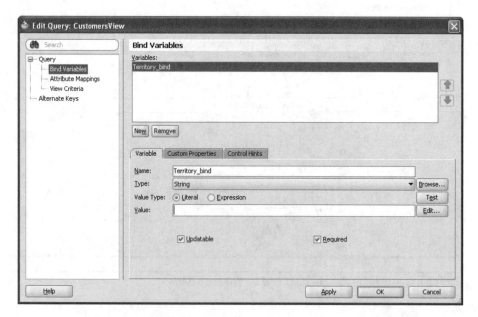

Now in your query set *Where* to "NLS_TERRITORY LIKE :Territory_bind ||'%'" and click OK. You can now test through the ADF Business Component Browser, and when you select CustomersView1 you will be prompted for a value for the bind variable. Try entering "ITALY" or "INDIA" to automatically filter the data.

Bind variables are an important feature of view objects and demonstrate how you can dynamically define parameters for a view object's query. However, for the purposes of this application, you are going to be working with all possible customers, so it's not required for this application.

View Object Lookups

So far your business service has had a one-to-one relationship between an entity object and a view object. The CustomersView view object maps to the Customers entity object, and only that entity object. However, the reality is that when dealing with information about a customer, the end user really requires information pulled from a number of different sources. For example, CustomersView has an attribute AccountMgrId, which is the identifier for the account manager assigned to this customer. The problem here is that the value of AccountMgrId is something like "145" and so really doesn't mean anything to the end user. Instead, the application should show the name of the account manager looked up from the Employees table using AccountMgrId.

ADF Business Components provides a feature that allows a view object to be based on more than one entity object and takes care of looking up the correct information from the various entity objects.

Creating a View Object Lookup

Continuing the previous example, open CustomersView in the view object editor, select the *Entity Objects* tab, and move "Employees" to the *Selected* list. By doing this, you are defining that this view object is based on both the Customers and the Employees entity objects.

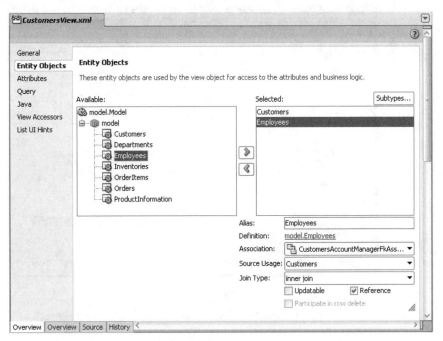

NOTE
At this point JDeveloper may display a warning that the query has a custom where *clause. This is to alert you that JDeveloper is about to alter the view object SQL statement and, if you have added a* where *clause, your custom edit may be overwritten. If this occurs, you should choose to overwrite your custom* where *clause. You can reapply it at a later point.*

At this point accept the defaults for the other values on this view object editor page.

NOTE
When you added Employees to the Selected list, you may have noticed that JDeveloper automatically picked up the association CustomerAccountManagerFkAssoc. This was the association created automatically based on the foreign key relationship between the tables Customers and Employees. The framework uses this association to ensure that you are looking up the correct employee information based on the AccountMgrId.

The next step is to define which attributes from the Employees entity object you want to include in the CustomersView view object. From the view object editor, select the *Attributes* tab, select the down arrow icon that is part of the green plus button, and select **Add Attribute from Entity**. Move FirstName and LastName from the *Available* list to the *Selected* list, noting that EmployeeId is automatically included as well since this is a key in this relationship. It's important not to remove this attribute because the framework uses both instances of EmployeeId for coordination.

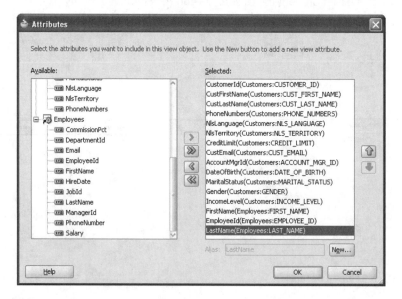

You can optionally set control hints for these attributes. For example, you might choose that EmployeeId from the Employees entity object should have *Display Hint* set to "Hide."

Run and test CustomersView in the ADF Business Component Browser. You will see that the AccountMgrId attribute value is being used to look up the name of the account manager from the Employees entity object. Furthermore, if you change the value of AccountMgrId to a valid value, the correct employee name is shown.

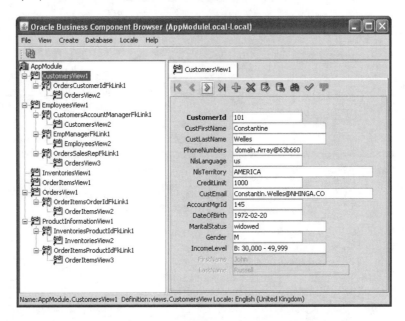

You will probably notice that attributes referenced from the Employees entity object are read-only. This is probably what you require in most cases; however, you can set these attributes to be updatable when defining the lookup.

TIP
Look at the query for CustomersView to see how the view object is implementing this lookup. You may also want to add lookups in other view objects where it might make sense; for example, OrderItemsView to look up product name and product description from the ProductInformation entity object.

Visualizing View Objects

Just like entity objects, you can visualize view objects on an ADF Business Components diagram by dragging them from the Application Navigator onto the ADF Business Components diagram. Figure 6-4 shows view objects and view links after some repositioning.

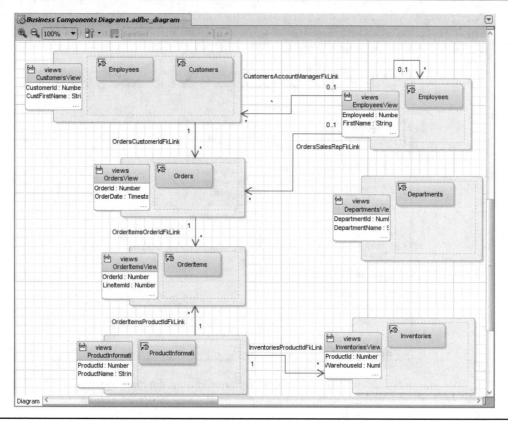

FIGURE 6-4. *Visualizing view objects*

Implementing Calculated Attributes

You have already been introduced to the concept of a transient attribute in an entity object. You can also have a view object transient attribute: one that is not based on a query or entity object attribute. This is a useful feature of ADF Business Components, allowing a view object to represent an attribute that has a value based on a calculation.

Calculating the Total for a Line Item

Consider the following example. The OrderItemsView view object includes attributes to represent the various line items within an order, including UnitPrice and Quantity. It is the data for these attributes that is persisted to the database; however, wouldn't it be useful to have an attribute that shows the total for each order item—that is, the product of UnitPrice and Quantity?

Creating the Attribute The first step is to create the transient attribute. Open the view object editor for OrdersItemsView. Select the *Attributes* tab and select the green plus button to create a new attribute. For *Name* enter "LineTotal," and *Type* should be "Number."

You now need to define that this attribute derives its value from the product of two other attributes. Select *Expression*, since this field is going to be based on an expression, and for *Value* enter "Quantity * UnitPrice."

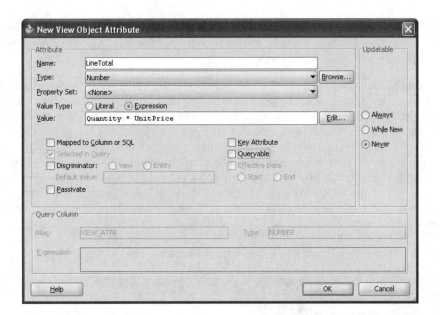

You will also want to define that LineTotal should be recalculated if either Quantity or UnitPrice changes. To do this, click Edit and select the two attributes into the *Selected* field to ensure an automatic recalculation.

You should also take the opportunity to look at the properties that are available for this attribute. For example, *Queryable* is set to false and *Updatable* is set to "Never." You would never want to query on this attribute, and you wouldn't want the end user to update it directly. Click OK.

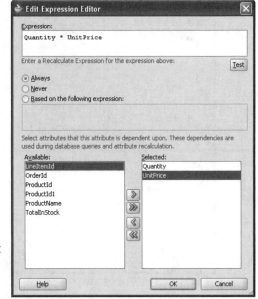

At this point you might decide to add some control hints to the attribute, such as a label and a format mask.

Again, you can test this new attribute through the ADF Business Component Browser. Notice that when you change either UnitPrice or Quantity, the framework automatically recalculates LineTotal.

Concatenating Attribute Values and Dependencies

Earlier in this chapter you implemented a lookup to bring FirstName and LastName from the Employees entity object. However, you might decide that you want to require this string to be concatenated into a single attribute. A single attribute might be more convenient if, for example, throughout the application you always display the first and last name together when dealing with an account manager.

In this case, you could introduce a transient attribute into CustomersView, whose value is a concatenation of FirstName and LastName, optionally choosing to set the control hint *Display Hint* for these two attributes to "Hide."

Creating the Attribute   Create a transient attribute AccountMgrFullName of type String in CustomersView and set *Value* to be an expression "FirstName + " " + LastName." You can now test using the ADF Business Component Browser. When testing, you might discover a problem. Although the new attribute seems to reflect the correct information, when you change the AccountMgrId for a customer, AccountMgrFullName is not updated. Why is that?

The reason is quite simple, and there is a simple solution. When you change AccountMgrId, the framework automatically looks up the FirstName and LastName from the Employees entity object and updates those attributes. However, AccountMgrFullName doesn't know it also has to refresh itself when this happens. You therefore have to explicitly mark that AccountMgrFullName should be refreshed when AccountMgrId is changed.

To do this, open the view object editor for CustomersView, double-click AccountMgrFullName, select the *Dependencies* tab, and move AccountMgrId from the *Available* list to the *Selected* list.

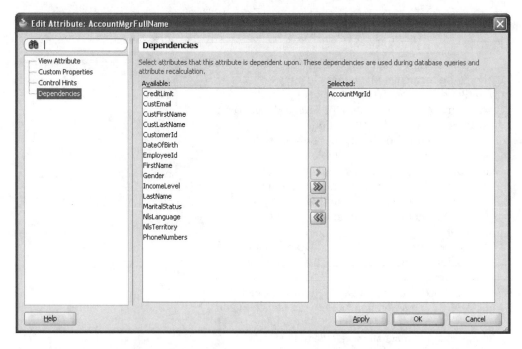

You can now retest and check that AccountMgrFullName is updated when you enter a new value for AccountMgrId.

Calculating Based on Attributes from a Different View Object
So far, the transient attribute values in the previous two examples have come from attributes in the same view object. However, what if you want to access an attribute in a different view object?

Suppose you would like to have information about the average order for a particular customer. That means you have to access OrderTotal in the OrdersView view object to perform this calculation. How can you access attributes of OrdersView from CustomersView? The answer is to use accessors.

A Quick Overview of Accessors   Chapter 5 briefly touched on the concept of accessors when introducing associations. An accessor, as the name implies, provides a means of accessing one view object from another view object. If you look at the view object editor, you will see a tab *View Accessors* where you can explicitly define which other view objects this view object can access.

However, view links implicitly define view accessors as the way of defining the master/detail link between two view objects. So, if you have view links linking two view objects, you shouldn't need to explicitly create accessors. View links and accessors are covered in more detail later in this chapter.

Creating the Attribute   Create a new transient attribute CustOrderAvg of type Number in CustomersView, and set *Value* to be an expression "OrdersView.avg("OrderTotal")."

So, what have you just done? Well, the expression you have just written is a notation called Groovy, which was touched on in Chapter 5 and will be more fully explored later, in Chapter 9. The notation has a built-in function `avg` that takes a parameter representing the name of the attribute to be averaged. To complete the expression, a view accessor name is used to indicate which view object is "accessed" from the current view object to perform the operation.

The view accessor is defined in the view link OrdersCustomerIdFkLink, and provides a handle to access the source or the destination view object at either end of a view link. So the OrdersView accessor allows CustomersView to access the OrdersView view object.

NOTE
By default the accessor, OrdersView, has the same name as the view object it refers to. Just remember that the expression you are using is based on the accessor name, not the view object name. If you were to change the name of the accessor to OrdersAccessor, then the expression would have to change to "OrdersAccessor. avg("OrderTotal")."

Run and test in the ADF Business Component Browser and check that the new attribute shows the average order for each customer.

Creating View Links

Now that you have fine-tuned your view objects to bring back the right data in the right order, the next step is to link these views together to give the correct hierarchy to the business service. View links provide the ability to describe a master/detail relationship between two view objects. The view link defines a source attribute in the master view object and the corresponding destination attribute in the detail view object. So you can have a view object OrdersView that shows all orders, but if you want to see only the orders for a specific customer, then you would require a view link to link OrdersView to CustomersView.

When you used the Create Business Components from Tables wizard in Chapter 4, JDeveloper created a number of view links based on the relationships between the tables. Referring back to Figure 6-4, you can see the view links, the view link names, and the view objects for which a relationship is defined. For this application, the Create Business Components from Tables wizard pretty much created all the view links required. In fact, there may be some view links you don't need. For example, OrdersSalesRepFKLink defines a master/detail relationship between EmployeesView and OrdersView. This would be useful if you want to see all the orders for which an employee is the sales rep, but this is not something that will be required in this application. You will probably want to delete any view links that are not required, but there is no harm in keeping them while you are still experimenting with the features of the framework.

However, there are two relationships for which view links don't currently exist. What if you want to view the employees in a specific department? Or what if you want to view the stock levels in your warehouses for a specific order item? Referring back to Figure 6-4, you can see that there is no view link linking DepartmentsView to EmployeesView or linking OrderItemsView to InventoriesView. This means that your business service, as it stands, can't show the employees within a specific department or the inventory level for a specific order item.

So let's have a look at how to create these view links.

NOTE
Using the Create Business Components from Tables wizard on the Employees and Departments tables would automatically create view links based on the foreign key constraints.

As you might have guessed, there are a number of different ways to create a view link; however, it doesn't matter which method you choose. Here are two options.

Creating a View Link from the Application Navigator

The first and most obvious option is to create a view link from the Application Navigator. Select **File | New** and, from the New Gallery dialog, select **ADF Business Components** and then **View Link**. This opens the Create View Link wizard. For *Name* enter "InventoryForOrderItemsVL" and then click Next. This page is where you define which view objects are to be linked. From *Select Source Attribute* select OrderItemsView and the ProductId attribute. From *Select Destination Attribute* select InventoriesView and the ProductId attribute. Click Add, then click Next.

The next page allows you to define whether you want an accessor exposed in the source or destination view object. By specifying an accessor, you provide the ability for a view object to programmatically "walk" to another view object and access attribute values from that view object. It is this functionality that was used to populate CustOrderAvg with the average order based on the OrdersView view object.

You can now either click Finish or click Next and accept the default values as you step through the remaining pages of the wizard.

You have just defined that there is a master/detail relationship between order items and inventories based on the ProductId. If you now look at the ADF Business Components diagram, as shown in Figure 6-5, you should see the newly created view link linking OrderItemsView and InventoriesView.

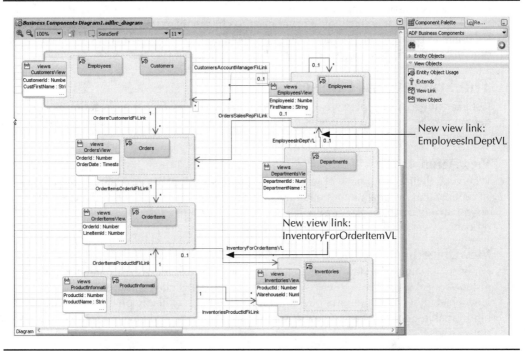

FIGURE 6-5. *ADF Business Components diagram showing newly created view links*

Creating a View Link from the ADF Business Components Diagram

Another way to create a view link is to draw a line between two view objects on the ADF Business Components diagram. With the ADF Business Components diagram open, go to the Component Palette and, under View Objects, select View Link. On the ADF Business Components diagram, click DepartmentsView. This drops an anchor for drawing a line and indicates that DepartmentsView is the master view object. Click on EmployeesView to complete the line and to indicate that EmployeesView is the detail view object. Enter the name "EmployeesInDeptVL." You can see this newly created view link in Figure 6-5.

So, using the ADF Business Components diagram, you were able to directly link two view objects and create a master/detail relationship. But how did JDeveloper know that this view link was to be based on the DepartmentId? Well, because there was already an association between the underlying entity objects, JDeveloper used that as the assumption for this view link.

View Object Classes

You've now gained some more understanding of and experience using view objects and their features and have built some more functionality into your application. Through the various wizards and dialogs, you have been defining information about your view objects and how they should function. When it comes to running your application, that information is read by a number of framework classes to implement the runtime behavior. Generally speaking, and certainly in these early days of learning, you'll never need to change these framework classes. Nevertheless, it's useful to be aware of the main classes involved and what they do. This section provides an outline of these classes, which are covered in more detail in Chapter 18.

The Framework Classes

Just like entity objects, there are a number of framework classes that are responsible for taking the definition of features you have built through the JDeveloper dialogs and turning that into runtime behavior.

ViewDefImpl

When you defined your view objects, JDeveloper assembled that information into an XML file. At runtime that metadata information about each view object definition is represented within an instance of `oracle.jbo.server.ViewDefImpl`. At this stage in your learning, you'll probably never need to alter the way this works.

ViewObjectImpl

For every instance of a view object in the data model, the framework instantiates a separate instance of `oracle.jbo.server.ViewObjectImpl`. This class is responsible for managing the view object query and the rows queried. Typical methods available on this class include setting bind variables, changing a `where` clause, executing a query, and navigating through the view object rows.

ViewRowImpl

Each instance of `ViewObjectImpl` manages a set of queried rows, each row being a pointer to the underlying entity object instance. Each of these view object rows is an instance of `oracle.jbo.server.ViewRowImpl`. `ViewRowImpl` provides methods for getting and setting view object attribute values.

TIP
If you are curious about these classes, you can enter the class name into the JDeveloper help system to find the Java documentation. You might find the number of methods daunting, but it is useful to know that the list of methods for a class can be found here.

Customizing View Object Framework Classes

Just like for an entity object, JDeveloper gives you the option of exposing a subclass of each of these framework classes if you want to augment or change the default framework behavior for a particular view object. Suppose that you are happy with the default functionality you've defined for your view objects, but you want to alter the rows returned by the CustomersView view object based on some runtime condition. In this case, you can subclass the framework class and add your own code to deal with this condition.

Exposing a Subclass of ViewObjectImpl

As you now know, `ViewObjectImpl` is the class that represents a view object and provides methods for managing instances of that view object.

Open the editor for the CustomersView view object and select the *Java* tab. Select the edit pencil icon to display the Select Java Options dialog. Select *Generate View Object Class: CustomersViewImpl* and also select *Include custom Java data source methods*.

This will generate a Java class `CustomersViewImpl`. So, what use is that to you? Well, this will be covered in more detail in Chapter 18, but for now you have a subclass that allows you to programmatically manage how your CustomersView view object behaves.

Go to the Application Navigator and double-click CustomersViewImpl.java. In the Java editor, locate the method `executeQueryForCollection()`. This is the method the framework calls to execute the CustomersView view object query. You can now programmatically alter the `where` clause of this view object by making a call to `setWhereClause()`, which is a method available through the parent `ViewObjectImpl` class:

```
protected void executeQueryForCollection(Object qc, Object[] params,
                                         int noUserParams) {

    //You could have some conditional IF statement here.
    setWhereClause("NLS_TERRITORY = 'ITALY'");
    super.executeQueryForCollection(qc, params, noUserParams);
}
```

Of course, this is a trivial example, but it demonstrates how you can use a subclass of `ViewObjectImpl` to programmatically control a view object at runtime.

Creating a Custom Service Method

Consider another example of where you may want to write custom code in a view object to address a business requirement and have that code exposed to the consuming client. Currently, the view object allows you to delete a customer order; however, rather than simply deleting the record, you want to retain the record but set the OrderStatus to indicate it has been cancelled. Furthermore, the cancelled order should now be assigned to a customer care representative for a courtesy call to the customer.

In this case, you can write a view object method to encapsulate the functionality, and then expose that method to the client in the same way the default methods such as delete and create are already exposed.

To do this, generate `viewObjectImpl` and `viewRowImpl` subclasses for OrdersView, choosing to expose accessors for `OrdersViewRowImpl`.

You can now add the following code to `OrdersViewImpl`. This will check whether the current order is live and, if so, will set the status to indicate it has been cancelled and assign the order to a customer care representative.

NOTE
JDeveloper may ask you to import `oracle.jbo.domain.Number`.

```java
public boolean cancelCurrentOrder() {

    OrdersViewRowImpl cr = (OrdersViewRowImpl)getCurrentRow();

    //Check to see if the order is currently "live" (orderStatus=1)
    if (cr.getOrderStatus().equals(new Number(1))) {
        //Set the order to cancelled by customer (status 3)
        cr.setOrderStatus(new Number(3));

        //Now assign to a new customer care rep.
        cr.setSalesRepId(new Number(101));
        return true;

    }
    return false;
}
```

Having written the method, you need to expose it through a view object interface. In the view object editor, select the *Java* tab, click the pencil icon to create a *Client Interface*, and select the method you have just created. This will create a Java class that will allow your method to be accessible from a client.

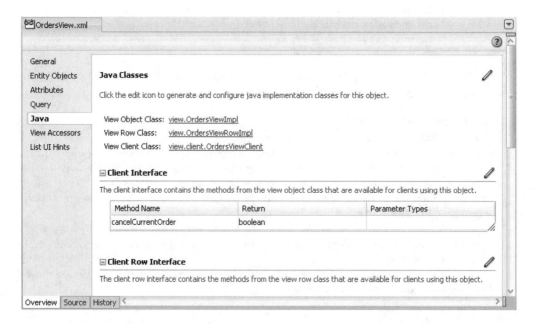

You can now test that this method can be called from within the ADF Business Component Browser. Select an instance of the OrdersView view object and then select **View | Operations**, which opens a dialog in which you can select and execute the custom method. Remember to select an order with an OrderStatus of "1."

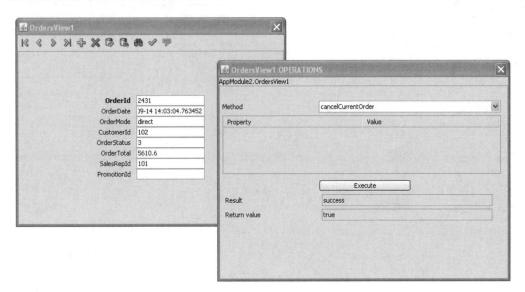

Summary

In this chapter, you have built view objects to represent application-specific views of your data and have learned that:

■ View objects are queries that select rows into your underlying entity objects.

■ A view object can represent a view of data based on a number of entity objects.

■ You can define an `order by` and `where` clause for a view object.

■ View object queries can be parameterized using bind variables.

■ View object attributes can be based on entity object attributes or on a calculation.

■ A view link defines a relationship between view objects to implement master/detail behavior.

■ View objects and view links can be visualized in a diagram.

■ View object classes can be subclassed and code can be added to the subclass to augment the framework behavior.

■ You can write custom view object methods and expose these to a consuming client.

Your mindset should now be that the view object, and the relationships between view objects as defined by view links, is your application-specific view of your data source. The next step is grouping these view objects into transactional containers called application modules.

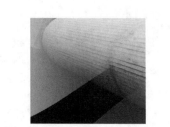

CHAPTER
7

The Application
Module

he preceding chapters took you through the process of creating a first-cut business service and gradually refining it to address more specific application needs. Now that you have fined-tuned the entity objects and shaped the application views of data, the next step is to take instances of these view objects and group them together to address specific application use cases.

In this chapter you will learn about the features of application modules and how you can create, edit, and use them. You'll also learn how the application module acts as the interface to the business service.

Understanding Application Modules

An application module represents a specific business use case, within which are instances of view objects required for that use case. But what is meant by a "business use case?" Well, there is no hard and fast definition, but you can think of a use case as a unit of work performed by a user or consumer of the service. That could be a use case like "manage customer order," "maintain employee details," or "inventory restock." Each of these use cases would typically be represented by a separate application module.

Furthermore, given that the business service is based on a relational database, the application module defines the database transactional boundary, meaning the point at which a rollback or commit happens. So "manage customer order," as represented by an application module, would be a separate transaction, and so rolling it back wouldn't affect the work the user had already completed when performing "maintain employee details." Conversely, if the whole of the business service was implemented as one big application module, then you would only have "commit everything" or "rollback everything."

Application modules can also be nested within other application modules. For example, "manage customer order" might involve the reuse of the "inventory restock" application module if the need to restock a product is deemed to be part of the management of a customer order. In this case, the nested application modules share the same transaction as the root application module.

Therefore, the granularity of the application modules and how you partition them will really depend on the use case you are implementing. Just as a view object defines an application-specific view of data, the application module describes the overall view of the business service and actions that can be performed on that business service. For this reason, an application module is sometimes referred to as a service façade, meaning it defines an interface that exposes only the data and actions with which a consuming client, such as a UI, can interface.

Managing Application Modules

In Chapter 4, the Create Business Components from Tables wizard created a default application module, and you've already been using the application module to test various features of the business service you've been building. We'll return to that in a moment, but first of all let's create a new application module.

Creating an Application Module

For this application you have identified a use case "maintain employee details." This requires the user to view and maintain information about departments and the employees within each of the departments.

Select the package in which you want to create the application module, select **File | New**, and, from the New Gallery dialog, select **ADF Business Components** and then **Application Module**. Enter a *Name* of "MaintainEmployeesAM" and click Next.

The next step, shown in Figure 7-1, is where you define which view objects are required for this application module. Move DepartmentsView from *Available View Objects* to *Data Model*. You now want to define that the data model should also include the employees for a particular department, rather than all employees. To accomplish this, select DepartmentsView1 in *Data Model* and move EmployeesView via EmployeesInDeptVL from *Available View Objects* to *Data Model*. You can optionally rename the view object instances within the application module. Click Finish to complete the application module creation.

TIP
It is important to emphasize the benefit of giving meaningful names to the view object instances within an application module. When it comes to building the UI, the view instance names can help guide the UI developer on their use.

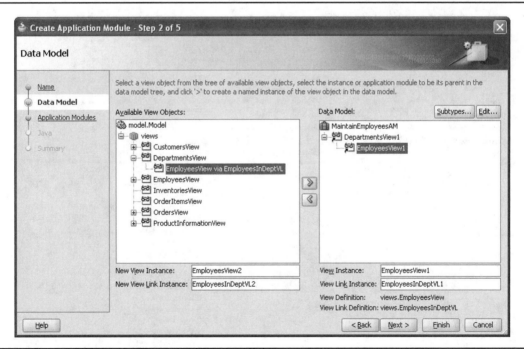

FIGURE 7-1. *Creating an application module to maintain employee information*

You've just defined an application module that encapsulates instances of view objects to implement the "maintain employee details" use case.

You can now test this in the ADF Business Component Browser.

Editing an Application Module

Now that you have created one application module, the next step is to fine-tune the default application module created earlier by the ADF Business Components from Tables wizard.

First, if you haven't already done so, right-click AppModule in the Application Navigator and select **Refactor** | **Rename**, and for *Rename To* enter "ManageCustomerOrdersAM." It obviously makes sense to name your application modules in a way that mirrors the use case they are implementing.

As with other ADF Business Components artifacts, double-clicking the Application Navigator opens up the appropriate editor. The default behavior for the Create Business Components from Tables wizard is to create an application module with an instance of every possible view object and view link. This is shown in Figure 7-2.

While this is useful for testing the view objects, the reality is that your application module will need to be refined to include only instances of view objects that are required for the business use case.

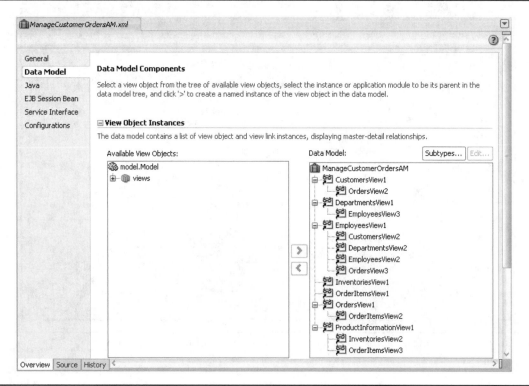

FIGURE 7-2. *Default application module created by Create Business Components from Tables wizard*

Of course, you could just delete this application module and create a new application module, but in this case we'll keep the application module and first remove all the view object instances from *Data Model*. You must remove the child nodes from *Data Model* before removing their parent nodes.

Having cleared the view object instances in the application module, the next step is to include only the view object instance required to manage a customer order. In this case, that will require the data model to include a view of customers, the orders for a customer, the order items for each order, and an inventory check for each order item.

NOTE
Remember, an application module contains instances of view objects and view links. This means that there may be many instances of the same view object. For example, there may be an instance of OrdersView representing all orders, and an instance representing orders for a specific customer. Each instance has its own current record indicator and state information.

Figure 7-3 shows the data model you are aiming to create.

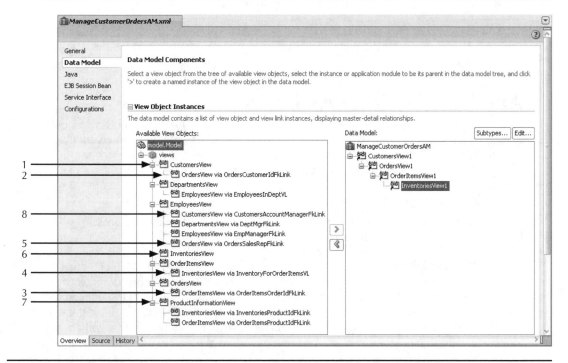

FIGURE 7-3. *Manage customer orders application module*

Available View Objects shows the various view objects and links between these view objects. For this data model you require the following:

- 1: View of all customers
- 2: View of orders for a specific customer
- 3: View of order items for a specific order
- 4: View of inventories for a specific order item

Move instances of each of the preceding view objects from *Available View Objects* to *Data Model*, making sure that in *Data Model* you select the parent node for which the *Available View Objects* should be a child. This gives you a data model that represents a master with three levels of detail: customers, orders for that customer, order items for that order, and inventory for each order item.

Although not required for this use case, some of the other view objects also give you the options of having

- 5: View of all orders for which an employee is a sales rep
- 6: View of all inventories
- 7: View of all products
- 8: View of customers for which an employee is an account manager

You can now test the application module in the ADF Business Component Browser to confirm you have the correct data model bringing back the correct data as per the defined relationships.

Application Module Classes

As you might have guessed, the declarative information defined for the application modules is backed by a number of framework classes. It is the responsibility of these framework classes to represent the definition of an application module and to create instances for each user.

At this stage, a brief introduction to the classes is pretty much all you need.

The Framework Classes

Just like entity objects, there are a number of framework classes that are responsible for implementing the features of the application module.

ApplicationModuleDefImpl

Just like for the other ADF Business Components artifacts such as view objects and entity objects, the definition of the artifact is held in XML. At runtime a single Java class is instantiated for each application module definition to hold information about that application module definition. This class is `oracle.jbo.server.ApplicationModuleDefImpl`. Given the fact that you are not looking to change the definition of an application module at runtime, you will probably not want to alter the default framework behavior.

ApplicationModuleImpl

Each instantiation of `oracle.jbo.server.ApplicationModuleImpl` represents an instance of an application module. Typical methods available in this class include getting information about the database connection and accessing and managing the view object instances.

Customizing Application Module Framework Classes

By default, the framework gives you methods to operate on the application module and the view object instances. You might not have realized, but as you were testing your application module in the ADF Business Component Browser, the buttons to navigate, commit, and rollback are firing these default methods.

What if instead of exposing these default methods, you wanted to expose a more business-oriented method. So, "remove department" would redistribute employees to other departments rather than just simply deleting the department record.

For each application module you define, you can ask JDeveloper to generate a subclass of `ApplicationModuleImpl` into which you can add your own code.

Exposing a Subclass of ApplicationModuleImpl

Open the editor for MaintainEmployeesAM and select the *Java* tab. Select the edit pencil icon to display the Select Java Options dialog. Select *Generate Application Module Class: MaintainEmployeesAMImpl*.

This generates a class `MaintainEmployeesAMImpl`, which is a subclass of `ApplicationModuleImpl`. It can do all the things that `ApplicationModuleImpl` can do, but it does it only for the MaintainEmployeesAM application module. Within this subclass are methods for accessing the view object instances.

So, what next? Well let's take a really simple example to show how you can access the various view object instances and navigate the selected data. In this case you'll create a method to access all the employees for the currently selected department, and perform an action on each of these records. To keep it really simple, that action will simply be to print out the employee's last name to the JDeveloper console.

Add the following code to `MaintainEmployeesAMImpl`:

```
public void printEmployeesInDept() {
    RowSetIterator rsi = getEmployeesView1().createRowSetIterator(null);
    while (rsi.hasNext()) {
        Row r = rsi.next();
        System.out.println(r.getAttribute("LastName"));
    }
    rsi.closeRowSetIterator();
}
```

NOTE
If you took the opportunity to rename any of the view object instance names, then you would have to reflect these changes in the preceding code as well.

Understanding the Code   So what does this code do? It's actually fairly straightforward. All you are doing is looping through a list of employees and printing out an attribute's value. To ensure that your programmatic accessing of the rows doesn't change the current record indicator, and so change the current record in the UI, you use your own instance of a pointer called a `RowSetIterator`.

So, reading from the first line, the code does the following:

1. Define a `public` method with no return.
2. Create a pointer, which is a `RowSetIterator`, to point to the rows in the EmployeesView1 instance.
3. While there are still more rows...
4. Go to the next row.
5. Print out the LastName attribute of the row.
6. When finished, close the pointer.

Of course, this is a trivial example, but it shows the basics of how you might write a method that programmatically accesses instances within the application module.

Creating a Client Interface

But isn't the application module acting as an interface to the consuming client? How do you expose this new method to the consuming client? For example, pressing a button should fire this method.

JDeveloper allows you to define that a method you have added to the `ApplicationModuleImpl` subclass should be exposed to the consuming client, just like the default actions commit and rollback.

In the editor for MaintainEmployeesAM, select the *Java* tab. Click the edit pencil icon for *Client Interface* to display the Edit Client Interface dialog. Select the method you just created from *Available* and move it to *Selected*. Click OK.

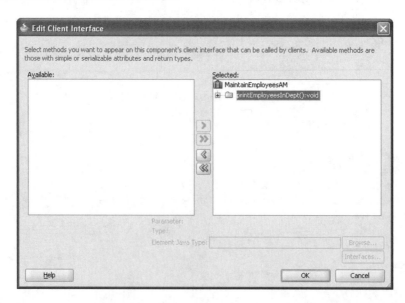

In doing this, you are telling JDeveloper that you want this method to be available through the application module interface.

NOTE
You may notice in the Application Navigator that JDeveloper has created a class to support this behavior.

Testing the Client Interface

Having added a new client method to the application module, how can you test this? Again, the ADF Business Component Browser allows you to test the application module, including the client method.

Run the ADF Business Component Browser in the normal way and select a department that has some employees. Right-click MaintainEmployeesAM in the ADF Business Component Browser and select **Show**. This displays a dialog containing the client method printEmployeesInDept(). Click Execute. This will execute the method, and in the JDeveloper console you will see the names of each of the employees in the selected department.

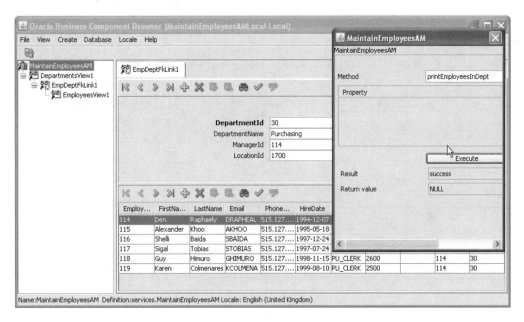

Summary

In this chapter, you have built application modules to implement business use cases using instances of the view objects you created earlier, and you have learned that:

■ An application module represents a specific use case.

■ The application module comprises instances of view objects.

■ The application module defines the boundary of the database transaction.

- ■ Application module classes can be subclassed and code can be added to augment the default application module behavior.

- ■ Methods added to the application module subclass can be exposed to the consuming client.

Now that you are more comfortable building application modules that closely mirror your business requirements, you can explore some of the more advanced features of ADF Business Components to extend the functionality of your business service. The next chapter introduces how you can add search and list of values features to your application.

CHAPTER
8

More View
Object Features

s you have progressed through the chapters, you've shaped your business service using view objects to bring back the right data in the right format. You've then assembled instances of these view objects within your application modules so that you now have a business service that is close to the finished product.

However, there are some more advanced features of view objects that you can use to enhance the application. In this chapter you will discover how view objects can be used to create predefined filters to allow users, and the framework, to dynamically refilter data. You'll also learn how you can set up a list of values for a view object attribute.

View Criteria

You already know that a view object defines a query to shape and filter your application data. You can also programmatically alter that view object by, for example, changing the `where` clause. However, if you find a business need, or user, that has the requirement to regularly filter on defined criteria, you might want to set up those filter criteria at development time and apply them as needed.

View criteria are a feature of view objects and allow predefined filters to be created that can then be applied when required. For example, while OrdersView selects all order records, you may find there is a requirement that the end user will often want to view only online orders that have been open for over one week. Or the end user might want to filter the list of customers provided by CustomersView to show only those customers based in the United States.

In each of these cases, you can define a view criteria on each of the view objects. These view criteria can then be applied programmatically, or they can even be exposed to the end user via a convenient search panel when dropped onto an ADF Faces page. You can also use view criteria to filter a list of values, as you will discover later in this chapter.

Creating a View Criteria

Open the view object editor for CustomersView and select the *Query* tab. Under the SQL query are two headings, *Bind Variables* and *View Criteria*. Click the green plus sign next to *View Criteria* to display the Create View Criteria dialog.

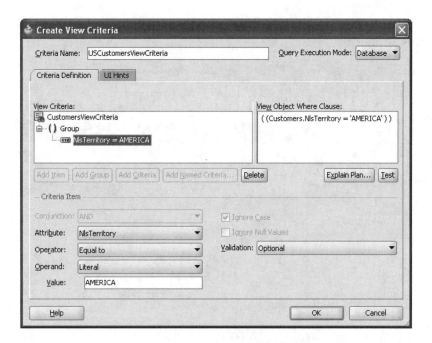

For *Criteria Name* enter "USCustomersViewCriteria." Click Add Item and set *Attribute* to "NlsTerritory," set *Operator* to "Equal to," set *Operand* to "Literal," and set *Value* to "AMERICA."

This defines a view criteria that, when applied, will filter CustomersView to show all customers who have the attribute NlsTerritory set to AMERICA. Of course, you can set up some more complex expressions by grouping conditions and then applying "AND" and "OR" between these groups. Furthermore, the view criteria expression can include bind variables, allowing the expression to be parameterized.

To test this view criteria, select the appropriate application module and run the ADF Business Component Browser. Open CustomersView1 and from the icon toolbar, click the Specify View

Criteria button, represented by the binoculars icon, and move USCustomersViewCriteria from *Available* to *Selected*.

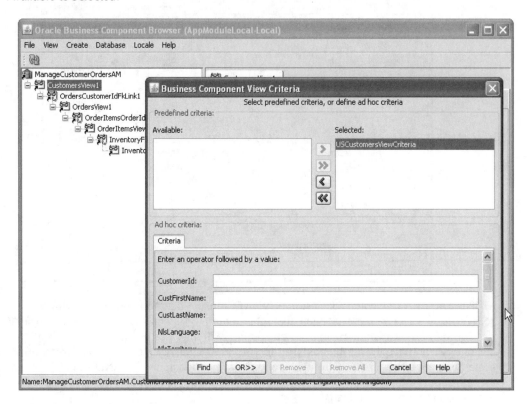

Click Find and check that the list of customers contains only U.S. customers. So, where can you now use this view criteria? Well, you can programmatically apply the view criteria as required; however, there are two other common uses for view criteria.

Applying a View Criteria to a View Object Instance

One area where you might decide to use this view criteria is on a view object instance. The definition of CustomersView defines a view of all customers, but assume that for the part of the application you are building, you only want to see U.S. customers. You can't change the `where` clause in CustomersView because that would change it for all instances. Instead, you can apply the view criteria to the view object instance in the application module.

Open ManageCustomerOrdersAM in the application module editor and select *Data Model*. Select the instance of CustomersView and click Edit.

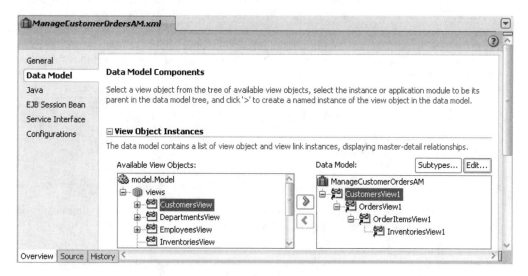

In the Edit View Instance dialog, you can now select that the view criteria you defined should be applied to only this instance of CustomersView. And, of course, if the view criteria was parameterized with bind variables, then the values for these bind variables could be set here.

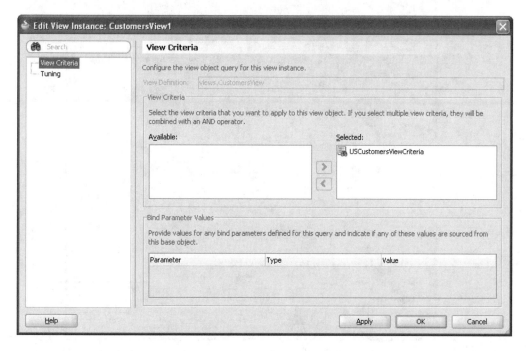

You can test this behavior in the ADF Business Component Browser.

Using View Criteria for User Searching

Another way to use a view criteria is by allowing it to be applied directly by the end user. Because the view criteria is acting as a filter, common user filter expressions can be defined as view criteria, and these view criteria can be exposed through an ADF Faces component called a query panel. This is covered in more detail later in the book, but here you can see an example of how the USCustomersViewCriteria view criteria is made available to an end user through a query panel at runtime.

The UI Hints tab in the Edit View Criteria dialog defines how this view criteria is displayed when used in a query panel, as shown in Figure 8-1.

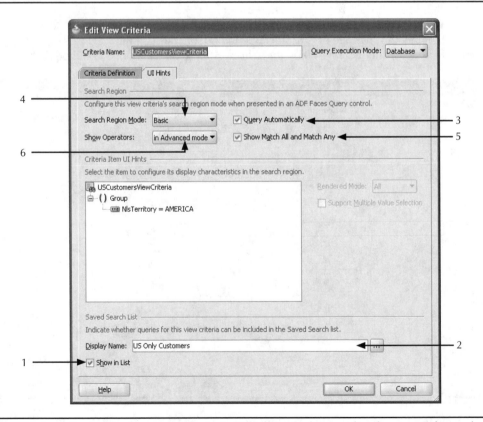

FIGURE 8-1.   *Controlling how a view criteria is displayed when rendered as a search panel*

Some of the options you have for controlling the layout are as follows:

■ 1: Indicates that this view criteria will appear in a drop-down list in the search panel as a predefined search

■ 2: Defines the label that will appear in the drop-down list for this view criteria

■ 3: Will automatically execute the query when the view criteria is selected from the drop-down list

■ 4: Defines the default mode for the search panel; in advanced mode the user has more options for controlling the search

■ 5: Determines whether to render a radio button to enable the user to choose to match either "all" or "any" attributes in a view criteria (equivalent to using either "AND" or "OR" conjunctions between the attributes)

■ 6: Defines if, and in what mode, you want to allow the end user to change the operator ("Equal to," "Contains," "Is not blank," and so forth) of the expression

TIP
If the user applies a view criteria from the search panel, then there is no way of unsetting the use of that view criteria without selecting another view criteria. To avoid this you may want to define a view criteria that shows all records defined by the view object. This allows you to "undo" any applied view criteria.

Model Driven Lists of Values

When building an application, you might find that instead of offering the user freeform data entry for some fields, it makes more sense to offer the user a list of valid values. For example, you might decide the valid values for income level should be presented in a drop-down list, or that a list of product codes should be displayed in a filterable dialog. As well as being a useful feature for the end user, it may also help protect your application from invalid data values.

ADF Business Components allows you to associate a list of values with a view object attribute. When that view object attribute is then bound to an ADF Faces page, it will be displayed with an appropriate UI component to present the list of valid values.

Creating a Model Driven List of Values

Model driven lists of values are defined on view object attributes. In this example, the CustomersView view object has an attribute IncomeLevel, and you would like the user to choose a value from a list of valid values.

Defining the List of Possible Values

The first step is to define the list of possible values. To do this, you need to use an existing view object or create a new view object. Create a view object, ValidIncomeLevelView, just as you did with MaritalStatusView, and define the static strings available for income level. Alternatively, you could create this new view object based on a read-only `select` statement such as

```
SELECT DISTINCT CUSTOMERS.INCOME_LEVEL INCOME_LEVEL
  FROM CUSTOMERS ORDER BY INCOME_LEVEL
```

At this point, it really doesn't matter which method you choose, so long as ValidIncomeLevelView is a view object that defines the list of possible values.

Defining a List of Values on an Attribute

You now need to define that this list of values is associated with an attribute. Open the view object editor for CustomersView, select the *Attributes* tab, select the attribute IncomeLevel, and click the green plus sign next to *List of Values:IncomeLevel*. This opens the Create List of Values dialog. By default, the name of this list of values is the attribute name prefixed with "LOV_."

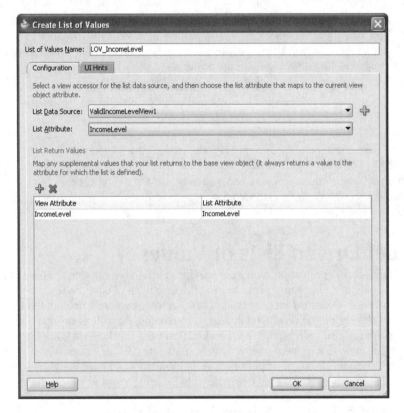

This first thing you have to do is define where the list of values is coming from. Click the green plus sign next to *List Data Source* and, from *Available View Objects*, select ValidIncomeLevelView and move it to *View Accessors*.

The next step is to define which attribute from ValidIncomeLevelView is to be returned from the list. For *List Attribute* choose "IncomeLevel." For *List Return Values* ensure that IncomeLevel is being returned into the correct attribute, which should be easy because they have the same name in this case.

Defining UI Hints for a Model Driven List of Values

Having defined the source for the list and the attribute mapping, you can now specify the default component used when the attribute is rendered on a UI page. There are a number of options available here:

- Choice List
- Combo Box
- Combo Box with List of Values
- Input Text with List of Values
- List Box
- Radio Group

For LOV_IncomeLevel, set *Default List Type* as "Choice List." You would also set *Display Attributes*, which allows you to define which attributes of the underlying list of values should appear in the choice list. Given there is only one attribute, IncomeLevel, select that.

As always, you can use the ADF Business Component Browser to test the changes you have made. Run the application module and confirm that IncomeLevel now appears with a list of valid values.

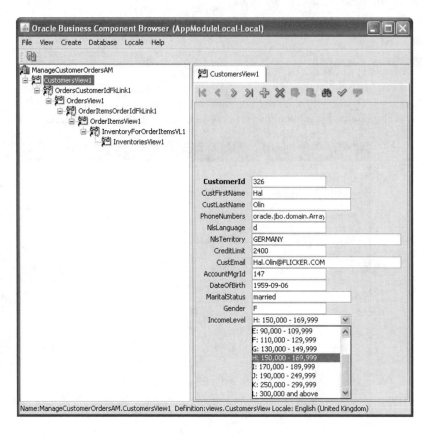

TIP
You might want to add some different model driven lists of values to your application now. For example, OrderItemsView has an attribute ProductId. Add a model driven list of values to show a list of products from ProductInformationView displayed as an input text field with a list of values. You can decide for yourself which attributes you want to display in the list of values and whether to include a search capability in the list of values.

Dependent List of Values

One feature in which model driven lists of values and view criteria can work together is a dependent list of values. A dependent list of values is one where the rows in the list of values are dependent on some factor. For example, the list of people who can be an employee's manager is limited to employees who are within that person's department.

In this case, a view criteria can be applied to a model driven list of values to filter the rows to show only employees in the selected department.

Creating a Dependent Model Driven List of Values

Let's implement the previously mentioned example in which a manager must be in the same department as his or her employee. So in this case, the DepartmentId of the selected employee limits the list of possible managers that will appear in the list.

Creating the View Criteria

The first step is to create a view criteria that will filter the view of employees based on DepartmentId. Open the view object editor for EmployeesView, select the *Query* tab, and create a new view criteria called "EmpInDeptViewCriteria." For this view criteria, the condition DepartmentId is equal to a bind variable of type `Number`. By using a bind variable, the view criteria can be parameterized by passing in the DepartmentId of the selected employee.

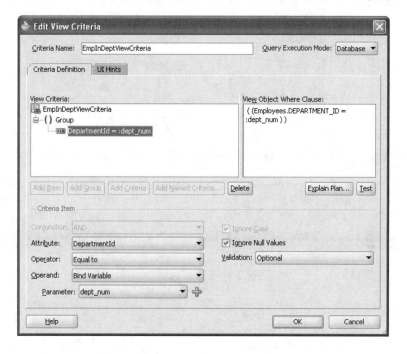

Creating the Dependent Model Driven List of Values

The next step is to create the model driven list of values. In this case, create a list of values on the ManagerId attribute of the EmployeesView view object where the *List Data Source* is EmployeesView and *List Attribute* is "EmployeeId." Select the *UI Hints* tab and set *Default List Type* to "Input text with List of Values."

It's at this point that the instance of the view object that is providing the list of values, *List Data Source*, should have the view criteria applied that will filter the list based on DepartmentId. To do this, click the green plus next to *List Data Source* to open the View Accessors dialog.

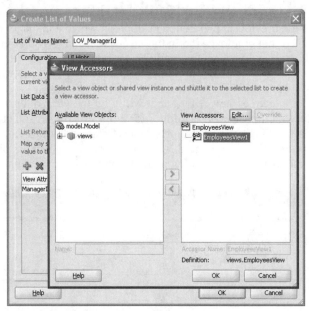

The View Accessors dialog allows you to apply the view criteria to the data that will appear in the list of values. Click Edit and move "EmpInDeptViewCriteria" from the *Available* list to the *Selected* list. The bind variable also needs to be set, so for *Value* input "DepartmentId." By doing this, you are defining that the bind variable, which is being used to filter the list of employees, should have a value, which is the currently selected employee's DepartmentId.

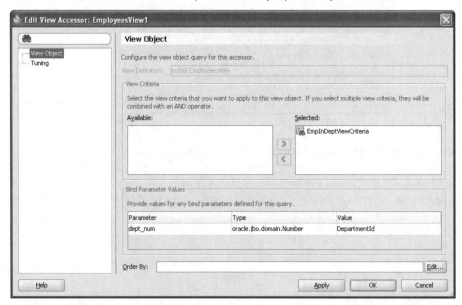

NOTE
The DepartmentId specified earlier is in fact a Groovy expression,
albeit a very simple one consisting of only the name of an attribute.

You can now select the appropriate application module and test it in the ADF Business
Component Browser. Select an employee and click the List of Value button to the right of
ManagerId. The list of values for a new manager is now restricted to only those employees in the
currently selected employee's department.

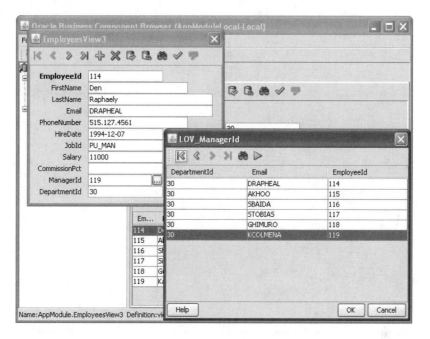

Summary

In this chapter you have utilized some of the more advanced features of view objects to
implement features for your application. You have learned how to:

- Set up filter conditions using view criteria.

- Use view criteria to filter instances of view objects within an application module.

- Use a view criteria as the tool for end user filtering of data.

- Define a list of valid values for a view object attribute.

- Filter a list of values based on a view criteria.

Now that you have finalized the shape of your business service, the final step is to add some
application-specific business rules. The next chapter guides you through the rich declarative
validation features of ADF Business Components and shows how you can start adding business
and data validation logic to your application.

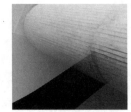

CHAPTER
9

Implementing Business
Service Validation

s you have been progressing through the chapters, you've built a rich business service for your application to read, write, and manage data from a database. However, you've not yet defined any validation rules for this application other than those that were already in the database. The next step is to add application-specific validation to the business service.

Your application is more than just the reading and writing of information to and from a database. Within that application you'll want to define rules on what the user can do and what data values can be input. Do you really want to allow the user to set a credit limit for a new customer to be a million dollars?

ADF Business Components provides a rich, declarative validation framework that allows user input to be validated against a static value, a list of values, a numeric range, and even values returned from queries. The framework also provides a convenient way to hook up the validation mechanism to a Java method if you choose to write more complex validation rules in Java.

In this chapter you will discover how ADF Business Components provides functionality for defining declarative and programmatic validation of data.

Creating Validation Rules

Validation rules, because they are working on data, are defined as part of the entity object and can be placed on an attribute or at the entity level. A validation rule defined on an entity object attribute fires when the attribute value is changed, whereas a validation rule defined at the entity level fires when changing rows or committing data. Entity-level validation rules are useful when the rule depends on more than one attribute value. For example, the maximum value for a customer's credit limit is dependent on their income level, and so it only makes sense to validate when both attribute values have been set.

Regardless of the style of validation, or whether it is defined at the entity level or at the attribute level, the steps are similar. Open the entity object editor and select the *Business Rules* tab. Figure 9-1 shows the attributes and any validation rules already defined. At this point you might notice that validation rules already exist for some attributes. These are the framework

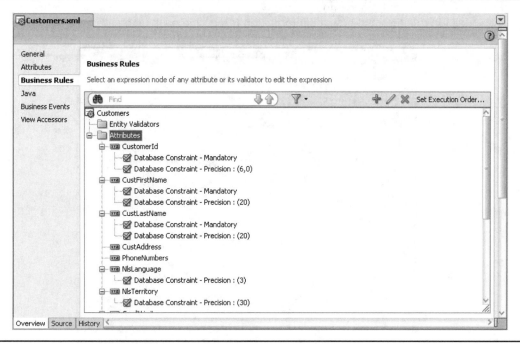

FIGURE 9-1. *Entity object validation rules*

implementation of the database constraints, such as defining that an attribute is mandatory, defined when creating the entity object.

Overview of Adding a Validation Rule

To add a validation rule, select an attribute or entity and click the green plus sign to display the Add Validation Rule dialog. From this dialog you can define the validation rule by clicking the

Rule Type drop-down list and choosing the type of rule. In addition, you can also define when the validation rule fires and how the information is reported back to the user.

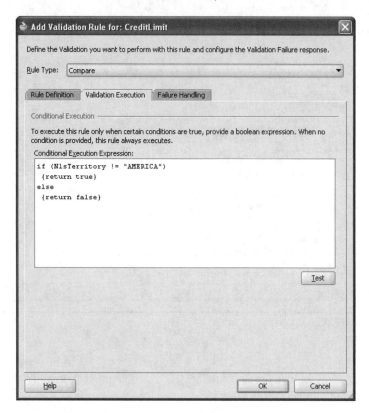

Conditional Execution of a Validation Rule

A powerful feature of the validation framework in ADF Business Components is that you can define a condition on which the validation will fire. For example, you might decide that the credit limit rule for a customer is only applied to non-U.S. customers. In this case you can add an expression, the result of which should return true if the validation rule is to fire and false if it is to be ignored. To set a conditional expression, select the *Validation Execution* tab on the Add Validation Rule dialog.

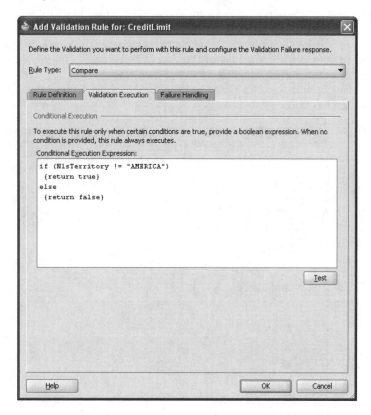

You can then add an expression, such as the one shown, that returns true or false.

Failure Handling

For any validation rule that fails, you can customize the message displayed to the user. Select the *Failure Handling* tab on the Add Validation Rule dialog. You can either directly type the message string or select it from a translatable message bundle. As well as defining the message text, you can also define whether the validation failure should be treated as a warning or as an error. If you set *Validation Failure Severity* to "Error," then the framework will not allow a value that fails the validation check. If it is set to "Informational Warning," then the message appears, but the new value is accepted.

Customizing Validation Messages

Rather than having validation messages that are static strings, ADF Business Components allows you to parameterize these messages using tokens that can refer to attribute values and properties that are resolved at runtime. For example, instead of defining a static error message "That credit limit is too high," you could define the message "You cannot set a credit limit of {x} for {first} {last}," which at runtime gets resolved to the more helpful "You cannot set a credit limit of 5000 for Constantine Welles."

In this case {x}, {first}, and {last} are simply tokens in the message, each of which can refer to an attribute name or a Groovy expression.

In this case, newValue refers to the new value of CreditLimit rather than the value the user was trying to change, while CustFirstName and CustLastName are attribute values.

A Quick Word About Groovy

The term Groovy has appeared a number of times in the book so far. So, what is Groovy?

Well, Groovy is a Java-like scripting notation that runs inside a JVM and has access to all the Java APIs, any custom classes and methods you write, as well as a few APIs of its own. Also, because it is interpreted at runtime, rather than being compiled, it can be customized on an application-to-application basis.

But hold on, aren't we supposed to be coding in Java? Yes, you are and yes, you will be. Nevertheless, ADF Business Components has a number of hooks into which you add Groovy expressions that give you the flexibility to write code without dropping into full-blown Java.

This works particularly well with numerous features of ADF Business Components, including validation and default values where Groovy expressions can be used to provide conditional processing or values derived from expressions.

For more information, search online for the Oracle White Paper "Introduction to Groovy Support in JDeveloper and Oracle ADF 11g" written by Grant Ronald.

Compare Validation

Probably the most common validation rule you will choose to implement is one that compares a new attribute value to a specific value. The compare validator allows you to define that the value you are comparing against is a literal value or one that is derived at runtime from an expression, query, or another attribute.

Comparing an Attribute Against a Literal Value

The simplest case is comparing an attribute to a literal value. Create a new validation rule on the Salary attribute of the Employees entity object. Set *Rule Type* to "Compare," *Operator* to "LessThan," and *Compare With* to "Literal Value." For *Enter Literal Value*, enter "25000."

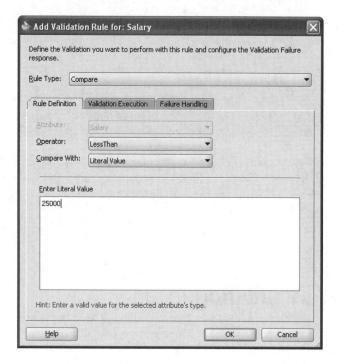

You have just defined that the salary for an employee must be less than the literal value 25000. You can also define a message to be displayed.

TIP
For each validation rule that you define, make sure you test it in the ADF Business Component Browser to ensure that it works as expected.

Comparing an Attribute Against an Expression

Rather than validating against a static value, you could validate against an expression. For example, a date of birth or an order date can't be in the future, but you can't hard-code the current date into your validation rule. In this case, you can define a validation rule to compare against an expression.

On the Customers entity object, add a new validation rule to DateOfBirth. Set *Rule Type* to "Compare," *Operator* to "LessThan," and *Compare With* to "Expression." Enter "adf.currentDate" into *Expression*.

The value "adf.currentDate" is a built-in Groovy expression that returns the current date.

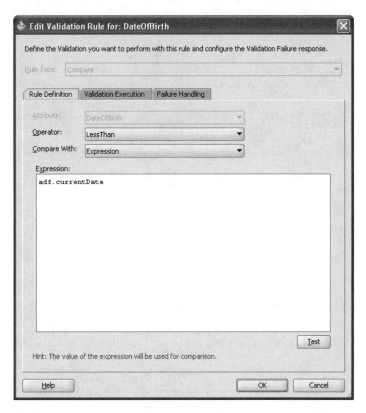

Comparing an Attribute Against an Attribute Value

But what if you want to compare against an attribute value defined somewhere else in your business service? For example, the selling price for an order item should never be less than the minimum price for that item. That requires you to look up the minimum price for the item and use that as part of the validation rule.

You could select the minimum price for an item via a database query, but that involves a trip to the database and you wouldn't find any changes that are still a part of the current transaction.

Instead, you can use an expression to reference the accessor defined by the association between the OrderItems entity object, and the ProductInformation entity object. In this case, the accessor is called ProductInformation.

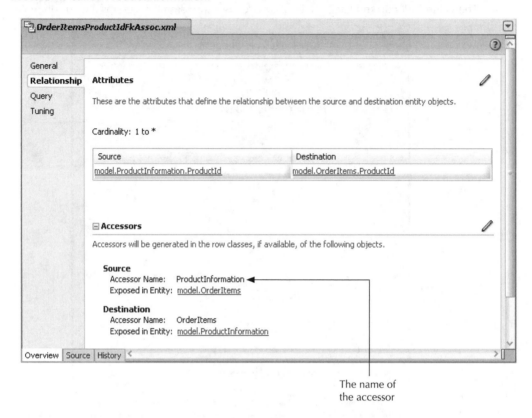

The name of
the accessor

On the OrderItems entity object, add a new validation rule to UnitPrice. Set *Rule Type* to "Compare," *Operator* to "GreaterOrEqualTo," and *Compare With* to "Expression." Enter "ProductInformation.MinPrice" into *Expression*.

You have just defined that the value of UnitPrice must be greater than or equal to the corresponding MinPrice for the product.

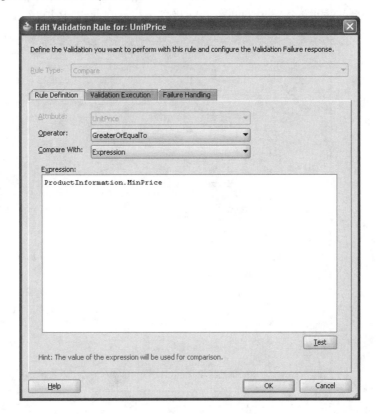

List Validation

An entity object attribute can also be validated against a list of possible values, where the list of possible values can come from a number of different sources.

Validating Against a Static List of Values

The simplest example is to validate an attribute against a list of static values. For example, in the Customers entity object the attribute Gender can only be one of two values: M or F.

Create a new validation rule for Gender by setting *Rule Type* to "List," *Operator* to "In," and *List Type* to "Literal Values." For *Enter List of Values*, enter "M" and "F." This ensures that only M and F will be accepted as valid values for Gender in this application.

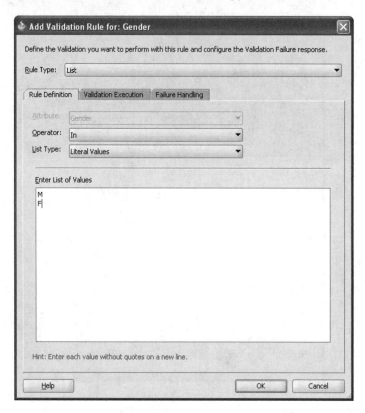

Validating Against a View Object Attribute

Rather than checking an attribute value against a list of static values, you can validate against a view object attribute. In Chapter 6 you defined a read-only view object of values: MaritalStatusView. You can set a validation rule that the valid values allowed for MaritalStatus are found in that view object.

Create a new validation rule for MaritalStatus, setting *Rule Type* to "List," *Operator* to "In," and *List Type* to "View Object Attribute." Then select MaritalStatusView and MarriedStatus to define that the only valid values for MaritalStatus are those that exist in the MaritalStatusView view object.

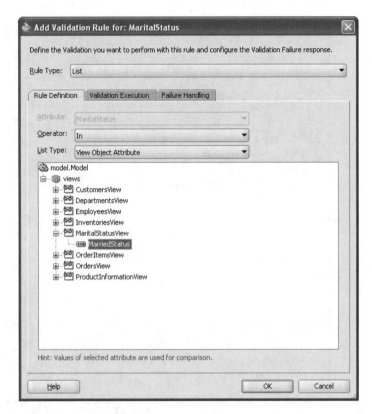

Validating Against a Query Result

A list validation can also validate against a query result. Generally speaking, you will probably want to avoid validating against large result sets in this manner. Furthermore, other validation rules, such as key exists (described next), may be more appropriate. However, for the purpose of demonstration, let's assume that the application is to prevent new customers joining from new territories because you've not yet set up the supporting management teams in those areas. Therefore, the value for NlsTerritory should be a value that already exists in the Customers table.

Create a new validation rule for NlsTerritory and set *Rule Type* to "List," *Operator* to "In," and *List Type* to "Query Result." *For Enter SQL Statement*, enter the following:

```
select distinct NLS_TERRITORY from CUSTOMERS
```

This defines that the valid values for NlsTerritory are ones that already exist in the Customers table.

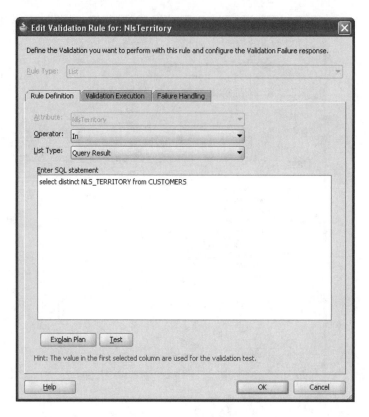

Key Exists Validation

A common use case for validation is to check that a value entered already exists as a key. For example, for an order item, you might decide that you want a different product and so change the product ID. In this case you want to ensure that the value entered is a valid product ID.

There are a number of advantages in using a key exists validation over something like a list validation using a query result. First, it doesn't always have to go to the database to find the key since it looks in the entity cache, and second, the key exists validation will find keys that exist in the current transaction that have not yet been committed.

Creating a Key Exists Validator

Open the entity object editor for OrderItems and create a new validation rule for ProductId. Set *Rule Type* to "Key Exists" and *Validation Target Type* to "Entity Object." JDeveloper should automatically recognize that there is an association between the ProductId of OrderItems and the ProductId in the ProductInformation entity object.

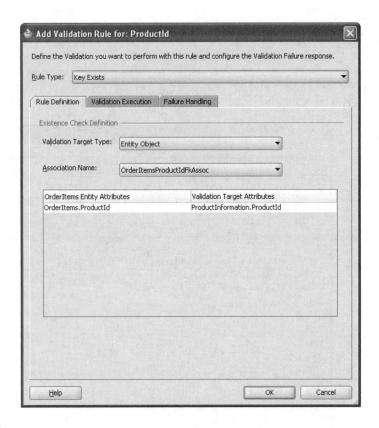

Regular Expression Validation

Another useful feature of the validation framework is the ability to validate input against a particular pattern; for example, a membership number should always be two alphabetical characters followed by ten numeric digits. ADF Business Components allows you to define a validation rule that uses something called a Java regular expression to define the data pattern. This is simply a string that defines what characters and symbols are allowed for a specific piece of data. For example, a Java regular expression `[A-Z] [a-z] {0,10}` defines that a piece of data should have an initial uppercase letter followed by up to ten lowercase alphabetical characters.

JDeveloper already provides some prebuilt expressions that handle U.S. telephone numbers and e-mail addresses, and there are numerous other examples of expressions posted online.

TIP

Searching the Web for `java.util.regex.Pattern` *is probably a good place to start to find out more information about regular expressions.*

Creating a Regular Expression Validator

Open the entity object editor for Customers and create a new validation rule for CustEmail. Set *Rule Type* to "Regular Expression," *Operator* to "Matches," and *Predefined Expressions* to "Email Address." Click Use Pattern, and JDeveloper displays a predefined pattern for an e-mail address. This prevents, for example, an e-mail address that does not contain the "@" symbol.

Script Expression Validation

You've now seen that ADF Business Components provides some powerful declarative validation features, but what if you require a little more flexibility? Script expression validation allows you to write a Groovy expression that returns either true or false to indicate whether the validation passed or failed. This gives you much more conditional control over your validation expression. For example, rather than validating credit limit against a single value, you might decide that the credit limit is based on the customer's income, and so if they have a higher income, then their credit limit is higher.

Creating a Script Expression Validator

Given that this expression is going to be checking both credit limit and income, then it makes sense to place it at the entity level.

Create a new entity-level validation rule and set *Rule Type* to "Script Expression." For the *Expression* enter the following Groovy code:

```
// Debug lines to check values
println(IncomeLevel)
println(CreditLimit)
//End of debug lines
if (IncomeLevel == "A: Below 30,000")
   {return CreditLimit < 1000}
else
   {if (IncomeLevel == "B: 30,000 - 49,999")
     {return CreditLimit < 2000}
    else
      return CreditLimit < 3000}
```

In this case the first two lines print out the values of the attributes that are being used in this validation rule. This is a useful technique to aid debugging, and you can view the values in the JDeveloper console window. The code then checks the value of IncomeLevel, and if the value is "A: Below 30,000" it evaluates whether CreditLimit is less than 1000. If the value of IncomeLevel is "B: 30,000 - 49,999" then CreditLimit must be less than 2000; otherwise CreditLimit must be less than 3000.

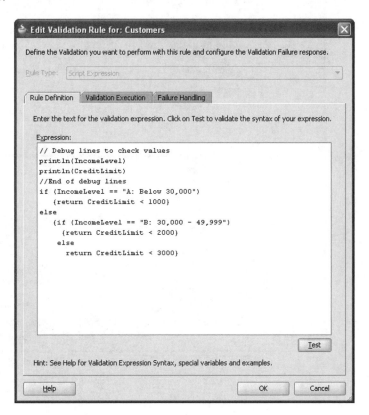

Method Validation

Of course, not all validation requirements can be achieved by using only the declarative features of the framework. In such cases, Java gives you the power and flexibility in code to access and manipulate data structures to do pretty much anything you want.

JDeveloper lets you write a validation rule in Java and indicate that that method should be called as part of the validation cycle. When creating a method validator, JDeveloper will automatically create an empty method in the appropriate Java class. So, for the Customers entity object the method will be created in the `CustomersImpl` class. The method should return either true, to indicate that the validation passed, or false, to indicate that the validation failed.

Creating a Method Validator

Let's assume that you want to define a more complex validation rule that high-income customers should have an account manager of an appropriately senior position.

Create a new entity level validation rule and set *Rule Type* to "Method." JDeveloper automatically suggests a method name, in this case `validateCustomers()`.

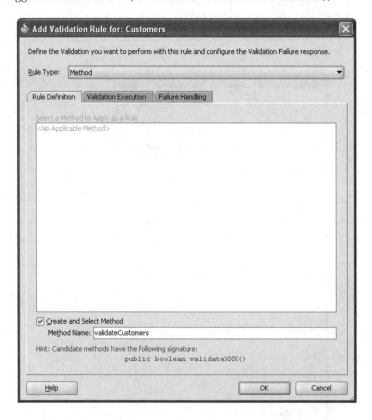

You can now go into the `CustomersImpl` class and add the following code to the validation method:

```
public boolean validateCustomers() {
    String job = (String)getEmployees().getAttribute("JobId");
    if (getIncomeLevel().equalsIgnoreCase("L: 300,000 and above") &&
        !job.equals("AD_PRES")) {
        return false;
    }
    return true;
}
```

The code uses the accessor to the Employees entity object to find JobId and ensure for high-income customers that the associated account manager, as identified in the Employees entity object, is a president.

NOTE

In the preceding code, `getEmployees()` returns an `EntityImpl` object and `getAttribute()` is called on that object. However, if you have generated an `EmployeesImpl` class, then you could cast the `EntityImpl` object to `EmployeesImpl` and then call `getJobId()` on that object.

Summary

Congratulations! You've now completed building your business services, although there is nothing to stop you from going back to fine-tune the details as you start assembling your application UI. Having completed this chapter, you should understand more about ADF Business Components validation and how:

- Validation rules are defined on entity objects.
- Validation failure can be treated as an error or as a warning.
- Validation messages can be parameterized.
- Comparison validators can compare against static values, expressions, and attribute values that are not part of the entity object.
- List validators can validate against static lists, queries, and view object instances.
- Data input can be validated to ensure it matches a specific pattern.
- Groovy can be used to evaluate more complex validation conditions.
- A Java method can be called as a validator.

With your business service development complete, the following chapters involve changing hats and becoming the developer who has to build the page flow and lay out the pages that interface into the business service.

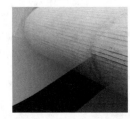

PART
III

Building the User Interface

CHAPTER
10

Introduction to ADF
Faces Rich Client

ow that you have built your business service, the focus of the book changes to how you can expose that business service to the end user. It can often be the aesthetic qualities and ease of use that shape a user's perceptions of an application, so it's important that the UI technologies not only are productive for the developer, but also can meet the expectations of the end user.

In this chapter you will be introduced to ADF Faces Rich Client and the library of components available for building your UI pages.

NOTE
The terms ADF Faces and ADF Faces Rich Client are often used interchangeably. Strictly speaking, ADF Faces is the name used to refer to the UI components in Oracle ADF 10g, with ADF Faces Rich Client being used to distinguish the visually and functionally richer components in Oracle ADF 11g; however, the term ADF Faces is now generally used for the Oracle ADF 11g component set. For the purposes of this book, when ADF Faces is mentioned, it refers to the Oracle ADF Faces Rich Client 11g components unless explicitly noted otherwise.

An Overview of ADF Faces

As you found out earlier in the book, Java Server Faces (JSF) is a standard for building web UIs. One of the advantages of JSF is that, as a developer, you are working with components, each of which compartmentalizes its behavior and how it renders itself. This means that as the developer using, for example, a JSF table component, you are protected from the implementation details of how that component handles the event processing when data is changed in the table or if a scroll bar is moved. Furthermore, how that table renders is handled by the component itself. It might generate HTML and JavaScript for rendering in a browser, but generate different markup if the component is being rendered on a handheld device like a mobile phone.

NOTE
There is also an element of future-proofing in using JSF components like ADF Faces. If, for example, some new markup language is invented for displaying web pages or a new browser comes on the market, the component developer would be responsible for handling the differences in the browser versions or rendering of the new markup. As the consumer of the component, you can expect the component to "do the right thing" when it comes to rendering.

Because JSF is a standard, different vendors can develop their own JSF-compliant components, with ADF Faces being Oracle's offering of JSF components within Oracle ADF. The infrastructure supports not only the visual UI components you would expect, like buttons and input fields, but also features like drag and drop, popup dialogs, and page templates.

The Building Blocks of ADF Faces

Although your first exposure to ADF Faces will probably be the catalog of UI components, ADF Faces has more to it than that. Let's briefly look at the main building blocks of ADF Faces.

UI Components

ADF Faces includes a palette of over 150 UI components ranging from basic buttons and input fields to highly interactive graphs and maps. Each UI component has properties, such as background color, and can have behavior as well; for example, a button can be clicked to initiate an action.

Managed Beans and Backing Beans

While your business logic code is encapsulated inside the business service, you may want to write UI-specific code related to a particular web page. Managed beans are simply Java classes that are managed for you by JSF and where you can write UI-specific code.

For example, on clicking a button, you might want to hide some components on the page. In this case you would use a managed bean to contain the code for implementing this UI behavior.

"Backing beans" is simply a naming convention for managed beans that are specifically associated with a UI page. While you are still learning, you'll probably have only limited need to use them, but it's good to know they are there and what they are for.

Expression Language

Later in this chapter when you create your first page, you might notice that some of the UI components contain a strange syntactical text. This is a feature of JSF called Expression Language (EL). EL is simply a notation that allows the UI component to refer to a Java bean associated with the application. Primarily, you'll see EL used to hook up the UI components to the framework Java class that implements the binding to the business service. So, for example, an input field might have its *Value* property set to "#{foo.firstName}." EL will look up a managed bean called "foo" and then call `getFirstName()` in that managed bean.

Navigation Cases

For any application that is more than just a single page, you will need to define the flow of the pages. JSF provides a feature to allow the flow of the application to be defined separately from the application pages, rather than hard-coding links or page references inside a page. The JSF page flow can be defined in a file called faces-config.xml. However, Oracle ADF extends the default JSF controller with the ADF Controller that adds functionality above and beyond the standard JSF page flow, including allowing page flow to be defined in any number of files. This means that the flow of the application can be broken down into different subflows that can be worked on in isolation and reused as required. The default ADF Controller page flow file is adfc-config.xml.

Life Cycle

Requesting a page or performing an action on a page requires a number of steps to be executed. This series of steps is collectively called the life cycle. For the most part, the various steps are not something you need to know in any depth at this stage in your learning. However, it is good to know that there are a number of steps involved in the request and response of an ADF Faces page, and as you become more experienced you can add your own custom code to augment the behavior of these steps.

Overview of ADF Faces Components

Throughout this book, and as you start to get more hands-on with JDeveloper, you will become more and more familiar with the full range of components, what they can do, and how they are best used. Many of the components will be created automatically for you as you drag and drop the business service onto pages. However, as a way of an introduction to the components, here are some of the more frequently used components with which you will become familiar.

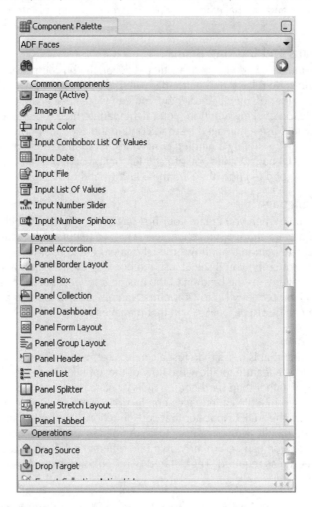

Visual Components

For the most part, you will be working with ADF Faces components that are used to visualize data from your business service. Some are best suited for direct data entry, while others are useful when dealing with lists of data.

Input Components

ADF Faces includes a number of different components for facilitating the input of data into your application. Some of the more common components are introduced here.

Input Text   The Input Text component is probably one of the most common components you will use for entering data into your application. The two principal properties associated with this component are *Value* and *Label*, which are used to define the data value of the field and the label that accompanies the component. You can also control the behavior of the component using properties such as *MaximumLength* to limit the number of characters that can be input.

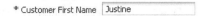

Input Date   Input Date is a component that combines a text input field with a date picker. By default, a date attribute in the business service will be displayed using this component. This allows a user to either enter a date directly in the field or select from a calendar that is automatically displayed by selecting the calendar icon that appears to the side of the input field. Like Input Text, the properties *Value* and *Label* are used to control the value and the label for the component; however, the component also supports the ability to limit the data values entered using properties such as *MinValue* and *MaxValue*.

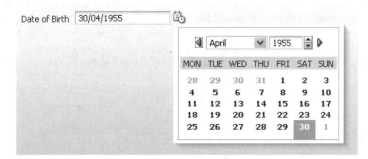

Input Number Slider   Input Number Slider provides a convenient component for inputting a numeric data value. The component includes a slider that allows a value to be selected by positioning the slider between a minimum and a maximum value. As with the previous components, Input Number Slider has properties for *Value* and *Label* as well as *Minimum* and *Maximum* to define the limits of the slider. *MajorIncrement* and *MinorIncrement* are properties to define the tick intervals on the slider scale.

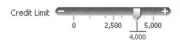

Input Number Spinbox   Like the Input Number Slider component, the Input Number Spinbox component provides a convenient way of entering numeric data. The user can either type a value directly into the component or use the spinbox to increment or decrement the value. The component implements the properties *Minimum* and *Maximum* to define the limits and *StepSize* to define how the component steps through the values when using the spinbox. The component automatically handles the display of an error message if a value input is outside the limits defined by *Minimum* and *Maximum*.

List Components

List components provide a convenient way of displaying and inputting data where you wish to guide the user to select from a list of possible values.

Select One Choice   Select One Choice is a component in which data can only be selected from a drop-down list of values. If you have defined a model driven list of values in the business service, then this is one of the components you can use to display the list of values for an attribute. In common with other components, it supports properties for *Label* and *Value*. The list of possible values for the component is provided by an instance of another component, called Select Item, which is automatically defined as a child of the Select One Choice component.

Select One Listbox   Select One Listbox works in similar manner to Select One Choice except the component itself is the list of possible values that you can select. As well as *Label* and *Value*, the component includes a property *Size*. This defines the number of values that are visible in the list; a scroll bar automatically appears if there are more possible values in the list.

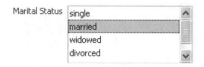

Select One Radio   Select One Radio allows the user to select one value from a number of choices displayed as radio buttons. As well as supporting *Label* and *Value* properties, the component also supports *Layout*, which defines whether the radio buttons are laid out horizontally or vertically.

Collection Components

A collection component is any component that is used to display a data collection rather than one specific data value.

Table   A Table component is used to display a collection of data as rows and columns. The Table component provides a rich set of features, enabling the user to resize and reposition columns as well as filter rows.

This component typically contains a number of child components, including a column component for each column of the table. The column component also has a child component, for example, an output text field in the case of a read-only table. The Table component contains a number of properties to control the look and behavior of the table. *ColumnStretching* defines which column should automatically be resized if there is any unused space in the component in which the table is placed. *FilterVisible* defines whether a filter field is placed above each column, and the visual aspects of the table can further be managed through the *HorizontalGridVisible* and *VerticalGridVisible* properties.

Tree   The Tree component is used to display hierarchical data in the form of nodes showing one level of hierarchical data that can then be expanded to show the related data for that node. For example, you can show a tree of departments where each department node can be expanded to show the employees within that department.

Layout Components

One of the challenges of building a browser-based UI is to be able to manage effectively the changing geometry when the browser window is resized. To aid the developer, ADF Faces includes a number of layout components. These components are containers that have one or more child components and are responsible for managing the layout of the child components. Many of the components also have specially named areas called facets. These are areas in the component for specific content. For example, a Panel Header component has a *toolbar* facet and, as you might expect, this is where you could put a toolbar.

It's fair to say that the power of these layout components can sometimes make it difficult to understand what they are going to do in any given situation, especially when layout containers are nested inside other layout containers. Nevertheless, the fact is that you get things like automatic geometry management when a page or container is resized, and consistent layout makes them an essential tool of UI development. The following is a guide to some of the more common use cases for layout containers.

* CustomerId	101		CustEmail	Constantin.Welles@NHINGA.CO
* Customer First Name	Constantine		Date of Birth	20/02/1972
* Customer Last Name	Welles		Marital Status	widowed
NlsLanguage	us		Gender	M
NlsTerritory	AMERICA		Income Level	B: 30,000 - 49,999
Credit Limit	1000			

FIGURE 10-1. *Panel Form Layout with two columns*

Panel Components

Most of the layout components you will use are called panel components. Each panel has a different look and behavior. For example, some panels have headers and borders, while others are unseen and are simply there to manage the layout of child components. Each of these panels can be, and often is, nested within other panels. You can drag and drop a panel component onto an ADF Faces page; alternatively, JDeveloper will often automatically insert layout components where it makes sense.

Panel Form Layout   Panel Form Layout (see Figure 10-1) lays out its child components in a form layout with labels and fields aligned vertically. The property *LabelAlignment* defines the alignment of the labels to be either above the field or at the start of the field. By using the properties *MaxColumns* and *Rows* you can define whether the form layout is single column or multiple column.

Panel Group Layout   The Panel Group Layout component lays out its child components in a simple pattern based on the *Layout* property. Typical values for *Layout* would be "horizontal" or "vertical." This layout component would typically be used for grouping components, such as a row of buttons.

Panel Box   The Panel Box component is primarily used to display content offset by a border and title. The title is defined by the *Text* property, and *Icon* can be used to define an optional icon. Panel Box has a built-in feature that allows the box to be collapsed, which is controlled by the property *ShowDisclosure*. This component also includes a toolbar facet that provides an area in the Panel Box header where a toolbar can be placed.

A panel box with a toolbar   Add   Remove
Content of panel box

Panel box with no dislosure icon
Customer First Name: Constantine
Customer Last Name: Welles

Panel Stretch Layout   Panel Stretch Layout is a layout component with five facets representing the center, start, end, top, and bottom. The size of the surrounding facets can be explicitly set using the properties *StartWidth*, *EndWidth*, *TopHeight*, and *BottomHeight*, with the center facet automatically stretching its child component to fill the rest of the available space. If no content is placed in a facet, then it will not be rendered.

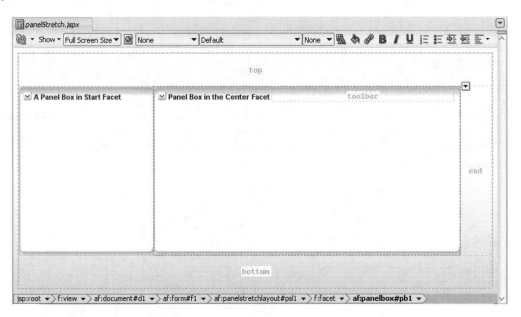

Panel Collection   Panel Collection is a component that manages collections of data such as Table and Tree components. What makes Panel Collection particularly useful for these components is that it includes facets for menus and toolbars.

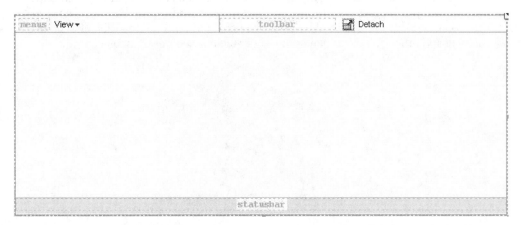

Panel Splitter   The Panel Splitter component is a panel with a divider that splits the panel horizontally or vertically depending on the *Orientation* property. Two facets are used to represent each part of Panel Splitter, with *SplitterPosition* defining the starting position for the divider, which the user can reposition at runtime.

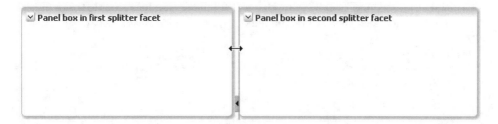

Panel Tabbed   Panel Tabbed is a component that manages one or more Show Detail Item child components, each of which appears as a separate tab. Selecting a tab brings the Show Detail Item component to the fore. Panel Tabbed has a *Position* property to define whether the tab appears above, below, or both.

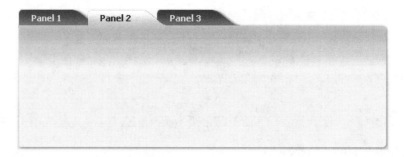

Panel Accordion   Like the Panel Tabbed component, the Panel Accordion component works in conjunction with Show Detail Item component to present a group of panels, each of which can be expanded or collapsed. The properties *DiscloseMany* and *DiscloseNone* define whether many panels can be visible at once and whether one panel must always be visible. Furthermore, users can drag and drop each of the panels to reorder them if *Reorder* is enabled.

Spacing Layout Components

The panel components will automatically manage their child components; however, sometimes you might want to fine-tune that layout by, for example, nudging a component so that it appears offset from the other components. The following components can be used for this purpose.

Spacer   Spacer is simply a component that occupies a fixed amount of space on a page and helps in laying out other components. The properties *Height* and *Width* can be used to control the size of the spacer.

A field with Spacer below	
A field with Spacer above	
No Spacer above	

Separator   Separator is a component that renders itself as a horizontal line to visually divide content.

A field with Separator below	
A field with Separator above	
No Separator above	

Group   The Group component is responsible for logically grouping content. It is particularly useful when used in conjunction with menus and buttons as it gives a visual indication that the child components are grouped using a separator.

Grouped Buttons	Button1	Grouped Button2	Grouped Button3	Button4

Building Your First Page

Now that you have a better understanding of a selection of the commonly used components, the next step is to create your first page and display some content on the page. Given you are now developing the UI of your application, all content should be created in the ViewController project of your application. This ensures a clean separation between the view and the business services.

Creating a JSF Page

To create a new JSF page, select the ViewController project, select **File | New**, and, in the New Gallery dialog, select **JSF** and then **JSF Page**. This launches the Create JSF Page dialog, as shown in Figure 10-2. At this point you only need to input a name for the page.

NOTE
Ensure that Create as XML Document *is checked. In fact, it shouldn't make any difference to the page you are about to create, but it's a good practice since there are a number of benefits, such as page customization, that you may wish to exploit as you become more experienced and build production applications.*

You will notice there are some other options on this dialog. For example, you can create the page based on a template or one of the supplied quick start layouts. At this time just create a blank page. Templates and the quick start layouts are covered later in the book.

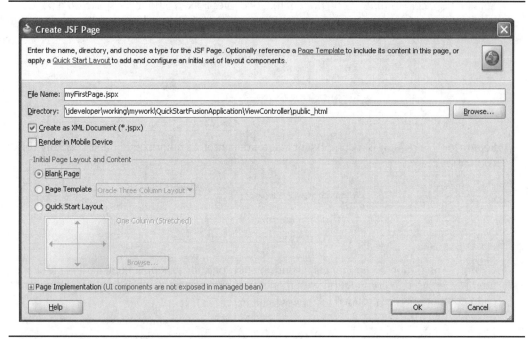

FIGURE 10-2. *Create JSF Page dialog*

Also, if you expand *Page Implementation*, you can define whether you want a managed bean to back this page and whether accessors to the UI components you create should be automatically created in the managed bean class.

Creating Content on Your Page

Congratulations, you've just created your first JSF page. However, you will probably want to put some data on this page now. You have a number of choices. You could simply drag and drop UI components from the Component Palette. But you would have to then specifically wire them up to your business service. Instead, JDeveloper provides a much more convenient way of quickly adding data-bound components on a page.

Data Controls Panel

The Data Controls panel is the ADF Model representation of the business service you created earlier. If you cast your mind back to Chapter 2, you may remember that ADF Model is the layer that provides a common abstraction over your business service. The Data Controls panel shows that representation. You can expand each of the nodes to view the structure of the business service; however, this is covered in more detail in the next chapter.

TIP
By default, the Data Controls panel is displayed in a collapsible panel in the Application Navigator below your projects.

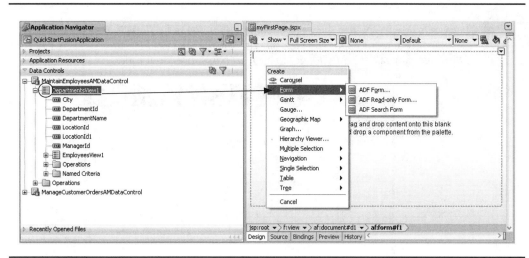

FIGURE 10-3. *Dragging from the Data Controls panel*

JDeveloper allows you to drag a node from the Data Controls panel directly onto the page. It then prompts you as to how you would like that part of the business service displayed, as shown in Figure 10-3.

Try this, and select that you want to display Departments as a read-only form. JDeveloper will automatically display all of the attributes of the underlying Departments business service, using appropriate visual components, in a form layout. The *Value* property of each of the components will automatically be set to the appropriate framework class in order to populate the component with data from the business service. Furthermore, if you defined control hints on the business service, then this information should also be reflected on the page.

You can also select whether to display navigation buttons on the page. If you choose to do so, these buttons will be bound to the business service methods for navigating the rows of data. And these are the same methods that were being called by the ADF Business Component Browser when you were testing the business service.

TIP
Use the Structure window and the Property Inspector to examine the various layout components and EL values that have been automatically created.

Running and Testing Your JSF Page

Having created a data-bound JSF page, you can now run and test it. Right-click the page and select **Run**. This will deploy the application to the integrated server, and the page appears in the browser.

NOTE
*The very first time you run the page, there are a number of actions that
JDeveloper has to automatically kick off. This means the very first run
of the page may take slightly longer to appear than subsequent runs.*

Summary

You now should have an understanding of the high-level concepts of ADF Faces and an overview
of some of the more commonly used components. You have learned that:

- ADF Faces includes components for data input and list selection.

- Collections of data can be displayed as a table or a hierarchical tree.

- ADF Faces includes layout components for helping to manage page layout.

- ADF Faces components can be dragged and dropped onto a JSF page.

- Business services can be directly bound to a page by dragging and dropping from the
  Data Controls panel.

You are now able to create pages and to add data-bound components by simply dragging and
dropping from the Data Controls panel. The next chapter goes into more detail on the ADF Model
and how it binds your UI components to the business service.

CHAPTER
11

Introduction to
ADF Model

hereas the business service layer implements the nuts and bolts of your application processing, the View layer provides the UI components for displaying and interacting with the data. However, there is one essential piece of the Oracle ADF jigsaw that is easy to overlook: ADF Model.

For any application based on the Model-View-Controller (MVC) architectural principle, where the business service is separated from the implementation of the UI, the two tiers need to be bound together. ADF Model provides this binding and is responsible for ensuring that a specific piece of data from the business service, such as an order item, is bound to an appropriate UI component, such as a table. Furthermore, if the user wants to delete an order item through an action like a button click, ADF Model ensures that the button is associated with the appropriate business service action to perform the deletion.

This chapter gives an insight into ADF Model and how it provides the binding between the business service and the UI.

ADF Model provides a number of significant benefits to the developer. The first is that it implements the physical binding of a UI component to a business service. ADF Model enables you to do this by providing a framework feature, called a binding container, that acts as the glue between a page and the business service.

The second benefit is that ADF Model provides a layer of abstraction over the underlying implementation. So, regardless of how the business service is implemented, such as ADF Business Components, web services, or simple Java classes, it is always presented to the UI in the same way. This means that the View layer can be developed in a consistent manner, since the integration and interaction with the business service is always performed through ADF Model.

The Data Controls Panel

You have already been exposed to ADF Model though the Data Controls panel of the Application Navigator in Chapter 10. This panel shows an implementation-agnostic representation of the business service, as shown in Figure 11-1. In this panel, you can drag data collections, individual attributes, or operations from the business service onto a page and JDeveloper will prompt for how you want that business service element displayed as a UI component. Once you have chosen the appropriate UI component, JDeveloper automatically binds that UI component to the underlying business service.

By using the Data Controls panel, you can quickly create data-bound pages without having to know much about the internal workings of ADF Model. However, by taking a closer look at the building blocks, you will be able to achieve much more.

FIGURE 11-1. *Data Controls panel*

The Building Blocks of ADF Model

There are essentially two halves to the binding problem: the business service has to be exposed in a consistent way, and a UI component has to know how to bind to that abstraction.

In nonsoftware terms, you can think of the solution as being analogous to two pieces of VELCRO® brand fasteners. One piece of Velcro, with loops, is attached over the business service, while the other piece of Velcro, with the hooks, is attached to the UI component. No matter how the business service is implemented, the UI component can always bind to it so long as it has the appropriately shaped piece of Velcro.

NOTE
As this analogy mentions, the UI component must use the appropriately shaped piece of "Velcro." This is because different UI components, such as buttons and tables, work with the data in slightly different ways, and so require a slightly different "shape" to the binding. For example, a UI component such as a table must be bound to many rows and columns of data, whereas a text field is bound to only a single piece of data. You will find out more about the different bindings later in this chapter.

But how does ADF Model implement the hooks and loops of the Velcro analogy? The answer is that ADF Model provides the two halves of the binding solution: data controls and bindings.

Data Controls

Data controls provide the abstraction of the business service. Like many artifacts in Oracle ADF, data controls are simply XML definitions of the underlying business services. The XML describes the business service, including what attributes it has and any operations it exposes.

So, how do you generate a data control for your business service? The good news is that for ADF Business Components, you don't have to. Because the definition of a business service developed using ADF Business Components, specifically the application module, is already XML, ADF Model knows how to work with that definition. Thus, ADF Business Components is already "data control ready." All the information defined in the application module, such as the view object instances, their attributes, and their operations, define the façade for the business service in a way that ADF Model already understands. This is what you see in the Data Controls panel shown in Figure 11-1.

Creating a Data Control

Suppose you create some part of your business service and don't use ADF Business Components; how do you create a data control for that? As you might expect, JDeveloper takes care of this for you.

Let's take the simple example of a Java class (note, however, that you would follow the same steps even for something more advanced like a web service). You decide to write a Java class in your business service that returns, for example, the duty manager for today's shift. This is an essential part of the business service and needs to be exposed on the UI via ADF Model.

First of all, in the Model project, create the class to implement the business functionality. Select **File | New** and, in the New Gallery dialog, select **Java** and then **Java Class**. Add the following code:

```
package services;
public class ManagementRoster {
    public String todaysDutyManager() {
        return "John Smith";
    }
}
```

Of course, this is a trivial example, but it demonstrates the point. Having created the class that implements your business function, you now want to create a data control for this Java class so that it can be made available through ADF Model. Simply right-click the class name and select **Create Data Control**.

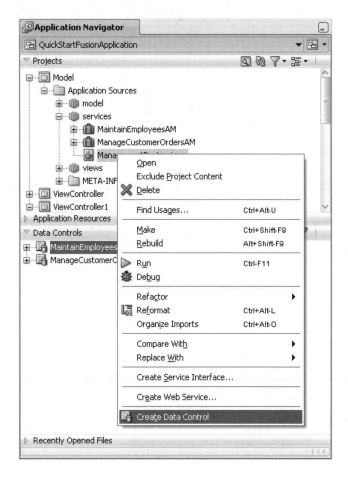

TIP
You can also drag and drop the Java class directly onto the Data Controls panel to create the data control.

JDeveloper creates the data control that describes the class to allow it to be accessed from the UI through ADF Model.

You should now see the associated data control definition file in the Application Navigator, and the data control itself should be visible in the Data Controls panel, as shown in Figure 11-2. You could now drag and drop this data control onto a JSF page if you wish to display the current duty manager.

TIP
You may need to click the Refresh button on the Data Controls panel to see the new data control.

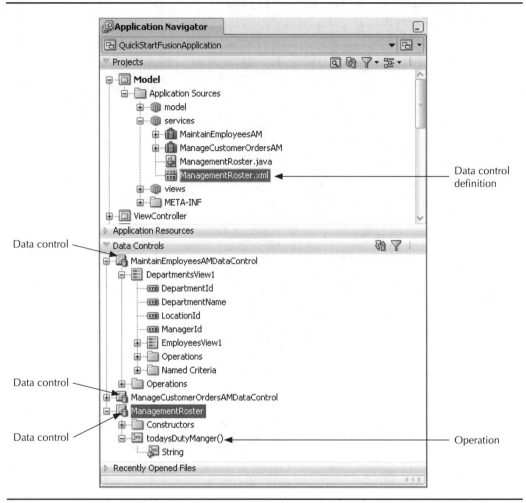

FIGURE 11-2. *Data Controls panel after adding a data control for a Java class*

With your newfound understanding of data controls, you should now recognize in Figure 11-2 that each of the application modules created in the business service is represented as a data control.

NOTE
The file DataControls.dcx is also created in your Model project. This file acts as an index for all non–ADF Business Components data controls.

Binding

So with data controls you have one half of the solution, providing a common abstraction of the business services. The second part of the puzzle is the binding, which is responsible for connecting the UI component to the data control.

The first thing to recognize is that there are different flavors of binding, because there are different types of UI components; a button requires a different kind of binding than a table component requires, since one is binding to an action and the other to a collection of rows of data.

When you create UI components by dragging from the Data Controls panel, JDeveloper offers a choice of UI components. This choice depends on whether you are dropping on the page a data collection, such as Departments, or a single attribute, like CustFirstName. After you make a choice, JDeveloper automatically creates the UI component on the page, creates the binding, and then wires up the various properties of the UI component, like *Value*, to the binding.

NOTE
The properties of UI components reference the binding by using Expression Language (EL). This is covered in more detail later in this chapter.

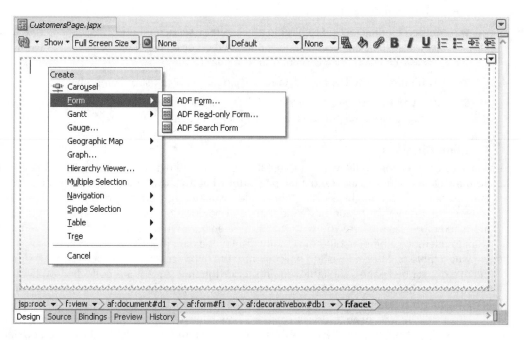

Also note that many UI components can reference the same binding. For example, the *Value* property of a text field and the *Text* property of a panel box could both reference the same binding; for example, the binding for the Customer's first name attribute. This would be useful if you wanted the name of the currently selected customer to also appear in the title text of the panel box.

NOTE
It is not only UI components that can reference bindings; you can also reference the bindings from code. Chapter 19 explains how you can programmatically access the UI component binding in order to access or change a value.

Types of Binding

For the most part you can expect JDeveloper to do the right thing with respect to creating the right kind of binding for the right UI component. However, it is useful to be aware of the different flavors of binding. Some of the more common binding types are noted here:

- **Attribute binding**   Used to bind to a single attribute value such as DepartmentId, typically using a component like an input text or output text field.

- **Tree binding**   Used to bind collections of data, such as Departments, using components like a tree control or a table.

- **Action binding**   Used for binding the default actions of an ADF Business Components service such as Create, Delete, Next, and Previous. This would typically be bound to a push button or a link.

- **Method binding**   Used to bind to any business service function implemented as a Java method such as an application module method or a Java class method. This would typically be bound to a push button or a link.

- **List binding**   Used to bind data lists, such as a choice list or combo box.

- **ListofValues binding**   Used to bind data to a list of values component. This component typically involves a pop-up dialog with search capabilities.

Creating Bindings

So far you are relying on JDeveloper to create the right bindings for you when you drag and drop from the Data Controls panel onto a JSF page. But what if you want to explicitly create a binding? The first question you might ask is, "Why would I want to create my own binding if JDeveloper is supposed to do everything for me?" And that's a good question; however, you will start to find more and more cases where you will want to create your own binding. For example, you might want to reference a binding but not actually display the data in a UI component. Or you might be viewing a table of data and wish to have an attribute of the currently selected record displayed as the title of a tabbed panel. The table requires a tree binding since it is a collection of data; however, the title for the tabbed panel requires only a single value. In this case, it would make sense to create an attribute binding to the same data control as the table is using.

The first thing you need to do is to create a new page to display a table of customers. Create a new JSF page and drop on a Panel Tabbed component and inside the Panel Tabbed component drop a Panel Collection. Inside the Panel Collection, drag and drop the customers data collection from the Data Controls panel as a read-only table, as shown in Figure 11-3. You can choose which attributes you want to display.

JDeveloper will automatically create the table UI component and the appropriate binding to the data control. You can view the bindings for this page by selecting the *Bindings* tab, as indicated in Figure 11-3. This page shows the bindings and the data control to which it is bound, as shown in Figure 11-4. The icon for the binding shows that this is a tree binding; however, placing the cursor over the binding will also display a hint that this is a tree binding.

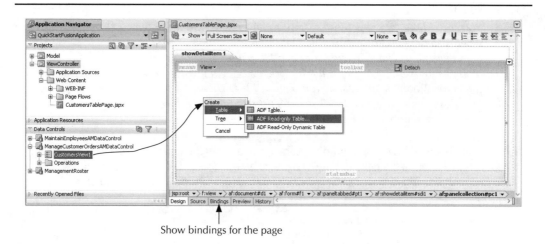

FIGURE 11-3. *Adding a table of customers to a page*

You will also notice that there is a middle column, *Executables*. For the moment you can assume one executable per collection. This executable is an iterator, or pointer to the current data object. So, in Figure 11-4 you have a tree binding CustomersView1; the pointer for that collection of data is called CustomersView1Iterator; and that references the CustomersView1 data control.

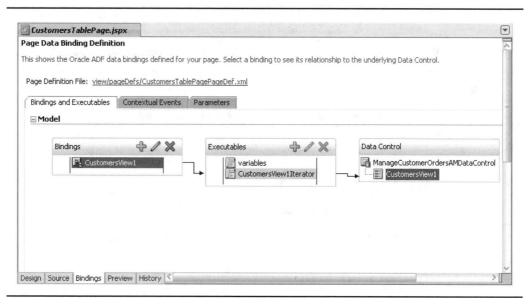

FIGURE 11-4. *Data binding for a page*

NOTE
You should see two new files created in the ViewController project when you drag and drop from the Data Controls panel. There is a file <PageName>PageDef.xml for each JSF page. This defines the bindings for each page and is the file you are viewing when you select the Bindings *tab as shown in Figure 11-4. There is also a file DataBindings.cpx, which holds information about which JSF page is mapped to which PageDef.*

You now want to create a binding to be able to show the currently selected customer's e-mail address in the tab of the tabbed panel. To create a new binding, click the green plus sign in *Bindings*. In the Insert Item dialog, select "Generic Bindings, select "attributeValues," and click OK.

In the Create Attribute Binding dialog, select the data control collection and attribute that the binding should reference. For *Data Source* select "ManageCustomersOrdersAMDataControl .CustomersView1" and for *Attribute* select "CustEmail."

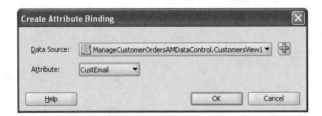

This will create a binding to the CustomersView1 data collection's CustEmail attribute. The resulting new binding is shown in Figure 11-5.

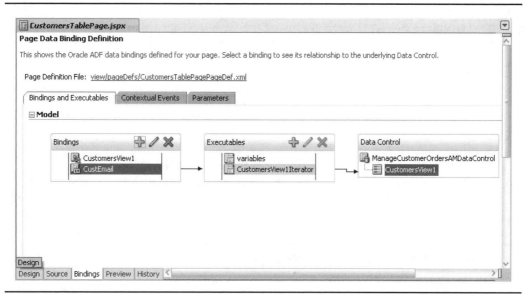

FIGURE 11-5.   *New data binding added to the page*

NOTE
Because the tree binding and the attribute value binding are referencing the same data control through the same executable, the CustEmail binding will correctly reference the currently selected data object. The executable is maintaining the pointer to the current row.

The final step is to reference that binding from the tabbed panel using Expression Language. This is explained in more detail in the next section, but if you wish to try this now, set the *Text* property of the showDetailItem subcomponent of the tabbed panel to "#{bindings.CustEmail. inputValue}." You can now test that selecting a row in the table displays the e-mail address for the customer in the tab title.

NOTE
*In order for the text in the tabbed panel to be refreshed, an action has
to happen on the page, such as switching tabs. However, if you want
to force the refresh automatically, select the CustEmail binding and set
its ChangeEventPolicy property to "ppr." This is a feature called partial
page refresh, which is covered later in the book. This will force the
component that references the binding to automatically refresh when
the binding has been updated.*

Understanding Expression Language

Expression Language (EL) is a feature of the View technology, that enables you to use an
expression to reference Java objects. This is particularly important for ADF Model because EL is
used in the properties of the UI component to reference the binding objects created by ADF
Model.

Using EL to Reference Bindings

For any UI component created by dragging and dropping from the Data Controls panel,
JDeveloper not only creates the binding, but also references that binding from the appropriate
properties of the component. For example, an attribute value binding would be referenced from a
text field component's *Value* property using an expression such as #{bindings.CustomerId.
inputValue}. This indicates that the value for the UI component should be derived from the
bindings object that ADF Model provides for the page; this is the reference to "bindings" in EL.
CustomerId references the name of the actual binding, and inputValue references the property
that should be returned from the binding.

However, bindings can return more than just data values. The *Label* property for a text field
could be set to #{bindings.CustomerId.hints.label}. This defines that *Label* gets its value from the
CustomerId binding in the bindings object and returns the label of a control hint. In Chapter 5
you learned that you can set up control hints in an entity object or view object; it is these control
hints that are being referenced, through ADF Model, by the UI components.

And, being an expression language, EL can use operators. An example is setting the *Disabled*
property, which controls whether the button is enabled or disabled, to "#{!bindings.Next.
enabled}." Note the exclamation mark, which negates the expression and thus sets the *Disabled*
property to false if you are able to navigate to the next row.

The Expression Builder

So, how are you supposed to ensure that you write correct EL? Well, for the most part, JDeveloper sets up the correct EL for you when you drag and drop from the Data Controls panel, so in the early stages of your learning, you will not be writing much, if any, EL. However, there is a dialog to help you build EL expressions if you require assistance. Each UI component property in the Property Inspector has a drop-down arrow to the right of the Property field that you can click to display a dialog for building EL.

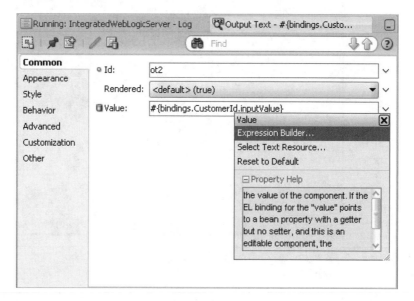

The Expression Builder dialog, shown in Figure 11-6, shows various features of the framework that you might choose to reference from EL. However, since you are only concerned with binding, the only node that is relevant at this point is the *bindings* node. When expanded, this node shows the binding container for the selected page; in Figure 11-6, you should recognize the names of the bindings created earlier.

Expanding one of the bindings, for example CustEmail, shows the various elements of the binding that can be referenced. Later in the book, and as you become more proficient, you will find out about some of the other framework elements you can reference from EL, but for now, the ones you are most likely to use and see are *inputValue*, *hints.label*, *hints.tooltip*, and *hints .mandatory*.

FIGURE 11-6. *Expression Builder dialog*

Summary

You should now have a clearer understanding of the role of ADF Model and how it helps you bind UI components to your business service. Specifically, in this chapter you learned that:

- The Data Controls panel is a technology-agnostic view of your business service.

- Data controls abstract the implementation details of business services.

- ADF Business Components are already "data control ready."

- Bindings allow UI components to reference the business service through data controls.

- There are different flavors of binding depending on whether the binding is to a single attribute value, a data collection, a list, a method, or an action.

- Dragging and dropping from the Data Controls panel automatically creates bindings for you.

- UI components reference bindings using EL.

CHAPTER
12

Building Typical ADF
Faces Pages

ou should now feel comfortable enough with the concepts of ADF Faces and ADF Model to start building some data-bound application pages. In this chapter you will be introduced to some of the more common ways of presenting business service data through UI components. You'll also learn about the features that these UI components offer.

Of course, how you design the look and feel of your application really comes down to individual preference; however, there is one important rule when designing your pages that goes beyond the choice of colors and fonts: work with the components, not against them. What does this mean? Well, each UI component, like a table, graph, or carousel, has a specific set of behaviors and a standard set of features. Before embarking on a development effort, you need to understand how these UI components work and, more importantly, how you can get the best results from the components. Simply designing a page without understanding what the UI components can do may lead you down the path of trying to force the proverbial square peg into a round hole.

This chapter looks at some of most commonly used UI components and layout strategies you will find yourself using again and again.

Table UI Component

One of the most common, and useful, UI components for displaying a collection of rows of data is the ADF Faces Table component. This component can be used to display tabular data and allows features like row selection, reordering, and filtering. The component itself is a parent component encompassing a number of column components, which are themselves parent components of components that render values such as an output text field.

Figure 12-1 shows an example of a Table component and highlights some of the inbuilt features of the component.

Using an ADF Faces Table Component

When you create a table on a page by dragging and dropping from the Data Controls panel, JDeveloper presents a Edit Table Columns dialog from which you can choose the columns and some options for the table, as shown in Figure 12-2.

Row Selection

By setting *Row Selection*, as shown in Figure 12-2, you are specifying a visual indicator of the currently selected row in the table. This means that the selected row in the table is synchronized with the current row in the business service.

NOTE
Selecting Row Selection, *as shown in Figure 12-2, sets three properties.*
RowSelection *defines the selection policy for the table; for example, "single" indicates a single row is selected at a time. The properties* SelectedRowKeys *and* SelectionListener *are also set to elements of the binding layer that will ensure the synchronization of the table with the underlying data. If you want to enable row selection on a table that was not previously set up for row selection, you can relaunch the Edit Table Columns dialog by selecting the Edit Component Definition button, shown with a pencil icon, on the Property Inspector for the table.*

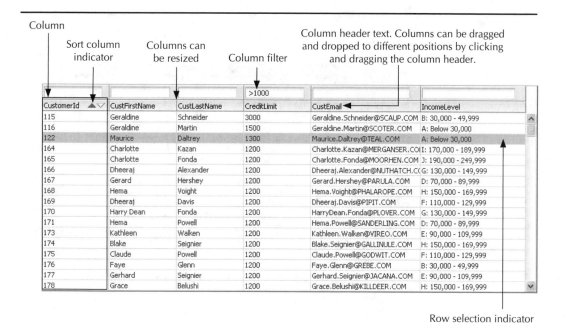

FIGURE 12-1.   *ADF Faces Table component*

Filtering

As shown in Figure 12-2, you can select *Filtering* on a table. Selecting this option places a text field at the top of every column and sets the column's *Filterable* property. This allows a user to enter an expression. An example is shown in Figure 12-1, which specifies that CreditLimit should be greater than 1000. This would refilter the data in the underlying business service to show only customers who have a credit limit greater than 1000.

NOTE
Setting Filtering *in the Edit Table Columns dialog sets the properties* filterModel, queryListener, *and* filterVisible.

Sorting

If you select the *Sorting* check box, shown in Figure 12-2, you give the user the ability to sort the table in ascending or descending order by selecting the column header. This sets the *Sortable* property on all columns of the table, which can also be specified on a column-by-column basis.

Table Columns

When you create a table by dragging and dropping from the Data Controls panel, you can specify which columns are displayed and which component is used. Figure 12-2 shows the red **✗** button

Row selection for the table   Table sorting

Table filtering

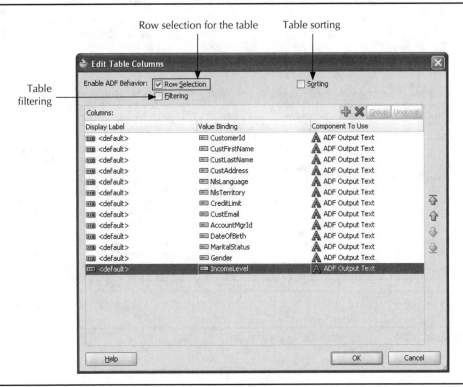

FIGURE 12-2. *Creating a read-only table from the Data Controls panel*

that you can use to remove selected attributes from the table. If you remove any attributes, they will not appear in the table or the binding that the table uses.

TIP
Having created a table, if you decide you want to change the columns or UI components within a column, select the Columns *tab in the Property Inspector for the table. Here you can edit the information the table displays.*

Other Table Properties
There are a number of other table properties that may be of interest.

Column Stretching   The *ColumnStretching* property of a table allows you to define which column should automatically stretch to fill the available space within the parent container. For example, it could be set to "last" to define that the last column in the table automatically stretches horizontally.

Column Selection   The *ColumnSelection* property of a table defines that the user can select a column. This is particularly useful in the case where the table is a child of a Panel Collection component (covered later in this chapter), which allows the selected column to be frozen. The rest of the table can then be scrolled horizontally, typically to show other columns, while the frozen column remains in view within the table.

TIP
You can also set the Frozen *attribute on a column to freeze a specific column rather than requiring the user to select a column and then freeze it.*

View ▾ Format ▾	📝	🞖 Freeze	📄 Detach	⏎ Wrap

CustomerId	NlsTerritory	CustFirstName	CustLastName
197	AMERICA	Gerard	Altman
198	AMERICA	Maureen	de Funes
199	AMERICA	Clint	Chapman
200	AMERICA	Clint	Gielgud
201	AMERICA	Eric	Prashant
202	AMERICA	Ingrid	Welles
203	AMERICA	Ingrid	Rampling
204	AMERICA	Cliff	Puri
205	AMERICA	Emily	Pollack
206	AMERICA	Fritz	Hackman
207	AMERICA	Cybill	Laughton
208	AMERICA	Cyndi	Griem
209	AMERICA	Cyndi	Collins
210	AMERICA	Cybill	Clapton
211	AMERICA	Luchino	Jordan
212	AMERICA	Luchino	Falk
214	AMERICA	Robin	Danson
215	AMERICA	Orson	Perkins
216	AMERICA	Orson	Koirala

Table Grids   The table properties *RowBandingInterval* and *ColumnBandingInterval* define the interval at which different color banding appears for rows and columns. *HorizontalGridVisable* and *VerticalGridVisible* also define whether horizontal or vertical grid lines are drawn for a Table component.

Layout Strategies for a Table Component
Experience and a certain amount of trial and error will guide you as to how best to use table components. However, there are a few simple pointers and best practices you can follow at this early stage in your learning to ensure that you get the best from the components.

Panel Collection
A Table component can reside within a number of different layout components; however, there is one component that is particularly well suited to managing a Table component: a Panel Collection.

The Panel Collection provides a number of useful features and facets that are commonly required for tables of data. The Panel Collection also automatically stretches its child component to fill the available space within the component.

Panel Collection View Menu   The Panel Collection includes a default menu, titled "View," that allows the table within the Panel Collection to be customized at runtime by the end user. The following are the menu options:

- **Columns**   Allows the user to select which columns are visible in the table.
- **Freeze**   For a table that has the property *ColumnSelection* set to "single" or "multiple," a column can be frozen such that it remains in view while other columns are scrolled horizontally. The table has to be wider than the parent container for the scroll bar to appear; otherwise, all columns are already in view.
- **Detach**   Detaches the Panel Collection so it appears as a floating pop-up window, thus maximizing the viewable area.
- **Sort**   Allows the user to sort the table in ascending or descending order based on a selected column, or to open a pop-up dialog and choose advanced settings for sorting columns.
- **Reorder Columns**   Displays a pop-up dialog that allows the user to reorder the table columns.
- **Query By Example**   Toggles the display of the filter fields that appear for each column where *Filterable* has been set to "true" on the column.

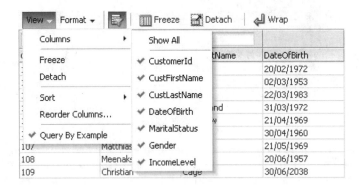

Panel Collection Facets   The Panel Collection contains the following facets that are useful when managing a Table component. Each facet is a named region of the Panel Collection component that has a suggested use.

- **afterToolbar**   A toolbar area that sits below the main toolbar facet.
- **menus**   A facet that can be used for a menu. Adding menus is covered in Chapter 14.
- **secondaryToolbar**   Provides a secondary area for a toolbar.
- **statusbar**   Another facet area that can be used for a toolbar or to display application messages.

- **toolbar**   Provides an area for a toolbar, which would typically include buttons. Toolbars and buttons are covered in Chapter 14.
- **viewMenu**   Allows you to define menu items that appear as part of the default "View" menu.

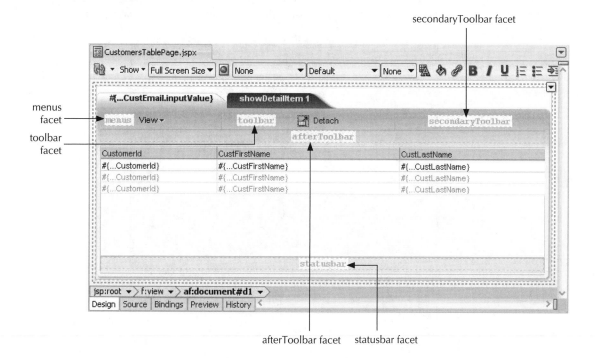

secondaryToolbar facet

menus facet

toolbar facet

afterToolbar facet   statusbar facet

Understanding Bindings for the Table Component

If you find yourself venturing beyond the drag-and-drop capabilities of the Table component, you might find that you need to adjust the binding. For example, if after creating the table you decide you want to show income level instead of credit limit, or you want to add a new column to the table, then you may need to adjust the binding. The first thing to understand is that a tree binding is used for table components. That might seem counterintuitive at first, but the reason is that a Table component behaves just like a Tree component, but with only one level of hierarchy. In both cases, a collection of data is rendered one row at a time, with each row, or node in the case of a tree, being represented by a number of attributes.

This tree binding uses a collectionModel, which you can think of as an object that includes all the attributes and rows you need for the binding. So, a Table component's *Value* property would typically be set to a value like "#{bindings.CustomersView1.collectionModel}."

Each field within a column must then reference the collectionModel in order to stamp out the value for each row of the table. To do this, the table has a property *Var* that has the default value "row." *Var* is just the name of a pointer that will loop through all the rows in the collectionModel object and return a row. Thus, the value of a field in a column of a table would be set to something like "#{row.CustFirstName}."

Viewing and Editing the Bindings for a Table For a JSF page with a Table UI component, select the *Bindings* tab to display the Page Data Binding Definition page. This shows the bindings for the page. Select the tree binding and then click the Edit Selected Element button, represented by the pencil icon. This opens the Edit Tree Binding dialog, where you can add a new attribute to the binding. So if you wanted to display income level instead of credit limit, you would add "IncomeLevel" to *Display Attributes*, which would create a new binding to that attribute.

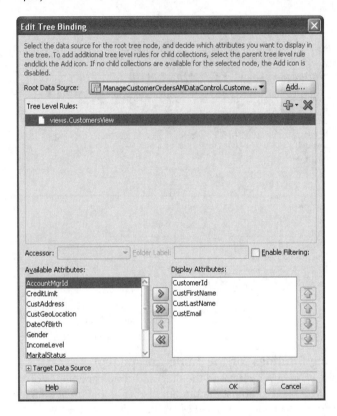

To reference this new binding in the actual Table UI component, change the *Value* property of the field within the table column to "#{row.IncomeLevel}."

TIP
The previous example shows how to create a binding and then reference that from the table. An easier way is to click the Edit Component Definition button, represented by the pencil icon in the Property Inspector, and add a new column to the table from there.

Adding and Editing Table Columns via the Property Inspector Another way to add columns and bindings to an existing table is through the Property Inspector. For the Table UI component, select the *Columns* tab in the Property Inspector. Here you can add new columns to the table by clicking the green plus button. Given that the collectionModel knows about all the possible attributes in the underlying data control, the *Value Binding* field presents a drop-down list of possible attributes that can be bound. This automatically creates the binding, adds the column to the table, and references the bindings in the column component.

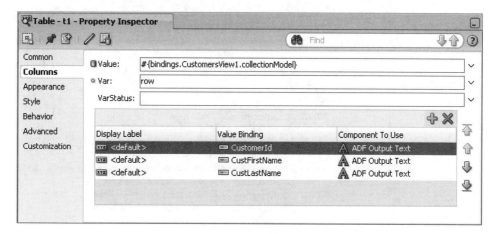

Form Layout

When you drag a data collection from the Data Controls panel, you also have the option of rendering the collection as a form. This is essentially a group of aligned labels and fields. There are three options when dropping a collection as a form:

- **ADF Form**   Lays out the data collection attributes using labels and input fields, or other selected UI components
- **ADF Read-Only Form**   Same as the ADF Form but all fields are read-only
- **ADF Search Form**   Same as ADF Form but with the ability to search for records depending on values entered into the fields

Strictly speaking, dragging and dropping a collection as a form does not create a single component called a form. Instead, JDeveloper is using a Panel Form Layout component to manage the display of the UI components that make up that form layout. You can see this in the Structure window, as shown in Figure 12-3.

NOTE
Looking at Figure 12-3, you may notice that there is a component called a form. But didn't the last paragraph say that there wasn't a single component called a form? In fact, `af:form` is at the root of all ADF Faces pages and is not specifically related to laying out a data collection as an ADF Form.

Creating an ADF Form

To create an ADF Form layout, simply drag and drop a data collection from the Data Controls panel onto a new page and, in the Edit Form Fields dialog, select the attributes that should appear in the form. You may also note at this point that attributes such as DateOfBirth and IncomeLevel

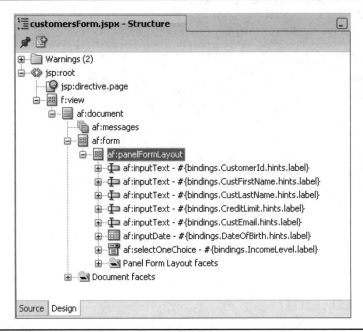

FIGURE 12-3. *Structure window showing an ADF Form*

have the UI component choice defaulted to an appropriate component because they represent a date and a list of values, respectively.

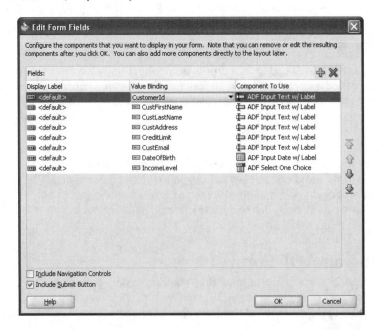

You can, of course, override this default choice for UI components and pick any appropriate component type you wish. Furthermore, you can select whether you want navigation buttons on the page to enable the user to navigate through the rows of the collection.

NOTE
Not every possible UI component is available through the Edit Form Fields dialog. If the component you wish to use is not available, you can convert or replace the UI component later. This is covered later in this chapter.

When you click OK in the Edit Form Fields dialog, the resultant ADF Form is displayed, as shown in Figure 12-4.

Editing an ADF Form
Having created an ADF Form, you can edit, change, and add to the layout. JDeveloper provides a number of different ways of doing this. Some of the common actions you might want to perform are covered here.

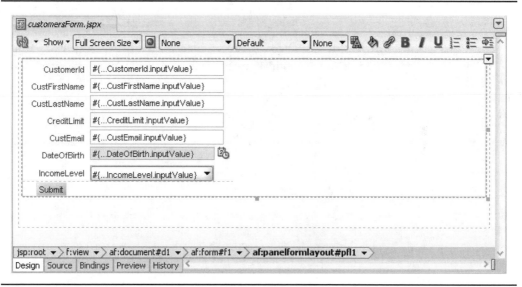

FIGURE 12-4. *ADF Form in the JSF visual editor*

Adding an Individual Attribute from the Data Controls Panel

As well as dragging and dropping data collections, you can also drag and drop individual attributes onto the JSF page. When you drop an attribute on a JSF page, JDeveloper presents a menu of appropriate UI components.

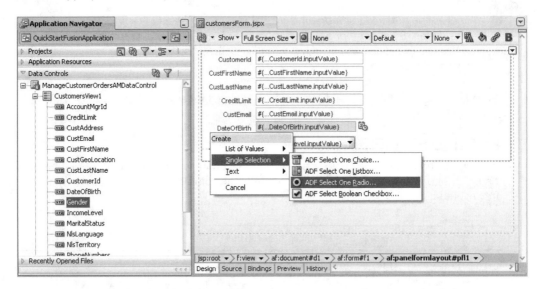

Depending on the UI component that you choose, JDeveloper may then display a dialog to allow you to define supplementary information about the binding. For example, for an ADF Select

One Radio, JDeveloper displays the Edit List Binding dialog to allow you to define the possible values of the Gender attribute.

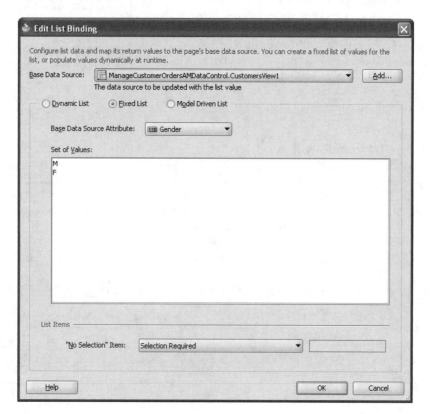

JDeveloper then creates the binding and the UI component and sets the appropriate properties of the UI component to reference the binding.

NOTE
The Edit List Binding dialog is the same dialog that appears if you edit a binding in the bindings editor, which is displayed by selecting the Bindings *tab on the JSF visual editor. This means you can easily change the binding whenever required.*

Converting an Existing UI Component

You may find that your page contains a UI component that, on reflection, you think would better be represented by a different UI component. Rather than deleting that UI component and then replacing it with a different component and having to rebind the new component, JDeveloper allows you to convert from one type of UI component to another.

In the JSF visual editor, right-click the field showing credit limit and select **Convert To**. The Convert Input Text dialog appears and you can choose a different UI component, such as Input Number Spinbox.

JDeveloper automatically maps the common properties between the old and the new component, such as *Label* and *Value*, so that you don't have to manually rebind the component. JDeveloper will flag any UI component properties that do not map to the new component.

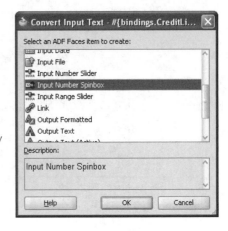

Binding a UI Component

The final option covered here is that you can drag a component from the Component Palette and drop it on the page. Then manually reference either a new or existing binding from the appropriate property of the component. This technique requires more experience with creating bindings, component properties, and EL.

However, there is one helper feature within JDeveloper that was touched on earlier. For a selected UI component, the Property Inspector includes a button Bind to ADF Control.

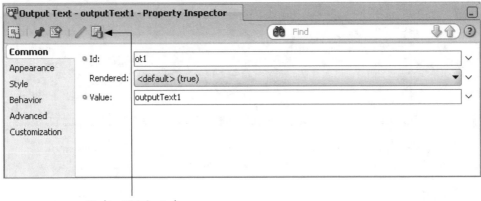

Bind to ADF Control

Clicking this button presents a dialog that allows you to select a data control. JDeveloper will then create the appropriate binding and reference that binding from the component properties. Note, however, that this feature is not available for all UI components.

Master Detail Layout

Your business service includes not only data collections, but also definitions of relationships between those data collections. This means that, for example, you can display the order items for a specific order. This master detail relationship is represented in the Data Controls panel as a hierarchy.

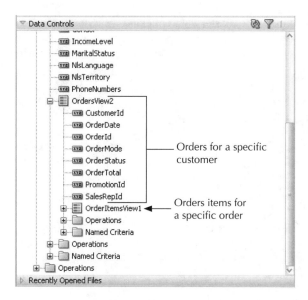

When you drag the detail node from the Data Controls panel onto a JSF page, JDeveloper recognizes this relationship and creates an appropriate page layout.

Creating a Master Detail Page

Assume that you have created a page containing a tabbed panel displaying a table of customers and you now want to show the orders and order items for that customer. Furthermore, you want to be able to navigate through each of the customer's orders.

To create a master detail layout, drag the child data collection—in this case OrderItemsView1—from the Data Controls panel onto the page. JDeveloper recognizes that this data collection is a detail for a master data collection and thus includes the menu option **Master-Detail**. In this case, select **ADF Master Form, Detail Table**.

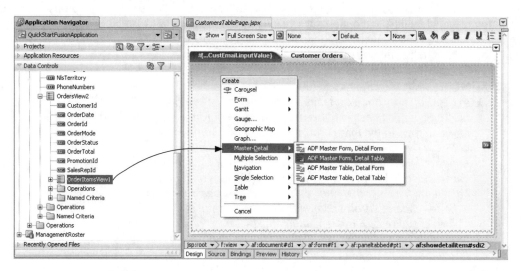

JDeveloper arranges the master data collection as a read-only form using a Panel Form Layout, and the detail data collection appears as a read-only table. If you wish, you can now fine-tune the UI components using the techniques described earlier in this chapter.

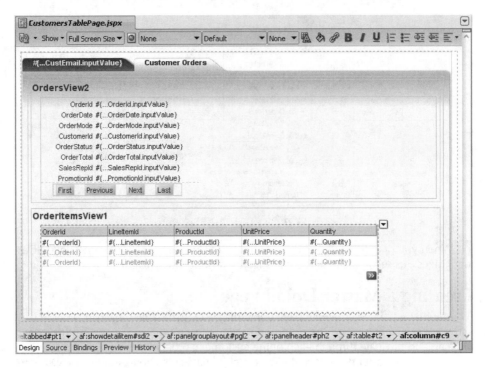

When you are ready, you can run the page and check the order items for a selected customer's order.

If you run and test this page, you might notice that the order items detail table doesn't stretch to fit its parent container. To get the table to stretch automatically, set the table property *StyleClass* to "AFStretchWidth" and optionally set *ColumnStretching* to "last." At this point you probably don't need to know much more than the fact that this is a useful feature for automatically enabling tables to stretch to fill horizontal space.

NOTE
In case you are curious, a feature called partial page rendering is helping your page achieve this master details coordination. When you navigate rows in the master form, the master UI components, or more correctly the binding executable used by the master UI components informs the detail table that it needs to refresh. It is called partial page rendering *because only these two groupings of components are talking to each other and so the rest of the page does not need to be re-rendered. A property on the binding executable called* ChangeEventPolicy *has been automatically set to "ppr" to inform the framework to implement this behavior. Partial page rendering is covered in more detail in Chapter 15.*

Search Functionality

Back in Chapter 8 you learned that view criteria could be used to set up filter conditions that could be exposed to the user in the form of a query panel. This would allow the user to quickly select, apply, or customize a filter for data being viewed on a JSF page.

Each view criteria defined is visible in the Data Controls panel under Named Criteria. There is also an addition filter "All Queriable Attributes." This is a "pseudo" view criteria that enables you to create a query panel that lets the end user query on any of the attributes of the underlying business service.

Creating a Query Panel on a Page

As you might expect, you can drag and drop a view criteria from the Data Controls panel directly onto a page, whereupon JDeveloper will display a menu indicating how that information can be displayed. Let's assume that on the customers page created earlier, you now want to add a query panel to allow the end user to filter the customers in the table.

Drag USCustomersViewCriteria from the Data Controls panel and drop it on the page and then select **ADF Query Panel**. You could have chosen an option to create a query panel and a table, but since the table of customers already exists, you only need to add a query panel.

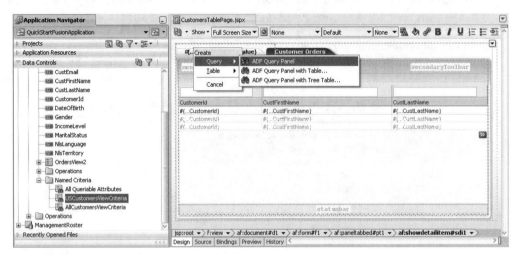

TIP
You might find it easier to drop onto the Structure window rather than the visual editor if you are trying to position the query panel at a specific point.

Depending on where you place the query panel, you might find that the Table component no longer sizes correctly. If this happens, it might be because you now have two child panels, the query panel and the table or Panel Collection, inside a parent container that would normally only size its first child. If this is the case, you may want to experiment by inserting other layout containers, or try setting *StyleClass* to "AFStretchWidth" on the table or Panel Collection.

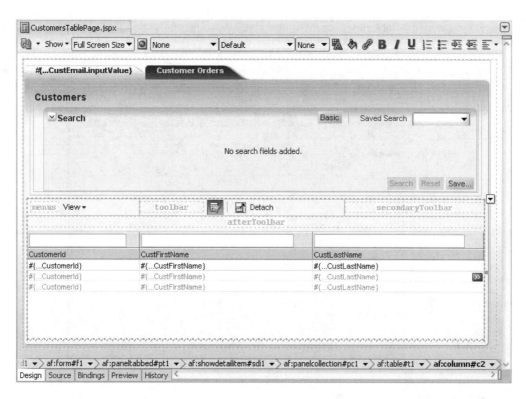

You should now have a query panel on your page. The query panel is automatically bound to the business service so that when a query condition is selected, it is applied to the appropriate business service. However, the query panel needs to know which UI component needs to be updated when a query is executed.

To enable the query panel to determine this, select the query component and, in the Property Inspector, find the property *ResultComponentId*. Using the property menu, accessed by clicking the drop-down arrow to the right of the field, select **Edit**. The Edit Property ResultComponentId dialog shows all the UI components within the page. Navigate to the Table component, select it, and click OK. This defines that this table is associated with the query panel.

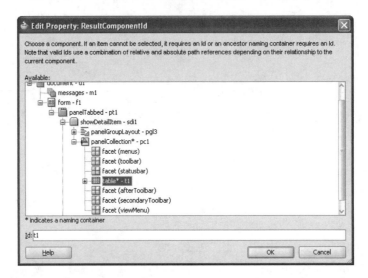

You can now run and test the search functionality by selecting a view criteria from the Saved Search list and clicking Search.

NOTE
The features of the query panel are controlled from properties on the component and also the UI Hints set up on the view criteria.

Summary

Having created some sample pages, you now have the core skills to create data-bound ADF Faces pages for your application. You should now know that:

■ You can drag and drop from the Data Controls panel to create different pages including a table and form layout.

■ Dragging and dropping from the Data Controls panel creates the UI component and the binding, and also references the binding from the UI component.

■ An ADF Faces Table component has built-in features such as row selection, filtering, sorting, column stretching, and repositioning.

■ A Panel Collection is a useful parent container for a table as it contains facets for toolbars, menus, and a status bar.

■ A data collection can be rendered as a read-only or editable form.

■ A data collection can be rendered in a master detail layout.

■ View criteria can be used to create a query panel.

Now that you can create data-bound pages, you need to understand how to link these pages together to provide the page flow for your application. The next chapter explains how task flows are used to define the flow of pages and business actions within your application.

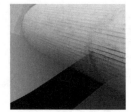

CHAPTER
13

Building Application Flow

ow that you are starting to build data-bound pages, you need to hook these pages together to provide a complete application. ADF Controller provides the ability to define application flow within reusable modules called task flows.

In this chapter you will learn about building task flows, discover different flavors of task flow, and gain an insight into some of the common features of task flows.

Introduction to Task Flows

Application flow typically involves the user navigating between application pages; however, ADF Controller goes beyond simply the flow of pages to include calls to business methods and features such as the conditional routing of application flow. Each of these definitions of application flow, called task flows, is easily reused, and at runtime the framework is responsible for reading the task flow definitions and implementing the appropriate sequence of pages and processes.

Figure 13-1 shows a simple example of a task flow depicting pages, flows between pages, a call to a business method, and a call to another task flow. Typically, each of the flows between pages would be associated with some user action, such as clicking a button on the page.

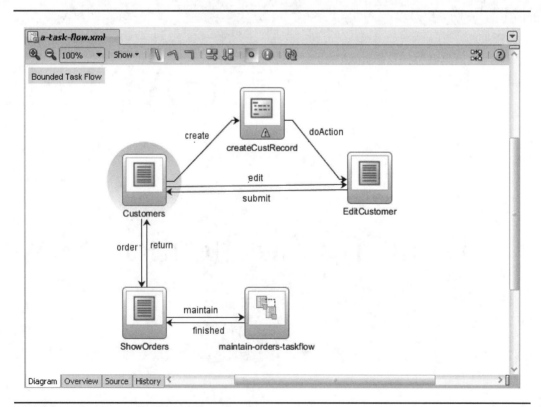

FIGURE 13-1. *Example of a task flow*

The specifics of the task flow diagram are covered later in this chapter, but for now, the task flow in Figure 13-1 can be interpreted in the following way:

- **Customers**   From the Customers page, for an *edit* action, navigate to the EditCustomer page.

- **Customers**   From the Customers page, for a *create* action, call a method createCustRecord before navigating to the EditCustomer page. Here the EditCustomer page is being used to enter details for a new customer as well as to edit an existing customer.

- **Customers**   From the Customers page, for an *order* action, navigate to the ShowOrders page.

- **EditCustomer**   On the EditCustomer page, if an action called *submit* happens, navigate back to the Customers page.

- **ShowOrders**   On the ShowOrders page, if an action called *return* happens, navigate back to the Customers page.

- **ShowOrders**   The ShowOrders page includes an action, *maintain*, that will call another task flow, maintain-orders-taskflow.

- **maintain-order-taskflow**   On completing the call to this task flow, control will return to the ShowOrders page via the *finished* action.

Each task flow is defined in its own file, so the application flow could be, and typically is, split into different task flows. There are a number of benefits in breaking application flow into different task flows, including: the ability to reuse task flows, simplified testing, development independence, and, of course, it just makes the application easier to understand if broken down into functional groups.

When it comes to building task flows, there are different approaches you might consider. You might start with a storyboard approach, where for a particular task flow you create placeholders representing pages to be created at a later point and draw control flows between those placeholders. This approach can be useful in allowing developers and end users to visualize the flow of the application before the job of building application pages actually starts. Alternatively, you might create a task flow by assembling existing pages into the task flow. And, of course, you may well take an approach that is a mixture of both. JDeveloper gives you the flexibility to choose whatever way suits your development project.

Creating a Task Flow

By default, the ViewController project in an Oracle ADF Fusion Application contains a task flow called adfc-config.xml; however, you can create further task flows by selecting **File** | **New** and, from the New Gallery dialog, selecting **JSF** and then **ADF Task Flow**. This launches the Create Task Flow dialog, as shown in Figure 13-2.

As you can see in Figure 13-2, there are a number of options for creating a task flow, more of which are covered later, but for now, let's address the fact that there are two types of task flow.

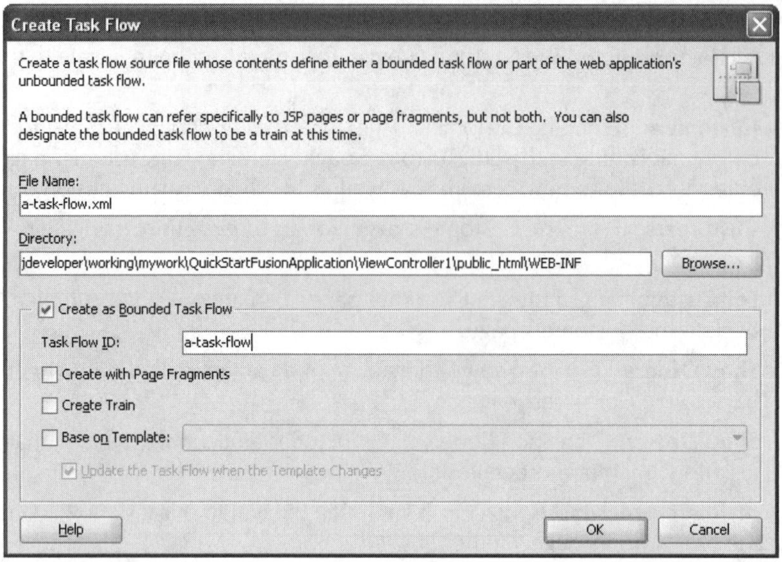

FIGURE 13-2. *Create Task Flow dialog*

Task Flow Types

When building task flows there are two flavors of task flow: bounded and unbounded. If you select *Create as Bounded Task Flow*, JDeveloper creates a bounded task flow; JDeveloper creates an unbounded task flow if you do not select that check box.

An application typically consists of one unbounded task flow and many bounded task flows, and fundamentally, both types of task flow do the same job aside from some slight differences.

Unbounded Task Flow

You can think of an unbounded task flow as the parent task flow from which your application is launched. With an unbounded task flow, any of the pages within the task flow can be the starting page of the application. If you want to have only one entry point into your application, such as always starting at the Customers page, then your unbounded task flow would contain only one page. If another page could be a starting point of the application, or is accessible from a bookmark or URL, then it would also appear in the unbounded task flow.

Typically, an unbounded task flow contains any page that can launch the application, and that page would reference further bounded task flows.

Bounded Task Flow

The bounded task flow is the task flow with which you will be working most often and represents a reusable application flow that can be referenced from any other task flow, whether bounded or unbounded. A bounded task flow has a single entry point and zero or more exit points. You can think of a bounded task flow as being similar to a subroutine call in a programming language: it can be called from different places but has only one entry point, it can be parameterized, and it can have multiple return points within its processing flow.

There are some other differences between bounded and unbounded task flows, which you will discover as you learn more about task flows, but for now you can think of the unbounded task flow as the top-level definition of your application flow, with calls to one or many bounded task flows.

Task Flow Diagram

Having created a task flow, you can then define the pages, called view activities, and the navigation between these view activities, called control flows, that characterizes that task flow. To do this, you will be working with the task flow diagram tool and dragging and dropping either pages or other task flows from the Application Navigator; or dragging and dropping task flow components from the Component Palette.

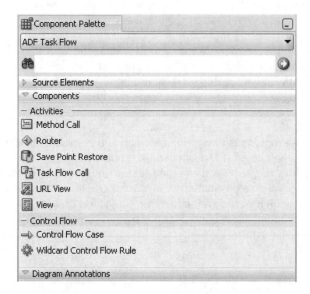

NOTE
Just like other artifacts in Oracle ADF, a task flow definition is simply an XML file. Feel free to view the source of the task flow to see the information created as you drag and drop onto the task flow.

Let's take a look at how you might create a typical task flow as shown earlier in Figure 13-1.

View Activity

A view activity represents a page within a task flow. You can either drag an existing page directly from the Application Navigator or create a placeholder for a page by dragging a view activity from the Component Palette.

When you drag a view activity from the Component Palette, a warning icon within the view activity alerts you to the fact that a page is not yet associated with this placeholder view activity.

Customers   EditCustomer

Having created a new view activity, there are a number of different ways to associate it with a page. If a page does not yet exist, then double-click the view activity to launch the Create JSF Page dialog. If a page already exists, then you can either drag it from the Application Navigator onto a view activity or select a page into the *Page* property of the view activity.

Typically, a view activity will have the same name as the page it represents, but that is not a requirement. The view activity properties *Activity ID* and *Page* define the name of the view activity and the page it references. By decoupling the navigation from the page name, it means not only that changes to the physical page name will not break the navigation, but also that a page can be reused in several contexts.

NOTE
If you are creating a bounded task flow, you may notice one of the view activities has a green halo. This indicates that this is the default activity, meaning it is the starting point for the bounded task flow. There is a button on the task flow diagram tool that allows you to change the default activity. You can also right-click the view activity and select **Mark Activity | Default Activity***.*

Control Flow Case

A control flow case represents navigation between two points in a task flow. To create a control flow, simply click the control flow case in the Component Palette and then click on the source point in the task flow diagram. You can then set the end point for the navigation by positioning the arrow and clicking on a destination point on the task flow. You can also set the name of the control flow case, which would typically reflect the action that causes the navigation to happen; for example, the following flow control case is named "edit."

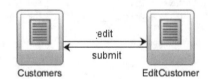

Once you have completed the preceding action, the control flow case properties *From Activity ID*, *To Activity ID* and *From Outcome* reflect the source, destination, and name of the control flow, respectively.

Initiating a Control Flow Case   So what triggers this control flow case? This is covered in more detail in the next chapter, but for the moment, the short answer is that a group of UI components, such as buttons, menus, and links, has an *Action* property. For this property, JDeveloper shows the possible control flow cases that can be initiated from the page on which the component is placed. If the *Action* property is set on the button, then the framework will automatically navigate, as defined by the control flow case, when that button is clicked.

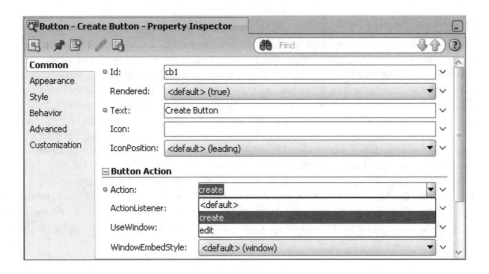

Method Call Activity

One of the key reasons we talk about "task flow" and not "page flow" is that a task flow is not limited to the navigation of only pages, but can also include calls to methods as part of the application flow. So, why might that be useful? Well, for example, when creating a new customer, you want to navigate to a new page to enter the customer details; however, you first want to call a method to create a new customer row.

You can either drag and drop a method directly from the Data Controls panel or create a placeholder by dragging and dropping a method call activity onto the task flow from the Component Palette. You can then use control flows to wire up the flow, just as you do with a view activity.

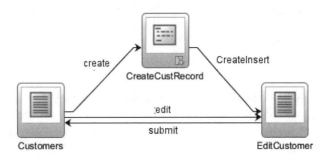

To associate a placeholder method call with an actual method, you can either drag and drop a method from the Data Controls panel onto the method call activity or explicitly set the binding using the *Method* property in the method call activity.

For a method call activity, the property *Activity ID* is the name of the method call activity in the task flow, which can be different from the method being called. The property *Fixed Outcome* defines the name of the control flow to be followed after executing the method.

Wildcard Control Flow Rule

So far, you have seen how to define the flow between specific pages and methods within a task flow. However, what happens if you have a page that is navigable from any other page, for example, a product catalog or a logout page? If you wanted to implement the navigation from every page, you would have to define a control flow from each view activity to the specified page. This would obviously make the task flow diagram much more complex.

Instead, a feature of task flows, called a wildcard control flow rule, allows you to define that a task flow activity can be accessed from any task flow activity whose outcome matches a particular wildcard. For example, if the product catalog can be accessed only from any of the customer pages, then you would define a wildcard "Customer*."

To implement this behavior, drag and drop a wildcard control flow rule from the Component Palette onto the task flow diagram and drag a control flow between it and the page to which you want to navigate. Now set the *From Activity ID* of the wildcard control flow rule to "Customer*" to indicate that this control flow can be called from any view activity whose name, defined by *Activity ID*, starts with the string "Customer."

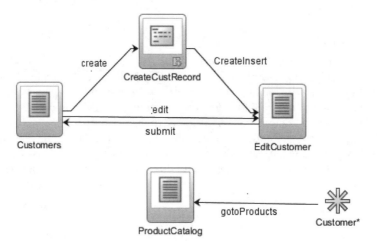

NOTE

If From Activity ID *is set to "*" then the task flow activity is available from all pages in the task flow. This might be useful if you want to have a help or logout page that can be navigated to from any page in the task flow.*

Now when it comes to setting the *Action* property for a button on a page, the option "gotoProducts" will be available on any task flow activity whose name meets the wildcard rule.

Router Activity

So far you have learned about static navigation, where, for a particular action, the control flow always navigates to the same task flow activity. You can, however, bring more flexibility into the task flow through the use of a router activity. This allows a rule to be evaluated and, depending on the result, navigate to different task flow activities.

Let's consider this simple example: On creating a new order, you gather different information for U.S. customers than you do for non-U.S. customers. You therefore want to navigate to one page for U.S. customers but to a different page for non-U.S. customers based on some information—in this case, the NlsTerritory of the customer.

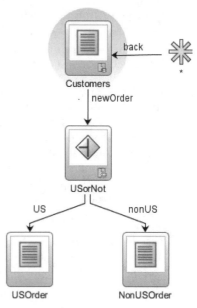

The router activity allows you to define expressions that are evaluated in order to decide which control flow the router will navigate. You can also define a default navigation case, specified by the *Default Outcome* property of the router activity.

So how do you define these navigation expressions?

Creating a Binding on the Router Activity Given that you want to create a routing expression based on information about a customer, you need to create a binding to that information so that the router activity can access it. Right-click the router activity and select **Create Page Definition**. This allows you to create an attribute binding to the NlsTerritory attribute of the customer.

You can then add an expression for each of the navigation cases. In the Property Inspector for the router activity, create two navigation cases, and, using the Expression Builder, enter an expression #{bindings.NlsTerritory.inputValue == 'AMERICA'} and define the *Outcome* to use if this expression is "true." Also enter the expression for the other *Outcome*, #{bindings.NlsTerritory .inputValue !='AMERICA'}, which checks for non-U.S. customers.

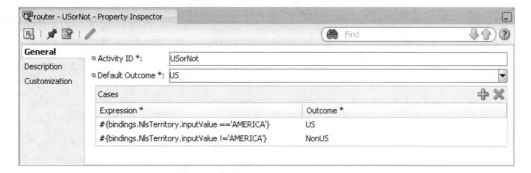

NOTE

A routing expression can also be based on information such as a parameter passed into the task flow, or from a managed or backing bean for a page. Task flow parameters are covered later in this chapter, while managed and backing beans are covered in later chapters.

Calling a Bounded Task Flow

The final example covered here is how you can call another task flow from within a task flow. There are two parts to this: calling the bounded task flow and defining what should happen when the called task flow completes.

Task Flow Call Calling a bounded task flow from within a task flow is similar to calling any other task flow activities: either drag and drop a bounded task flow from the Application Navigator, or drop on a task flow call activity from the Component Palette and then select the task flow into the task flow activity *Document* and *ID* properties. You can then define control flow cases to and from this task flow call.

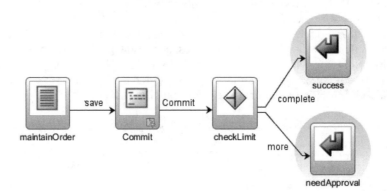

Task Flow Return For a bounded task flow, you also need to define where control should be passed when the bounded task flow exits. This is done by dropping a task flow return onto the bounded task flow.

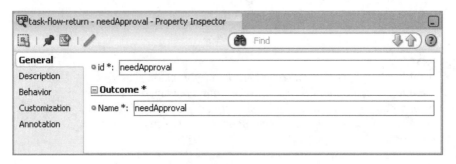

You need to indicate to which control flow in the calling task flow control should be returned. To do so, set the *Outcome Name* property of the task flow return to a control flow on the calling task flow.

Task Flow with Page Fragments

Until now, the purpose of a task flow has been to manage the navigation of application flow, including pages. However, there is another side to ADF Controller. Rather than navigating distinct pages, a task flow can navigate page fragments. What are page fragments? As the name suggests, these are fragments of a page. So, rather than navigating to a new page, the task flow would be embedded inside a region of a page, and only that region would change as the task flow steps through its defined fragments.

This might be useful if, for example, you want to remain on the orders confirmation page as you step through the various page fragments to enter details of the shipping address, billing information, and payment details.

Defining a Task Flow with Page Fragments

When you create a task flow, there is an option *Create with Page Fragments*, as shown in Figure 13-2. This sets up the task flow to deal with page fragments. You can then build the task flow exactly as you did before. The only difference is that when you double-click a view activity, JDeveloper will display the Create New JSF Page Fragment dialog. To all intents and purposes, this is exactly the same as the JSF pages you have been creating already, but these are subpages with a .jsff extension.

You can also create a page fragment by selecting **File** | **New** and, from the New Gallery dialog, selecting **JSF** and then **JSF Page Fragment**.

TIP
You can convert an existing task flow, based on pages, to one based on page fragments. To do this, right-click in the task flow visual editor and select **Convert to Task Flow with Page Fragments**.

Consuming a Task Flow with Page Fragments in a Region

Having created a task flow with page fragments, the next step is to embed that task flow within a region on a page. To do so, simply drag and drop the task flow from the Application Navigator onto the appropriate area on the page and select **Region**.

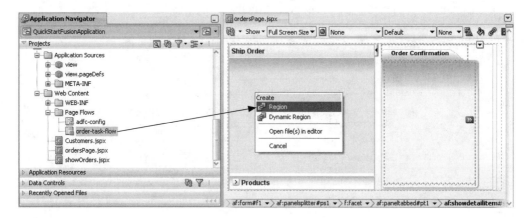

This will create a region on the page that references the task flow, and it is within this region the task flow navigation will happen at runtime.

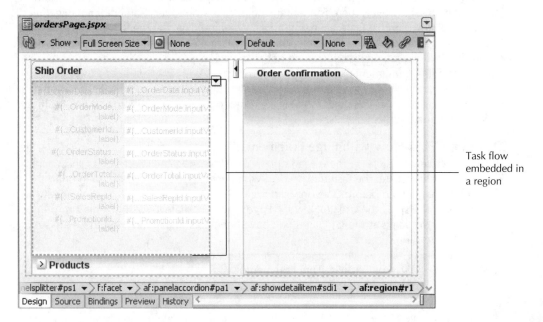

Task flow embedded in a region

Task Flow Trains

A common use case with application flow is where a task requires the user to step through a sequence of pages, or fragments, possibly allowing the user to navigate back to a previous page or to jump ahead in the page sequence. For example, entering the details for a new customer might involve separate pages for entering the name, contact details, and credit details before committing the data. After entering the name and contact details, the user might want to navigate back and correct the name before jumping ahead to the credit details page. This behavior can be implemented in a special type of task flow called a train.

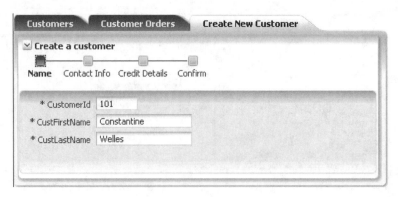

Creating a Task Flow Train

To create a train, as shown in Figure 13-2, use the *Create Train* option. Selecting this option defines the task flow as a train, and will automatically create control flows between the view activities when they are dropped onto the task flow. Having created the task flow train, you can call it, or embed it as a region, just like any other task flow.

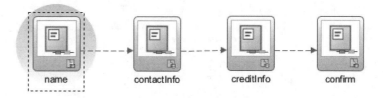

Train Navigation

Having created the page or fragment for each train stop, you will want to display a train navigation component to allow the user to move between the different train stops. To do this, drag and drop an ADF Faces Train component from the Component Palette onto the page. This is a UI component that can be found on the Component Palette when designing a JSF page. You need to do this on each page that is a train stop. JDeveloper will automatically bind the component so that it performs the navigation to the appropriate page when selected.

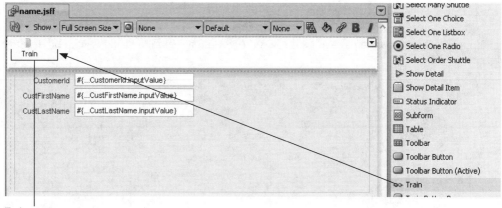

Train component

    The final step is to define the display name for each train stop as it will appear in the train navigation component. You might expect to set a property on the view activity for this, but at the time of writing, this has to be done through the Structure window. Right-click the train-stop and insert a display-name and set the *Text* property on this component.

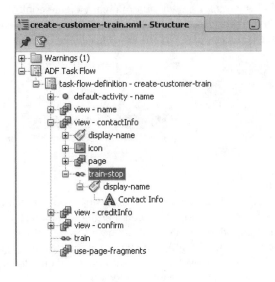

Task Flow as Dialogs

A further option for using task flows is to display a task flow as a pop-up window. So, instead of appearing as a separate page in the browser, or within a region, a task flow can be displayed in a modal dialog.

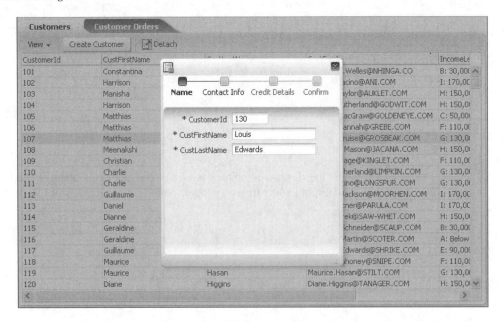

Displaying a Task Flow in a Dialog

In order to display a task flow in a modal dialog, you need to set two properties on the task flow call activity. By setting *Run As Dialog* to "true" and *Display Type* as "inline-popup," you can define that this task flow will be displayed inside an inline dialog.

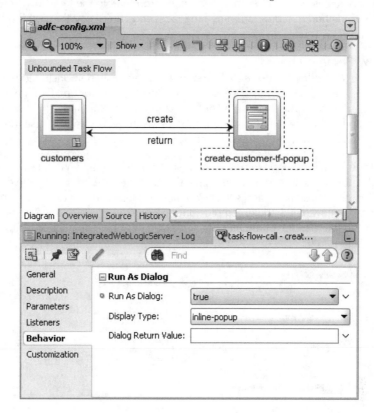

You also have to set *UseWindow* to "true" on the button that will launch the task flow. Now when the task flow is called from, for example, a button click, instead of appearing in a new window, it will appear in the pop-up dialog.

NOTE
After editing information in the task flow dialog, you might notice on returning to the calling page that the data is not reflected in, in this case, the table of customers. Even if you set ChangeEventPolicy *on the binding to "ppr," this only updates the customers table when you click on a new row. The reason is that the current implementation of task flow dialogs does not automatically refresh the calling page. To force a refresh, you have to write a method that forces the refresh when the dialog closes. This is covered in Chapter 19.*

Task Flow Parameters and Scope

Just like the analogy of a subroutine, a bounded task flow can have in and out parameters. This allows you to build task flows that are more loosely coupled, where information from outside the task flow can be passed in rather than referenced from within the task flow. And just like a procedure or method in a programming language, you can define the visibility, or scope, of these parameters.

Task Flow Parameters

Let's consider the following use case based on the previously demonstrated bounded task flow for creating a new customer. In this case, you want the task flow for creating a new customer to be parameterized. It could be that you want to pass in information about the user who is creating the new customer, or maybe default values for the fields; however, in this case the value of the parameter will be a string to be used in the heading on the task flow page.

Defining the Task Flow Parameter   The first step is to define what parameters the task flow should take. On the task flow diagram, click the *Overview* tab to display the overview information for the task flow, and select *Parameters*. Here you can define parameters, both in and out, for the task flow. Click the green plus button to create a new *Input Parameter Definition*. You can define the name of the parameter, its type (which if blank defaults to String), and whether the parameter is required.

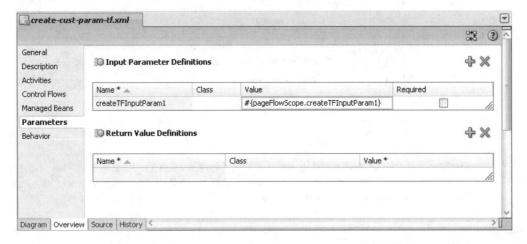

You also have to define where the parameter is stored while the task flow is executing. The field *Value* should default to #{pageFlowScope.createTFInputParam1}, which is a page flow scope parameter with the same name as the task flow parameter, or you can select this value from the Expression Builder dialog. This means that the parameter is being held in a special piece of memory called pageFlowScope, which is available while the task flow is running.

To reference the parameter within the task flow pages, in this example, the text for a header, set the appropriate property to reference this special piece of memory where the parameter is being stored: #{pageFlowScope.createTFInputParam1}.

A Brief Word About Scope   So what is scope and why is it important to task flows? Well, continuing the procedure and method analogy, these subroutines have visibility, or scope, as we call it in task flows. A variable declared inside a procedure cannot be accessed by another procedure; it is private to that procedure. And for a Java method, a private member variable cannot be accessed from other classes and, furthermore, is private to each instance of an object instantiated from that class.

The same is true for task flows, or more specifically, ADF Controller, where you can define objects, such as managed and backing beans, to have a scope. You can think of scope as being a piece of memory that you lease for a period of time. Objects within that memory can be referenced for the period of the lease. Once this lease is up, the memory is cleared. There are different scopes available, some of which are

- **Page Flow**   Available for the duration of a task flow
- **View**   Available for the duration of a single page or page fragment

Passing Parameters to a Task Flow   Having defined the parameters of the task flow and where they are to be stored, you need to pass a value to the parameter. When dragging a bounded task flow with page fragments onto a page, JDeveloper displays the Edit Task Flow Binding dialog. This allows you to define the value you want to pass into the task flow parameter using Expression Language. In this case, we'll just pass in a static string using the EL expression #{'A static String'}.

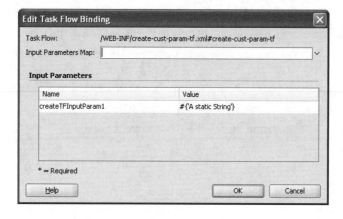

TIP
Having defined the value to be passed to the instance of the task flow in the Edit Task Flow Binding dialog, if you decide you want to change this and bind to a different value, you can do so from the Bindings *tab for the page in which the task flow is used.*

The result is that when the task flow is called, the parameter is passed into the task flow and is referenced by a label on one of the pages of the task flow.

Summary

Task flows are a powerful feature of Oracle ADF, allowing application flow to be easily partitioned and reused. You should now have an understanding of the role of task flows and how they are used to define the flow of your application. In particular you have learned that:

- Task flows are reusable modules that define application flow.
- Task flows allow navigation not only to pages, but also to method calls and other task flows.
- A task flow can be based on page fragments, which can then be embedded within a region on a page.
- A sequence of pages or page fragments can be defined as a task flow train.
- A task flow can be displayed in a pop-up dialog.
- You can define parameters to be passed into a task flow.

CHAPTER
14

Buttons and Menus

n order to bring your application to life, you will want to add buttons, links, and menus to allow navigation between pages and to initiate business service actions. This chapter will take you through some of the common uses of buttons and menus and the features they support.

Buttons and menus provide a means by which the end user can initiate actions such as deleting a customer record or navigating to the next order item. Both buttons and menus have properties that define what action should be initiated when clicked and, as you might expect, properties to control features such as label, icon, and whether the component is disabled.

There are essentially two flavors of buttons available on the Component Palette: the Button component and the Toolbar Button component. Typically, the Toolbar Button component is used within an application toolbar and includes features such as a hover-over icon and the ability to show toggled state. The Button component is generally used for initiating page navigation or submitting a business service action. However, these are only guidelines.

There are also different flavors of menu items such as a top-level menu bar, submenu, and the actual menu item that will initiate an action.

A Word About Toolboxes and Toolbars

You can pretty much drop your buttons and menus wherever you please; however, there are some guidelines on how you can make the most of your application buttons and menus. Some layout components, such as Panel Collection and Panel Box, have facets that are specifically designed for menus and buttons. Where you can, use these facets, given they are designed for that purpose. Furthermore, there are parent container components, such as Toolbar and Toolbox, that are also designed to work with buttons and menu components.

For example, a Toolbar Button component would typically appear inside a Toolbar component, and the Toolbar component is responsible for managing the layout and stretching of the components within it. The Toolbar component also shows an overflow icon if the page has been resized and not all components in the toolbar are visible.

If you require a stack of multiple menus and toolbars, then you can use a Toolbox component to group the required menu and toolbar components.

Adding Buttons to Your Application

As with other UI components such as text fields and tables, you can either drop a button onto a page from the Component Palette and wire it up to an action, or drag a business method from the Data Controls panel as a button.

Buttons Associated with Business Service Methods

The business service developed in the earlier chapters provided, by default, business service methods for navigating the rows of data and performing actions on that business service. You could also define your own custom business methods and expose them through ADF Model. To initiate any of these methods from a button click, simply drag and drop the business service method from the Data Controls panel onto a page and choose the appropriate kind of component.

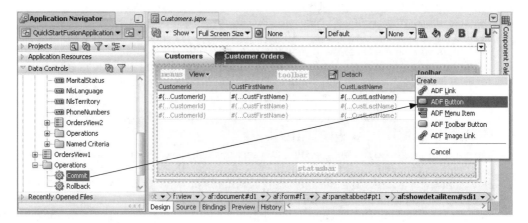

JDeveloper creates the appropriate UI component and action binding and sets the *ActionListener* property of the button to point to the binding; for example, #{bindings.Commit.execute}.

Clicking this button will now execute the commit operation on the associated data collection.

NOTE
Any default business service actions, such as next, previous, commit, and rollback, are bound to the buttons using action bindings. Custom methods such as todaysDutyManager are bound using a method action binding. The reason for this different binding is that the custom method could return a value.

Buttons for Application Navigation

You will probably want to define that the navigation of your application pages should be initiated from buttons, menus, or links. As you discovered in Chapter 13, ADF Controller takes care of application flow using named control flows between activities in a task flow. To initiate one of these control flows from a button click, drop a button onto your page and set the *Action* property of the button to the name of the control flow case.

NOTE
You might be wondering why a button has two properties for initiating an action: Action *and* ActionListener. Action *is used for application navigation, whereas* ActionListener *is used for invoking an action that does not require navigation. Also,* ActionListener *is called before* Action, *since it makes sense for navigation to be the final action. If you wanted to initiate a method call and also navigate, then you could set both properties. Alternatively, use a method call activity in a task flow to initiate the method call as part of the navigation.*

Buttons Calling a Method

The two cases outlined in the preceding two sections will cover most of your early learning requirements for initiating actions from buttons; however, there is one further case of which you may want to be aware. Consider the example where you want to perform some UI-specific processing on a page rather than calling a business method or page navigation. For example, if an order billing address is the same as the shipping address, then on clicking a button you want to copy values from the billing address field to the shipping address field. In this case, you can write some code to copy the values between fields using a Java class that is associated with the page and call that code from the button click. This code would be placed in a special Java class called a managed bean. Managed beans are covered in Chapter 15, but the outline of how to hook managed bean code to a button is as follows.

After dropping a button onto your page, double-click the button. This displays the Bind Action Property dialog. Select *Method Binding* to indicate you want to bind to a method, and click New to create a new managed bean. Enter a *Bean Name* of "myBean," a *Class name* of "MyBean," and set *Scope* to "request." This will create a managed bean for your UI-specific code that will be instantiated whenever the button is clicked. You can then define the name of a *Method* that will be called when the button is clicked.

JDeveloper will set the *Action* property of the button to point to the method using an EL expression such as #{myBean.cb2_action}. Now, when you run the page, clicking this button will execute the method in the managed bean.

TIP
If you want to try a simple example, put a System.out.println("Hello world"); statement into the method. Then, when you run the page, you can confirm the method is being called by observing the message on the JDeveloper message window.

Button Labels and Icons

There are a number of properties that you can set to control features like icons and labels. For example, on a Button component, you can define *Text*, *Icon*, and *IconPosition*, as shown for the Previous and Next buttons in Figure 14-1. You can also set *AccessKey* to define a quick

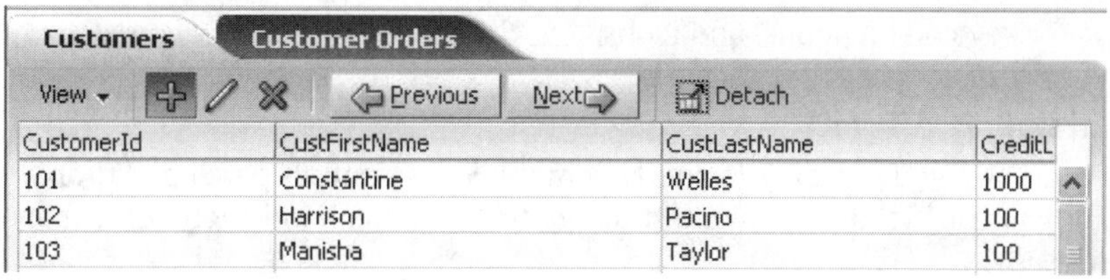

FIGURE 14-1.   *Label and icons for buttons*

access key to the button. In Figure 14-1, P and N are access keys for the Previous and Next buttons.

For a Toolbar Button component, you can define *Text, Icon, HoverIcon, DepressedIcon,* and *DisabledIcon,* as shown in Figure 14-1, where the icons represent adding, editing, and deleting a customer.

TIP
When you define icons for your buttons, JDeveloper prompts you to copy each icon into the project. However, if you import all your icons into your project, you can select the icons from a drop-down list instead of manually selecting and importing each icon. Select **File | Import** *and then select Web Source. You can now import all the required icons into the ViewController project.*

Adding a Menu to Your Application

Menus are another way of allowing your users to initiate business functions and navigate through the application. As with buttons, a menu item has an *ActionListener* property to allow the selection of the menu item to trigger a method, and an *Action* property for initiating control flow navigation to a new page or page fragment.

As noted earlier, many of the layout components, such as Panel Collection, have facets specifically for menus. Figure 14-2 shows an example of a menu within the menus facet of

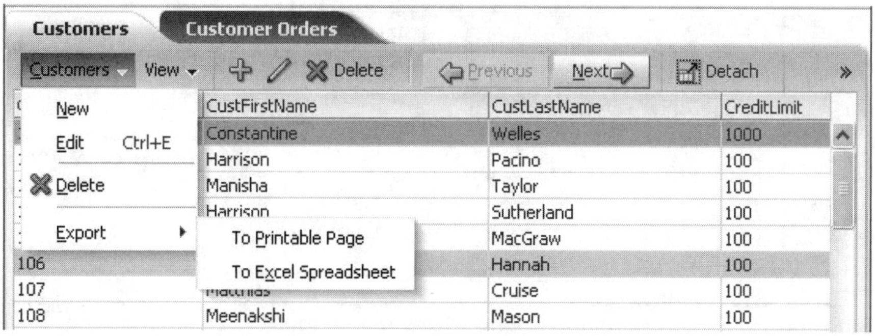

FIGURE 14-2.   *Using a menu in an ADF application*

a Panel Collection. Here you can see some of the features of menus, including submenus, accelerator key combinations, and icons.

Creating a Menu

As with buttons, you can drag methods from the Data Controls panel and drop them as menu items, or you can create your menu structure first and then bind each of the menu items when you are ready.

TIP
If you create a menu first, you can drag and drop methods from the Data Controls panel onto a menu item, and JDeveloper will automatically bind the existing menu item to that method. JDeveloper will display the Confirm Component Rebinding dialog to allow you to choose which properties should be overridden.

The typical structure of a menu is shown in Figure 14-3. Depending on the facet in which you place the menu, you will start with either a Menu or a Panel Menu Bar, represented by the tags `af:menu` and `af:menuBar`, respectively. If you want a menu bar with many top-level items, then you would use `af:menuBar`; however, because this menu is within a facet that only allows one

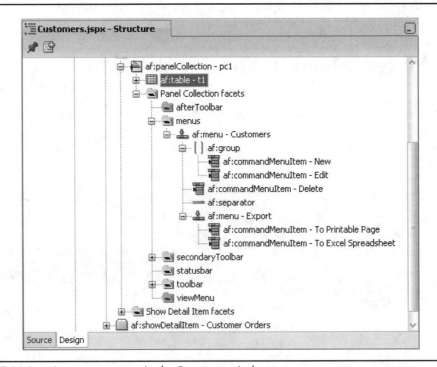

FIGURE 14-3. *A menu structure in the Structure window*

top-level menu item, `af:menu` is used. This represents the menu item that opens up a drop-down menu. Each of the menu items within the Menu component is a Menu Item component, represented by the tag `af:commandMenuItem`, as shown in Figure 14-3.

TIP
If you are unsure what component to insert inside a facet, or as a child of a component, then right-click the component or facet and select **Insert Inside**. *JDeveloper will guide you as to which component makes sense to insert inside this current facet or component.*

Within `af:menu` you will typically have one or many instances of `af:commandMenuItem`. These are the menu items that are used to initiate an action. As shown in Figure 14-3, you can also nest many instances of `af:commandMenuItem` within an `af:group` tag. This is used to group related menu items and automatically includes a visual separator.

You can also create submenus by using an instance of `af:menu` inside another `af:menu`. Figure 14-2 shows the runtime behavior and Figure 14-3 show the associated design time.

Menu Item Labels and Icons

Menu items include many of the same properties as buttons. *Text* defines the label for the menu item, and *Icon* is the associated icon. *AccessKey* defines the quick key mnemonic for the menu item, signified by an underscore of the appropriate character in the menu item label. *Accelerator* defines a key combination for immediate access to the menu item. So, setting *Accelerator* to "control E" allows access to that menu function through the key combination CTRL-E, and also adds the key combination to the menu label, as shown for the Edit menu item in Figure 14-2.

Summary

Buttons and menus allow you to bring your application to life by calling business service methods and application navigation. In this chapter you have learned that:

- Buttons and menus allow you to initiate actions through the *Action* or *ActionListener* properties.

- Some components have facets specifically for menus and toolbars.

- Toolbars and toolboxes can be used to help manage the layout of buttons and menus.

Now that you have an understanding of some basic ADF Faces components, task flows, buttons, and menus, your application should really start to take shape. The next step is to look at some of the more advanced features of ADF Faces and how you can use them to enhance your application.

CHAPTER
15

Advanced UI Techniques

ith the knowledge gained from the earlier chapters, you should be able to build a functionally rich data-entry application with various pages, navigation between those pages, and an assortment of different UI components. The next step is to build on top of those core skills and introduce some of the more advanced features of the ADF View layer that can be used to take your application to the next level.

This chapter explains pop-up dialogs, drag and drop, calling Java, how UI pages are refreshed, and other ADF Faces gems.

Partial Page Rendering in ADF Faces

Like most Internet users, you probably have had the experience of entering your details into an online application, clicking Submit, and then having the application tell you that you forgot to enter a required field, such as which country you live in. So you enter your country and click the button again, and it then tells you that your selected order date is not correct. Why didn't it tell you that the order date was wrong when you entered it? Surely the application could have checked when tabbing out of the field?

Part of the reason for this kind of behavior is that in a traditional HTML web application, nothing really happens until the page is submitted, typically through clicking a button. Only when that button is clicked will all the data on the page be posted to the application server, where the various validation checks will be run and the business service updated. Furthermore, a whole new page will be returned just to alert you of an error on the page.

So how can you build a Fusion application with a more responsive UI experience?

Oracle ADF provides a solution to this common problem by implementing a feature called partial page rendering (PPR). With PPR, a UI component can be flagged to indicate that as soon as data is input into the component, that data should immediately be submitted to the application. Then, if an error message needs to be displayed, for example, only the relevant component, or part of a page, will be updated to show the error message.

Generally speaking, this behavior is turned off by default, so let's look at an example where you might want to enable this behavior.

Immediately Validating Employee Salary Using PPR

Let's consider the following example. In Chapter 9, you created a validation rule that the salary for an employee must be less than $25,000. If you create a JSF page to edit the details for an employee, then you will notice that if you enter an employee salary of 30000, no error is shown until you submit the page via a button click.

If you require the data in the field to be automatically submitted when leaving the field, then set the property *AutoSubmit* to "true" on the UI component.

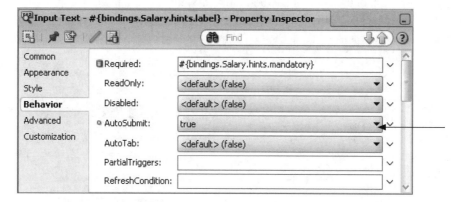

Now when the user enters a value into the Salary field, the value is immediately submitted when the user moves out of the field and, in this case, an error is displayed stating that the data failed the validation rule.

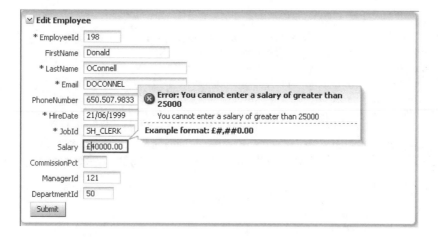

Responding to Changes in Other UI Components

Another example of where PPR can be useful is the case in which changing data in one field should force the update of data in another field. Earlier in the book you saw that for an order item, a line total could be calculated from the quantity multiplied by the price. If you create a page to allow the editing of an order item and then you change either the quantity or the price, you will notice that the line total is not recalculated until the page is submitted.

In order to force the line total to be updated immediately, you have to set *AutoSubmit* to "true" on both the Quantity and Unit Price fields to force the immediate submission of the data changes. However, you also have to indicate that the Line Total field should update itself to reflect the automatically submitted data. To do this, you need to set the property *PartialTriggers* on the Line Item field. This is a space-delimited list of the UI component identifiers that should trigger the refresh of the component. So in this case, the line total will be triggered by the update of either the Quantity or the Unit Price.

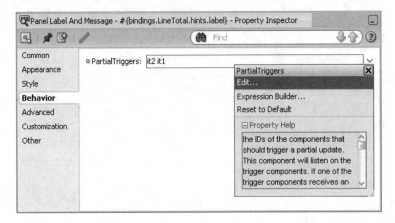

TIP
The component identifiers are specified by the Id *property of a UI component. The* PartialTriggers *property offers a dialog that you can use to select the UI component identifiers from the page hierarchy as an alternative to typing directly. Using this dialog ensures that if the target component is inside a container component, such as a Panel Collection, then that container component ID is also included.*

Now when the value of either the quantity or price is updated, the line total will automatically be refreshed without the user having to submit the whole page.

Automatic PPR

While features like AutoSubmit and ParitalTriggers (explained in the preceding section) have to be explicitly set, there are cases where JDeveloper will automatically enable PPR when it makes sense to do so. For example, when you drag and drop a data collection from the Data Controls panel as a form with navigation buttons, JDeveloper will automatically set PPR on the binding executable. Figure 15-1 shows the binding for a page, and you can see that *ChangeEventPolicy* is set to "ppr." This means that when the user clicks a navigation button, all components bound to that executable will be refreshed.

So why does JDeveloper do that? Well, let's assume you have a page displaying departments and their employees in a master/detail layout. As the user navigates through the employees data by clicking a button, only the fields that relate to that binding executable, in this case employees, will be refreshed and not the whole page. This is much more efficient than refreshing the whole page.

But hold on. Didn't we say earlier that clicking a button submits a whole page? Well, it does; but a button has a property called *PartialSubmit*. If *PartialSubmit* is set to "true," as is done automatically in this case, then the page is submitted, but the only components that will be refreshed are those that either have their *PartialTriggers* property set to reference the button or are bound to the same executable with *ChangeEventPolicy* set to "ppr."

So the combination of *PartialSubmit* on the button and *ChangeEventPolicy* on the binding executable ensures that when the page is submitted, only specific components are refreshed.

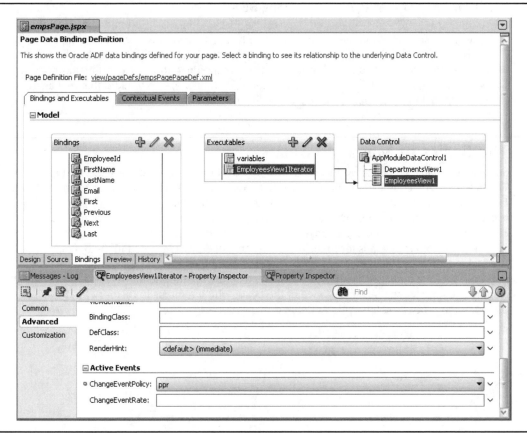

FIGURE 15-1. *Partial page rendering on a binding executable*

NOTE
You would still have to use AutoSubmit *if you want to force the business service to be updated immediately on data being changed in the UI. However, any business service attribute that changes as a result of that submit would automatically be refreshed, since PPR is set on the binding executable.*

Managed and Backing Beans

For the most part, the nuts and bolts of your application code will exist within the business services layer. This means that in the majority of cases, and certainly in these early stages of your learning, you will probably never need to create, or write code in, a managed bean. However, that doesn't mean that there won't be situations that require you to write code to address a specific UI requirement. Therefore, managed beans are covered here to show their basic principles and how they are created.

A Word About Managed and Backing Beans

You might see the terms "managed beans" and "backing beans" used interchangeably. They are, in fact, one and the same thing: simply a Java class in which UI-specific methods can be written. Strictly speaking, there are only managed beans. The reason for the two terms is that if a managed bean has a one-to-one mapping with a page and includes methods to access the UI components on that page, then you can think of that managed bean as "backing" that page—hence, a backing bean.

The Basics of Managed Beans

So what are managed beans? Managed beans provide a mechanism to register a Java class in which UI-specific code can be placed. The methods in the class can then be referenced, using Expression Language (EL), from the various trigger points or properties of UI components. These trigger points, called component listeners, might relate to an action, such as when a button is clicked or the value in a field is changed.

The configuration details for managed beans are generally registered in the default unbounded task flow file, adfc-config.xml, but can also be registered in any other task flow if required. When a managed bean method is called by a UI component, the framework is responsible for instantiating an instance of the bean, which remains in memory for a specific period of the processing life cycle as defined by its scope.

Creating a Managed Bean

As you might expect, there are a number of different ways you can create managed beans. One option is to create the managed bean through the *Overview* tab of the task flow editor. This is also the place where you can edit and fine-tune the details of the managed bean.

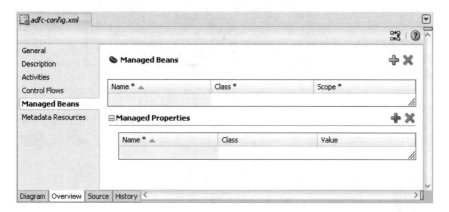

You can also create managed beans directly from the Property Inspector for a UI component.

Component Listeners

As well as having visual properties such as color, font, and label, ADF Faces UI components also have a built-in feature to listen for a particular event and then initiate some code when that event happens. You have already come across one of these component listeners in Chapter 14, where you found that a button has an *ActionListener* property, which listens for the button being clicked. Similarly, an Input Text component has a *ValueChangeListener* property that will be triggered when the data in the field is changed.

So, let's look at an example of where you could use a component listener to call a managed bean method.

Assigning a Managed Bean Method to a Component Listener

Consider the case in which the creation of a new employee should automatically disable the Commission field if the employee is not a salesman.

The first step is to go to the *ValueChangeListener* property for the Job field. This property defines the method that should be called when the value within the field changes.

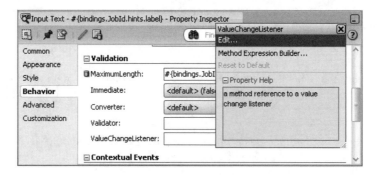

Click the down-arrow icon to the right of *ValueChangeListener* and select **Edit** to launch the Edit Property dialog. Either select an existing managed bean and method or create a new one.

JDeveloper will create the Java class for the managed bean and register that information in the appropriate configuration file. It will also create a placeholder method within the Java class and reference that method from the UI component. So, you should now see that the *ValueChangeListener* property is set to "#{editEmp.salesman_valueChanged}," meaning that when a value is changed in this field, this method will automatically be executed.

Exposing UI Components in the Managed Bean

If you look at the managed bean class you created, you will see the method that will be called when the value changes in the job field:

```
public void salesman_valueChanged(ValueChangeEvent valueChangeEvent) {
    // Add event code here...
}
```

It is in here that you will write your code to disable the Commission field depending on the value in the Job field. But how do you access the commission field from this code? How can you programmatically set the field to be enabled or disabled?

You can do this by asking JDeveloper to expose methods to access the UI components in the managed bean. A good rule to remember here is to only expose the UI components in the managed bean that you actually need. You can do this on a case-by-case basis using the *Binding* property for each UI component. This allows you to define the managed bean in which the component should be exposed.

If you do this for the Commission field, you will see methods in the managed bean class that allow you to access the component. You can now modify the method to be

```
public void salesman_valueChanged(ValueChangeEvent valueChangeEvent) {
    // Add event code here...
    getCommission().setDisabled(true);
    if (valueChangeEvent.getNewValue().equals("SA_REP")) {
        getCommission().setDisabled(false);
    }
}
```

This means that when a value is changed in the Job field, this method will fire and will only enable the Commission field for a sales rep.

TIP
Managed beans that include component references like this should have Scope set to "request" or "backingBean."

Ensuring Changed Components Are Refreshed

The final stage is to ensure that when this code is executed, the page knows that it has to refresh the Commission field. As you found out earlier in this chapter, *AutoSubmit* and *PartialTriggers* are required to implement this behavior; otherwise, any change to the field would not be visible until the page is submitted.

Set *AutoSubmit* on the Job field and set *PartialTriggers* on the Commission field to reference the component ID of the Job field. Now when you create a new employee, the Commission field will be disabled for those who are not sales reps.

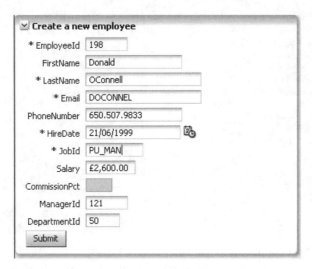

NOTE
This example serves two purposes. First, it outlines the basic feature of a managed bean and how it can be used for UI-specific code. Second, as noted earlier, it shows that in many cases you can achieve the same result without the need to write code in a managed bean. In this example, by setting the Disabled *property on the Commission field to "#{bindings.JobId.inputValue!="SA_REP"}," you can achieve the same behavior.*

Advanced ADF Faces Components

By now you should have an understanding of some of the more commonly used ADF Faces components such as buttons, input fields, and layout components. However, ADF Faces also includes a range of components that provide more advanced functionality. The good news for you is that, as a new Fusion developer, the experience of adding these more advanced features into your application is pretty much the same as how you add buttons and input fields. These more sophisticated ADF Faces components also exist in the Component Palette and can be dragged and dropped onto the appropriate facet or position on the page and have properties set.

Let's take a look at some of these features.

Pop-ups

You have already seen how a task flow can be displayed in a pop-up window, but there is a more general requirement to have UI information displayed in a separate window. The ADF Faces Popup component is a parent container for UI content that gets displayed in a separate pop-up window.

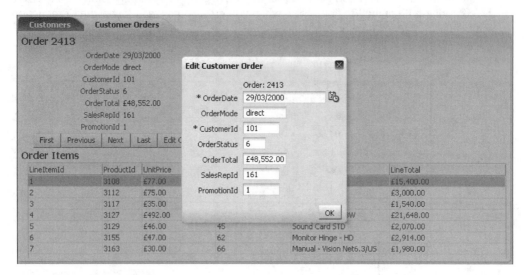

Creating a Pop-up Dialog

Let's assume you want to create a pop-up dialog in which you can view and edit details about a customer's order. To do this, drag and drop a Popup component from the Component Palette onto the page. You can drop the Popup component anywhere on the page, since it doesn't really matter where the pop-up dialog lives in the hierarchy of the page, but it is generally good practice to position the Popup component near the component that will initiate its launch.

On dropping the Popup component onto the page, the visual editor will switch to allow you to edit the Popup component. Note that you can also use the Structure window or, on the visual editor, right-click and select **Edit Popup** to edit the Popup component.

The Popup component is an invisible container. You would, therefore, typically drop a Dialog component as a child of the Popup component. The Dialog component provides a frame, title, and various options for displaying buttons. You can then design the pop-up dialog as you would any other page.

Displaying a Pop-up Dialog   Once you have created a pop-up dialog, the next step is to define the action that should display the dialog. Again, ADF Faces provides a component, called Show Popup Behavior, that has a property *PopupId* to define which pop-up dialog should be displayed. If you drop a Show Popup Behavior component as a child of a button (either a Button or Toolbar Button component), then clicking the button will automatically display the pop-up dialog as referenced by *PopupId*.

Context Info with a Note Window

Another option for using a Popup component is where you want to show some additional information to help the user, but feel that a pop-up dialog with a window title and buttons is more than you really need. In this case you can use a Note Window component as a child of the Popup component. This is particularly useful if, for example, you want to display some additional information about a product and don't require the visual overhead of a pop-up dialog.

You also have some options on how you display this pop-up note window. Rather than displaying the pop-up note window when a button is clicked, you might want to define that it be displayed when the user hovers over, or clicks in, a specific field.

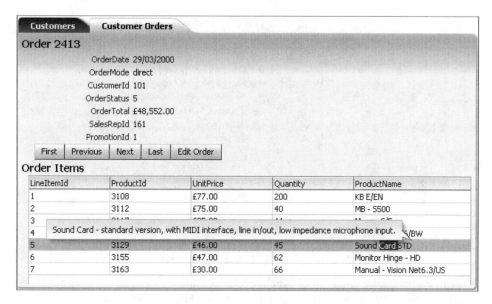

Drop a Show Popup Behavior component as a child of the component that should launch the pop-up note window, and set the *PopupId* property. You can now define *TriggerType* to indicate that this pop-up note window should be displayed when, for example, the user double-clicks the field of which the Show Popup Behavior component is a child.

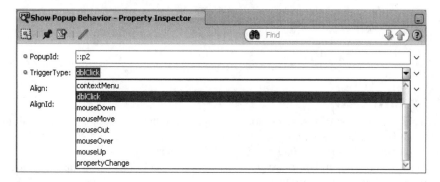

NOTE
The Popup component has a property ContentDelivery *that defines when the data within the pop-up dialog is refreshed. If you want to ensure that the data is refreshed every time the pop-up dialog is displayed, then you need to set* ContentDelivery *to "lazyUncached."*

Context Information   The preceding example shows how you can show a pop-up note when the user double-clicks on the product name; however, it might not be very clear to the end user that this feature exists. Wouldn't it be nice if there was a visual indicator to show the user that there is more information associated with the field? Well, there is a simple way to provide such an indicator. The Context Info component can be dropped into the context facet of a component, such as an Output Text component.

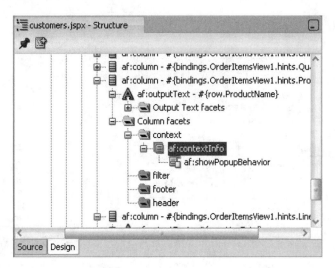

This component gives a visual indication (by default, a small orange square that changes shape when the mouse moves over it) that there is additional information associated with this field. The Show Popup Behavior component can then be defined as a child of the Context Info component and *TriggerType* set to display additional context information.

LineItemId	ProductId	UnitPrice	Quantity	ProductName
6	3			Manual - Vision Net6.3/US
1	3	Set consisting of a mouse and wrist pad, with corporate logo		Mouse C/E
2	2761	£79.00	112	Mouse +WP/CL
3	3127	£488.40	114	LaserPro 600/6/BW
4	3134	£17.00	115	Screws <B.32.5>
5	3143	£15.00	129	Screws <B.28.5>

Drag and Drop

You have already seen that some components, like an ADF Faces Table, include built-in functionality to drag and drop columns within the table. However, you can add further drag-and-drop behavior to your application by using the drag-and-drop ADF Faces components.

The basics of drag and drop are generally the same: ADF Faces provides a number of operation components that can indicate the source of a drag operation and the drop area. Each of these components would be a child of the UI component for which the drag or drop operation applies. In the simplest case, you don't require any additional coding to implement drag and drop; however, for more complex cases like shopping carts, where you might be storing a collection of items, you can also define a managed bean that can be used to handle the collection of dropped data.

Drag-and-Drop Attribute Values

Let's take a look at a simple example of how to implement drag and drop. In this example, you want to give the end user the ability to drag and drop the customer's first or last name into the E-mail Address field. Given that the customer's e-mail address is nearly always based on their first or last name, this might save the end user a few extra key presses.

Simply drag an Attribute Drag Source component from the Component Palette onto each of the First Name and Last Name input fields. JDeveloper then prompts for which attribute of the component you want to drag. For example, you could drag the label, but in this case you want to drag the data value in the input text field, so select "value."

You can then drag and drop an Attribute Drag Target component as a child of the E-mail Address input text field, again, choosing "value" as the attribute you want the drop operation to act upon.

Figure 15-2 shows the attribute drag-and-drop components.

TIP
If you have trouble locating any of the ADF Faces components in the Component Palette, you can type the name, or part of the name, into the search panel at the top of the Component Palette.

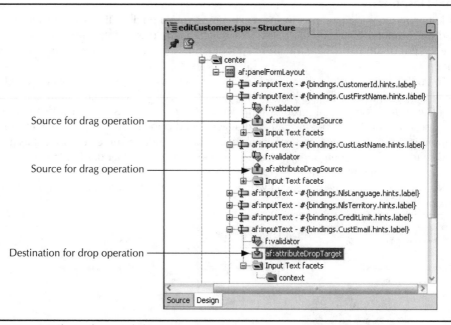

FIGURE 15-2. *Attribute drag-and-drop components*

Now when you run the application, you can drag the data from the customer's First Name and Last Name fields into the E-mail Address field.

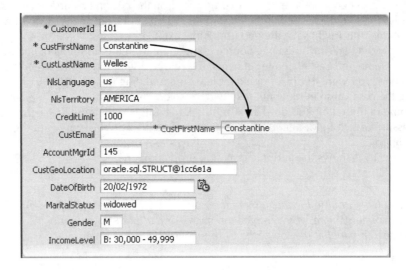

Panel Dashboard

In addition to allowing you to drag and drop values from a field, ADF Faces also lets you drag and drop components around the page. This is particularly useful if you are looking to implement some kind of dashboard where the user can reorganize content within the dashboard to meet his or her preference.

To do this, you need to use the Panel Dashboard component. This is a special layout container that will allow the repositioning of components that are placed within it. Inside the Panel Dashboard component, drop in some Panel Box components. You now need to indicate that these Panel Box components can be dragged and dropped within the Panel Dashboard component. To do this, drop an instance of a Component Drag Source component as a child of each of the Panel Box components. You don't have to specify a drag destination since the Panel Dashboard component already takes care of this.

Now when you run the page, you will see that you can reposition the panel boxes by simply dragging them.

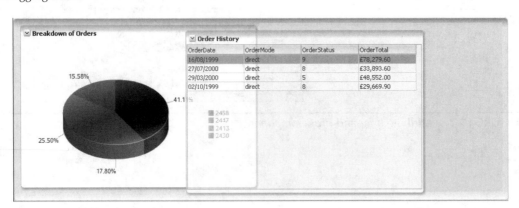

UI Component Validation

With any application development, there is a philosophical debate on where the best place is to perform user input validation. Should it be in the database, in the business service, or up front in the UI when the user enters data? In any case, Oracle ADF gives you the flexibility to define validation at many different levels.

You have already seen how ADF Business Components provides validation features at the business services layer, but if you require more immediate validation, ADF Faces also gives you the opportunity to define validation rules at the UI component level. This means that validation happens in the client and doesn't require a round trip to the application server to fire the validation rule.

Date Validation

You may have already discovered that when displaying a date attribute using an Input Date component, the component already implements some validation by default. For example, entering a date "tomorrow" will throw an error as soon as the user tabs out of the field. This is because the component is checking that the value entered can be converted to a date.

You can also set up some validation on the Input Date component. For example, if you want to define range limits for a date, then you can set *MinValue* and *MaxValue* to the lower and upper values for a date. This will display an error on exiting the field if the data entered is outside the allowed date range.

You can also define that for an Input Date component, certain days of the week are not selectable. For example, you might decide that a shipping date for an order can't be on Saturday or Sunday. Setting *DisabledDaysOfWeek* to "sat sun" will disable the selection of all Saturdays and Sundays in the associated date picker.

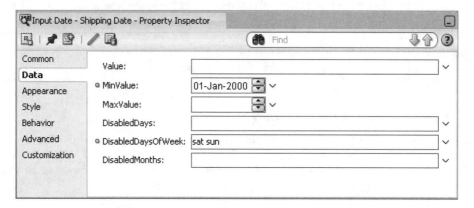

Furthermore, when the page is submitted, if the user has directly entered a date that is a disabled date, then an appropriate error message will be shown.

However, there are also other ADF Faces components that can be added to input components to provide further validation.

Validate Date Restriction   Dropping a Validate Date Restriction component as a child of a date component allows you to define dates that should be regarded as invalid input but, unlike the previously explained feature, will validate immediately on the user leaving the field.

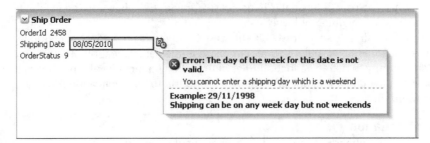

To implement this behavior, you need to set the property *InvalidDaysOfWeek* to "sat sun," to mark Saturday and Sunday as invalid days, and use *HintInvalidDaysOfWeek* and *MessageDetailInvalidDaysOfWeek* to define the appropriate messages.

Validate Regular Expression

One incredibly valuable validation feature in ADF Faces is the Validate Reg Exp component. This component allows immediate client-side validation of data against a Java regular expression. This could be useful for validating data that adheres to a particular format, like a UK postcode, IP address, or credit card number.

Drop a Validate Reg Exp component as a child of an input component and set the property *Pattern* to a valid Java regular expression such as "[A-Z][a-z]{0,10}." This defines that the field must have an initial uppercase letter followed by up to ten lowercase alphabetical characters.

TIP
If you search online for "Java regular expression," you can find various examples such as "UK postcode" and "US zip code." Try some of these.

Other Useful ADF Faces Operations

As you can see, ADF Faces is not just about visual components, but also includes some useful operations. This section looks at some additional operation components. As with any other ADF Faces component, you can drop them onto a page and set appropriate properties as required.

Export to Excel

On viewing a table of data, wouldn't it be useful to be able to allow the user to export that data into an Excel spreadsheet? ADF Faces has a component to handle this for you.

Drop an Export Collection Action Listener component onto your page as a child of a button or menu item. JDeveloper then prompts you for the identifier for the component that should have its data exported; in this case, the customers table component. You should also set *Export Type* to "excelHTML," which is the only currently supported value.

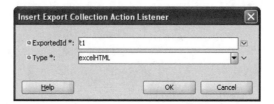

Now, when the button or menu item is clicked, the data in the table will be exported into an Excel spreadsheet.

Printable Page

Another common use case is to allow the end user to create a printable version of an application page. Drop a Show Printable Page Behavior component as a child component of a button or menu item. On clicking the button or menu item, a printable version of the page, minus command components such as menu bars and buttons, will be opened in a new browser window.

Summary

In this chapter you have explored some of the more sophisticated features of ADF Faces that allow you to design application pages with richer user interaction. Specifically, in this chapter you have learned that:

- Oracle ADF implements partial page rendering, meaning that not all of the page needs to be refreshed.

- Setting *AutoSubmit* and *PartialTriggers* on a UI component allows data to be immediately submitted, and for components to refresh based on that submitted data.

- Setting *ChangeEventPolicy* on an executable binding to "ppr" alerts all bound components to refresh themselves whenever the data model to which they are bound is updated.

- Managed beans can be used for writing UI-specific code.

- ADF Faces includes a Popup component for displaying UI content in a separate window or container, launched using a Show Popup Behavior component.

- ADF Faces allows you to define a drag source and a drop target for supporting drag-and-drop operations.

- You can implement immediate client-side validation using ADF Faces.

- ADF Faces includes operation components for exporting data to Excel and creating printable pages.

Now that you have gained an insight into some of the more advanced features of ADF Faces, the next chapter will introduce the components used for displaying data visually through charts and graphs.

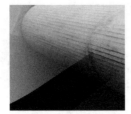

CHAPTER
16

Data Visualization
Components

t is often said that "a picture paints a thousand words," and this is especially true if you are trying to understand and view trends in huge collections of data. For this reason, you may find that presenting information using graphs or other visual means is a requirement for your application.

This chapter introduces the data visualization tools (DVT) and components that allow you to visualize your application data using graphs, charts, maps, and gauges.

ADF Faces includes graphs, gauges, and map components for visually representing and interacting with application data. As with other ADF Faces components, a data collection can be dragged from the Data Controls panel onto a page, whereupon JDeveloper will present a menu of UI component options, including DVT components, which can be bound to the data.

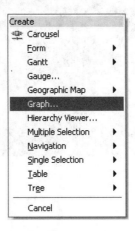

TIP
The secret to using these DVT components lies in the view object. If you ensure the correct aggregation of information in the view object, then it is relatively straightforward to bind the DVT components to that view of data.

On selecting a DVT component, such as a graph or gauge, JDeveloper displays a dialog allowing you to define how that data collection should be bound to the component. Different components will require different information, given the differences in how they will display that data collection. On completing the required information, as you would for a table or a form, JDeveloper creates the appropriate binding, references that binding from the component, and displays the component on the page, where you can fine-tune the properties through the Property Inspector.

Let's start by taking a look at some of the commonly used DVT components.

Graphs

ADF Faces provides over 50 different graph types, as shown in Figure 16-1, including bar graphs, pie charts, line charts, and scatter charts. Each of the graph categories may have a number of different options for that graph. For example, a bar graph could be stacked, based on percentages,

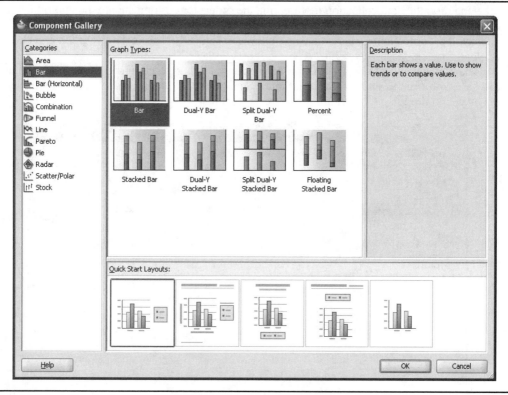

FIGURE 16-1. *Graph Component Gallery*

or have a dual Y-axis. Furthermore, JDeveloper also includes a number of quick start layouts that define whether the graph displays features such as a legend or title, and their position. Regardless of the flavor of graph or the layout chosen, the concept is similar for most of the graphs, where a set of data values is plotted against a series of reference points.

You can peruse the different types of graphs at your leisure, but for now, let's focus on two of the more common graphs: bar and pie graphs.

Bar Graph

The example presented in this section shows you how to design a page to display the order history for the currently selected customer. Given that a customer may have many orders, it would be good to see if there has been a trend to the order history. It might be beneficial to see if the value of the customer's orders have been increasing or decreasing over time, or if any peaks in their order history coincide with a sales campaign or a special offer. A bar graph plotting order totals over time might be useful.

Assuming you already have a table on the page showing customers, then displaying this order information is akin to adding a detail to the customer master table. From the Data Controls panel, drag and drop the data collection representing the orders for customers onto the appropriate area of the page. On choosing that you want to display this information as a graph, JDeveloper displays the Component Gallery dialog, as shown in Figure 16-1. Select a bar graph and choose one of the quick start layouts.

You then have to supply information as to how this data collection should be displayed. In this case, you want to set *Bars* to "OrderTotal" and *X Axis* to "OrderDate." You can do this by dragging and dropping the attributes onto the correct field.

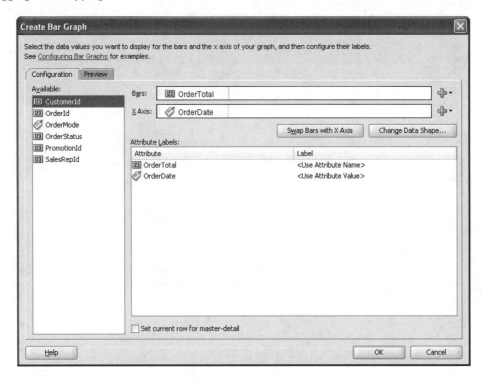

TIP
Since you are plotting the data based on an order date, it makes sense to ensure that the data collection is ordered based on order date, in which case you may want to ensure you have an order clause added to the appropriate view object.

You can now run and display the graph.

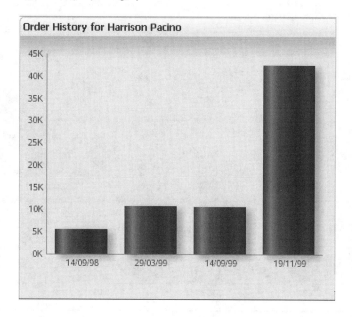

NOTE
Depending on how you have built your page, you may find that selecting a customer from the table does not update the graph. Why would that be? Well, the graph component is not aware that you are changing rows in the table, so you need to tell the graph that it should refresh itself when the data model changes to point to a new row. To do this, you can either set PartialTriggers *on the graph to reference the customer table, or set* ChangeEventPolicy *to "ppr" on the binding executable for the orders graph.*

Now that you have a basic bar graph up and running, let's take a look at some of the options for fine-tuning the graph.

Setting Graph Properties

Just like any other ADF Faces component, the graph you have created has a number of properties that can be used to control various features of the component. For example, the properties *3D Effect* and *Style* can both be used to change the look of the graph, as shown in Figure 16-2.

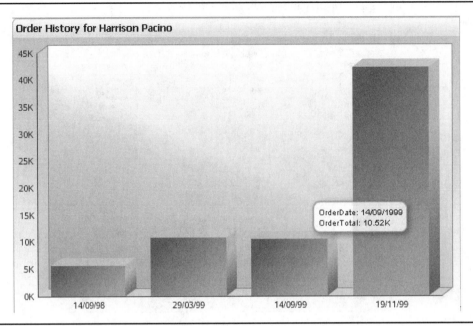

FIGURE 16-2. *Using the graph properties to control the features of a graph*

The graph can also be animated using *AnimationOnDisplay* and *MarkerTooltipType*, the latter of which can be used to display information as the mouse is moved over a bar, also shown in Figure 16-2.

Other properties such as *EmptyText* can be used to define a message if there is no graph data, and *DynamicResize* will automatically stretch the graph within its parent container.

Adding Graph Child Tags

As well as the graph having properties, special DVT components, called graph child tags, can be added as child components to the graph to represent different graph features such as titles, legends, and reference lines.

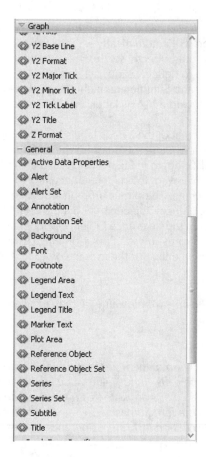

Just like other ADF Faces components, graph child tags can be dragged and dropped from the Component Palette, and each of these graph child tags also has its own set of properties. Alternatively, right-click on the graph to see a menu of options that will automatically set the appropriate graph child tag properties.

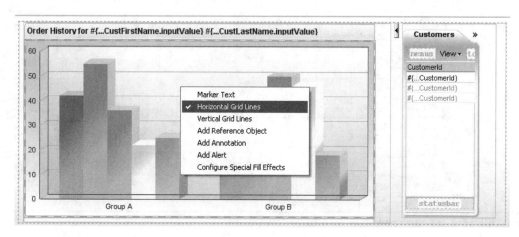

For example, as shown, you can define that the graph should have horizontal grid lines. Selecting this menu option will automatically set the *Style* property of the Y1 Major Tick graph child tag. Of course, you could directly set this property yourself through the Property Inspector.

You might also choose to define various labels for the graph, as shown in Figure 16-3. In this case you need to add Title and Subtitle graph child tags to the graph to represent a graph title and subtitle. And if you want to add a Y-Axis label, then drop an instance of the Y1 Title component onto the graph.

You can also set the format of the Y-Axis labels by dropping a Number Format component as a child of a Y1 Axis component and set *NumberType* to "NUMTYPE_CURRENCY."

As a final example, also shown in Figure 16-3, you can add reference information to the graph. For example, you may want to add a reference line to show whether this customer's orders are above or below an average. To do this, drop on a Reference Object Set component as a child of the graph and add a Reference Object component as a child to that component. You can now set the *LineValue* property of the Reference Object component to a numeric value, or you might choose to bind it to an EL expression such as "#{bindings.CustOrderAvg.inputValue.value}," which would show a reference line for the average order for the customer.

TIP
You will have to create an attribute value binding to reference the CustOrderAvg attribute.

NOTE
The current implementation of the Reference Object component requires that an EL value calls "inputValue.value" rather than just "inputValue." There also exists an issue that if the attribute being bound to LineValue *has a format mask associated with it, such as a currency, then an exception is thrown. Both these issues may be addressed in future releases.*

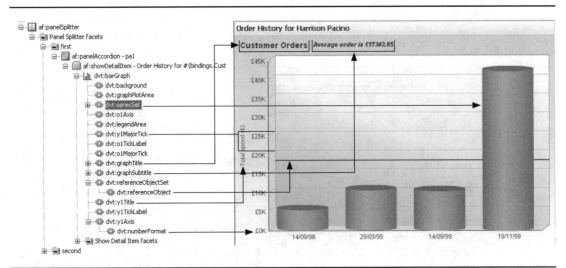

FIGURE 16-3. *Graph child tags on a bar graph*

Pie Graph

A pie graph is a particularly useful way of representing relative proportions, or percentages, of a whole. Let's consider the example where you want to display a pie graph showing the geographic proportion of your customer base.

NOTE
If you want to follow this example, you will have to create a new view object based on the following select statement and add it to the application module:

```
SELECT
    COUNT(CUSTOMER_ID),
    CUSTOMERS.NLS_TERRITORY NLS_TERRITORY
FROM
    CUSTOMERS
GROUP BY CUSTOMERS.NLS_TERRITORY
```

As before, drag and drop the data collection, but this time choose to display it as a pie graph. JDeveloper will prompt for the relevant information to create a binding. In the case of a pie graph, *Pie* represents the data you want to display, "CountCustomerId," and *Slices* defines how that data set is proportioned, "NlsTerritory."

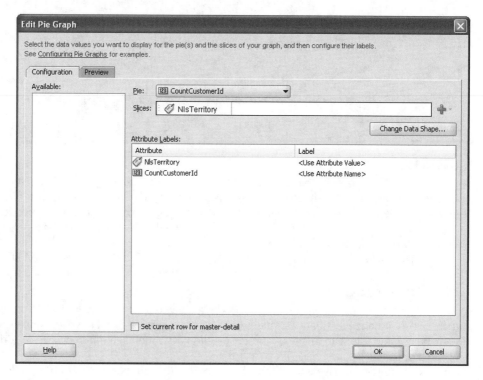

Properties on the pie graph such as *3D Effect* and *Style* can be used to control the look and feel, while setting *InteractiveSliceBehavior* to "explode" will allow slices to be offset from the pie when clicked by the user.

As with the bar graph, graph child tags can be used within the pie graph to show labels, legends, and other features.

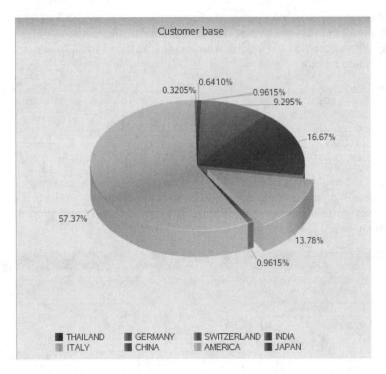

Gauges

A gauge is a DVT component that can be used for visualizing a quantity within a range, such as stock levels, temperature, or speed. The gauge itself depicts a data value and various thresholds. So, for example, stock levels might be represented in a gauge component as a number, but the gauge might also give a visual indication of whether that value is above or below a certain threshold, like a stock reorder limit.

Figure 16-4 shows the various gauge options, including a dial, status meter, and LED gauge.

Creating a Gauge

As with other components, you can drag and drop a data collection from the Data Controls panel and choose to visualize that data as a gauge, as shown in Figure 16-4. However, since you should already be comfortable with this drag-and-drop action, let's look at a different way of adding a gauge to a page.

In this example, you have a table that shows information about order items for a selected order, including a column showing the total in stock for each order item. This column is based on

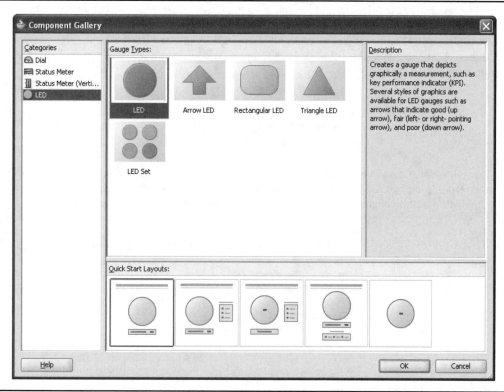

FIGURE 16-4. *Component Gallery for a gauge*

a transient attribute in the OrderItemsView view object that has its *Value* set to "InventoriesView .sum("QuantityOnHand")."

| Customers | Customer Orders | | | | | | |

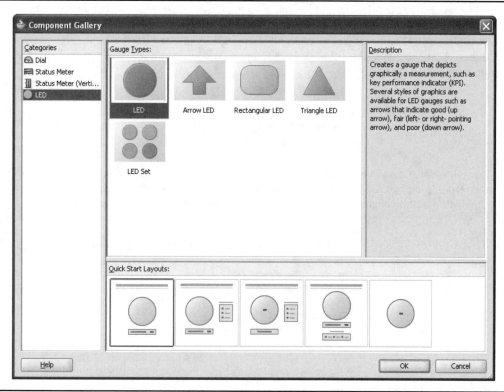

FIGURE 16-4. *Component Gallery for a gauge*

a transient attribute in the OrderItemsView view object that has its *Value* set to "InventoriesView .sum("QuantityOnHand")."

Orders

OrderId 2413
OrderDate 29/03/2000
OrderMode direct
CustomerId 101
OrderStatus 5
OrderTotal 48552
SalesRepId 161
PromotionId 1

First | Previous | Next | Last

Order Items

LineItemId	ProductId	UnitPrice	Quantity	ProductName	LineTotal	TotalInStock
1	3108	77	200	KB E/EN	15400	742
2	3112	75	40	MB - S500	3000	747
3	3117	35	44	Mouse C/E	1540	752
4	3127	492	44	LaserPro 600/6/BW	21648	387
5	3129	46	45	Sound Card STD	2070	762
6	3155	47	62	Monitor Hinge - HD	2914	
7	3163	30	66	Manual - Vision Net6.3/US	1980	

However, what you would like to do is give the user a clear indication of whether the current stock levels are enough to fulfill the order. To do this, you will replace the text field TotalInStock with a gauge that shows the stock level and shows red if the stock level is below the quantity required. You can locate the TotalInStock Output Text component in the Structure Window and simply delete it.

Having deleted this field, drag and drop a gauge as a child of the column, selecting the LED gauge type. In doing this, you have replaced the output text field with a gauge. You now have to set the value of the gauge to point to the correct binding and set the threshold levels.

Since the gauge is displaying a single value, just like the output text field it replaced, you can use the same binding. Set the *Value* property of the gauge to "#{row.TotalInStock}."

NOTE
At the time of writing, the current implementation is that if the gauge tries to display an attribute value that is null, then a default value of 63 is displayed. To work around this problem, you can make a slight change to the EL to check for a null value. If you set Value to "#{empty row.TotalInStock? 0 : row.TotalInStock }" this will check whether the value of TotalInStock is empty. If it is, then the value 0 will be used. This is standard EL and demonstrates the flexibility of EL.

You might want to fine-tune the look and feel of the gauge, such as setting *ImageHeight* and *ImageWidth* so that the gauge fits comfortably in the table row. Setting the *Position* property on the Metric Label component allows you to define where the data value appears. You may also choose to add a Number Format component and a Gauge Font component as child tags to the Metric Label component. The Number Format component allows you to set features like the scale and format of the number, while the Gauge Font component allows you to define font properties such as *Name*, *Bold*, and *Italic*.

Setting Gauge Threshold Values

You can run and test the page; however, the gauge doesn't yet give an indication of whether the value is above or below the threshold. To do this, you need to set the Threshold component. By default, the LED gauge is created with three of these threshold levels. In this example, set the first threshold's *ThresholdMaxValue* to "#{row.Quantity.value}" and select a color such as red as *FillColor*. This means that if the value is below the value of the current row's quantity, then the gauge will show a red alert. For the second threshold, set *FillColor*, maybe to green, but you don't have to explicitly set *ThresholdMaxValue* because this is the upper limit of the threshold. Since you are only indicating two threshold levels, you can delete the third threshold tag.

Now when you run the page, the user can quickly ascertain if there is enough stock to fulfill the order item. If the gauge is showing green, then it can; if it is showing red, then there are not enough items in stock.

Hierarchy Viewer

The hierarchy viewer is a DVT component for viewing hierarchical data. The classic example is a company organization chart showing departments, which can be drilled into to show employees within each department. Each node within the hierarchy viewer can contain output components such as output text fields and images, and each level of the hierarchy can display different information. For example, the department node may show only the department name but the employee node may show the full contact details for the employee. Furthermore, the hierarchy viewer can be configured so that different information is displayed depending on the zoom level. So for a high-level view of employees in a department, you may want to display only the employee's name and job title, but when you zoom in on an employee, you may want to see their phone number, location, and e-mail address.

The hierarchy viewer also includes features to allow the user to zoom and pan, as well as change the layout of the hierarchy component.

Creating a Hierarchy Viewer

When creating a hierarchy viewer, the most important fact is to ensure the data model being visualized is correctly defined. If it is, then setting up the hierarchy viewer is relatively straightforward.

Using the classic departments and employees example, you should have a data model that defines departments and the employees within that department. Furthermore, you could also define that for an employee within a department, you want to see which employees, if any, that person manages. If you have not already done so, you should be able to set this model up using ADF Business Components.

From the Data Controls panel, drag and drop the departments data collection onto the page as a hierarchy viewer. JDeveloper displays the Component Gallery dialog, where you can select from the different hierarchy viewer layouts.

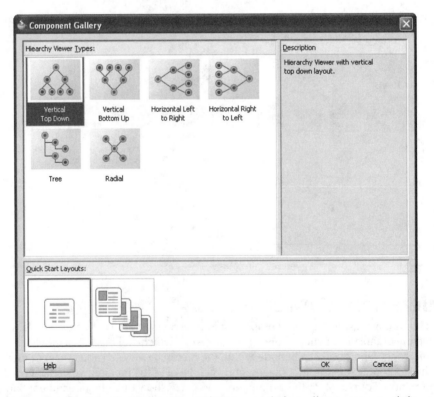

JDeveloper then displays the Create Hierarchy Viewer dialog, allowing you to define what information is to be displayed. As you can see in Figure 16-5 in the *Hierarchy* panel, this hierarchy viewer will display three levels: departments, employees in those departments, and

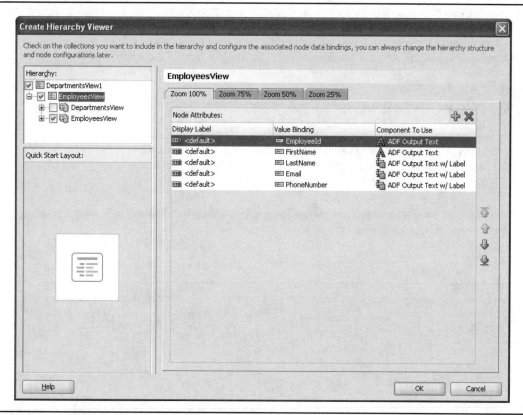

FIGURE 16-5.   *The Create Hierarchy Viewer dialog*

employees who report to an employee. You can also define what information is displayed at the different zoom levels.

You can now run and test the hierarchy viewer, although the first thing you might notice is that, because of the number of departments, there is really too much information to make this useful. Let's look at how the attributes of the hierarchy viewer can be changed to more closely fit the business need.

Fine-Tuning the Hierarchy Viewer

There are a number of attributes that allow you to fine-tune the layout details of the hierarchy viewer. For example, on the hierarchy viewer you can set the *Descendent Levels* and *Nodes Per Level* properties. Setting the first to "0" means that none of the children of the top-level nodes will be shown until the user explicitly expands a top-level node. Setting *Nodes Per Level* to a value of "6" will display only six nodes at each level. If there are any other nodes at this level—for example, there are more than six departments—then the hierarchy viewer automatically shows navigation controls to allow the user to display the other nodes.

You can set node attributes such as *Height*, *Width*, and *Shape* to alter the node, and you can also fine-tune the layout of each of the nodes, since each node is simply a collection of ADF Faces output components. If you want to add a picture of the employee at each node, drag and drop an image item onto the node and set the *Source* attribute of the image.

TIP
Since the schema you are using does not store images in the tables, you will have to read an image for each employee from the file system. You could have images on your file system named using a convention such as <employeeId>.jpg. You could then import the images into your project and set the Source *of the image item to the EL expression "images/#{node.EmployeeId}.jpg."*

You can now run and test the hierarchy viewer, as shown in Figure 16-6, where you can expand nodes, change layout, and zoom in and out.

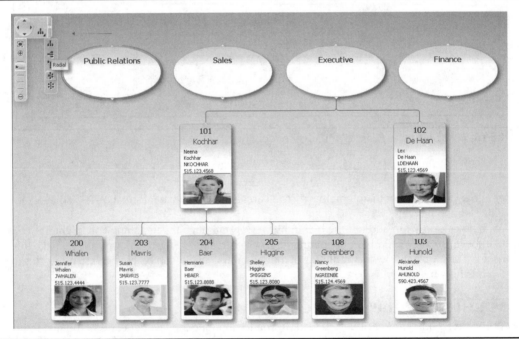

FIGURE 16-6. *The ADF Faces hierarchy viewer*

Geographic Maps

The final DVT component example is the geographic map. This component allows spatial data, such as latitude and longitude, or an address, to be plotted on a map. At each point on the map, the component can show different information such as data values or even graphs.

At the heart of this feature is the requirement for a map server, such as Oracle MapViewer, to serve up the maps on which the data will be plotted. In this example, we will use http://elocation.oracle.com/mapviewer to serve up the maps.

Preparing the Business Service

The OE schema used in this book has spatial data as part of the Customers table. This is the attribute CustGeoLocation, which is an object type. This object type contains the spatial information for a customer's location, specifically the longitude and latitude. At the time of writing, the geographic map can't bind directly with this complex object type. However, there is a simple trick to "flatten" out the object into its simplest constituent types. You need to create two new transient attributes of type Number in the CustomersView view object and select *Mapped to Column or SQL*. You can now map each of these new attributes to an SQL expression. Set *Expression* to "Customers.CUST_GEO_LOCATION.sdo_point.x" and "Customers.CUST_GEO_LOCATION.sdo_point.y" respectively. This will allow the view object to use its SQL statement to select the flattened-out object type into two separate transient attributes.

If you want, you can look at the view object query to see how this behavior is being implemented. Refresh the Data Controls panel and you will see these two extra attributes. The map can easily be bound to these "simpler" values.

Creating a Geographic Map

Having prepared the business service, you can drag and drop the customers data collection from the Data Controls panel and select **Geographic Map | Map and Point Theme**.

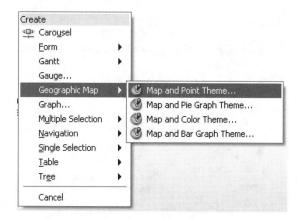

Before you can start binding the data collection, JDeveloper prompts you to configure the link to the map server. In the Create Geographic Map dialog, click the green plus button and create a *MapViewer URL*. This displays the Create URL Connection dialog. Enter the information as shown in the following illustration and test the connection.

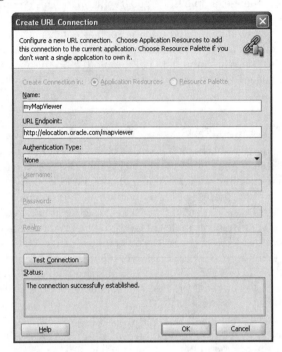

Now that JDeveloper knows where the maps are coming from, the next step is the binding. Click OK in the Create Geographic Map dialog and JDeveloper takes you to the Create Point Map Theme dialog. Select that your data is *X & Y (Longitude & Latitude)* and set *X (Longitude)* and *Y (Latitude)* to the two new attributes based on the flattened object type.

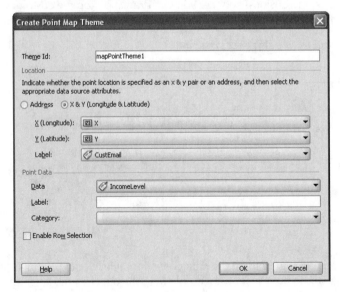

You can also set *Label*, which will display a label for the point on the map, and *Data*, which will show information when the point is clicked.

By default the map will be zoomed out to show the whole world; however, you can set the property *AutoZoomThemeId* to the value of *ThemeId*, which in the preceding case is "mapPointTheme1." This will then cause the map to automatically scale to a level that will include all the data points.

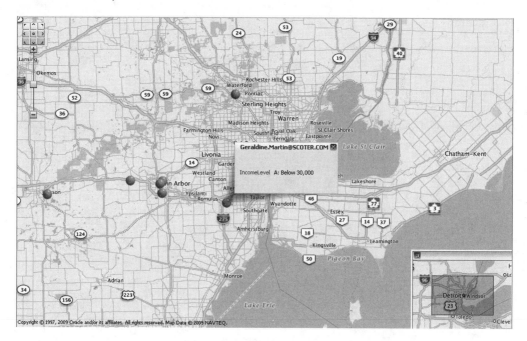

Summary

The ADF Faces DVT components are a valuable aid in building rich applications. Using graphs, gauges, hierarchy viewers, and other components, complex data structures and relationships can be easily visualized. This chapter has introduced some of these components and explained how:

- Bar graphs can be used to plot data points against a series.
- Reference lines can be added to a bar graph.
- Pie graphs allow you to visualize data as a proportion.
- Gauges can be used to represent a data value within a range or against threshold limits.
- Hierarchical information can be shown using the ADF Faces hierarchy viewer.
- ADF Faces provides a component for plotting spatial information on a map.

CHAPTER
17

Building a Reusable UI

hapter by chapter you have been learning about the building blocks of a Fusion application, and by now you should have a solid grounding in how to build a relatively functionally rich application. However, when moving from learning mode to building an application "for real," there are some additional considerations, such as potential reuse, ensuring consistency, and defining a look and feel for your application.

This chapter introduces how you can ensure that your application has a consistent look and feel by using page templates and reusable UI components.

Page Templates

Until now, you have been building pages in an ad hoc manner with no real thought to consistency of look and feel. This problem is exacerbated when you move into a team environment, where everyone may have differing opinions on what constitutes good page layout.

In order to promote consistency across the UI, Oracle ADF includes a feature called templates. As you might expect, a template allows a page designer to define a page layout, including elements such as a company logo or copyright information, and to apply that template to all application pages. The template designer would also define areas within the template where the consumer of the template can add their own content. This means that the developer using the page has well-defined areas where UI content can be placed, but anything outside these defined areas cannot be edited.

When a page designer uses a page template as the basis for a page, the page template is referenced from the page (rather than it being a copy). That means that if the template designer makes a change to the page template, then the page that uses the page template will automatically reflect that change because it is referenced.

Creating a Page Template

The page template itself is really just a special kind of JSF page with areas, known as facets, indicating the places where the consumer of the template can add their own content. So, creating a template is just like creating any other JSF page.

To create a new page template, select **File | New** and, in the New Gallery dialog, select **JSF** and then **JSF Page Template**. This displays the Create JSF Page Template dialog, as shown in Figure 17-1, where you can enter a name for the template. You can also define a number of features of the page template, as described next, before you click OK.

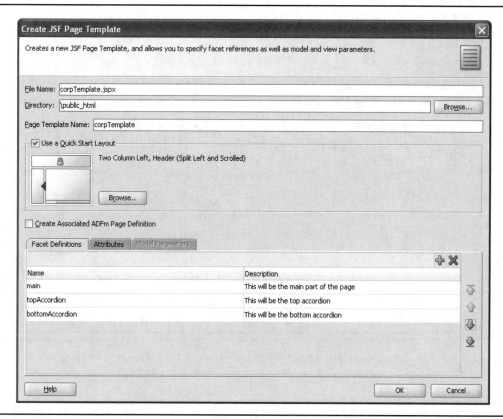

FIGURE 17-1.   *Create JSF Page Template dialog*

Quick Start Layout

An incredibly useful feature of JDeveloper is that when you're creating a page or template, JDeveloper offers a selection of predefined page layouts, called quick start layouts. These are simply common layout patterns implemented using ADF Faces layout components.

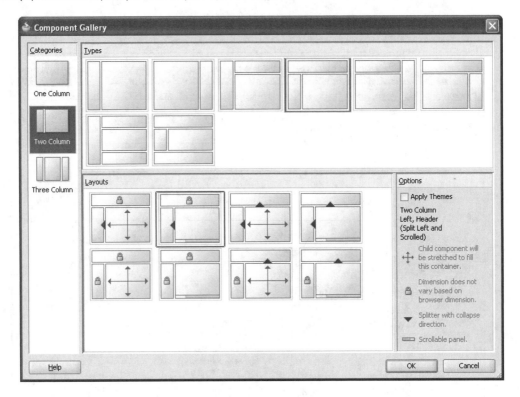

For this template, choose any one of the two-column layouts. This will create a template using a Panel Splitter component to represent each of the two columns.

Facet Definitions

When designing a page template, you need to define areas on the page where the consumer of the template can place his or her page content. These special areas are called facets and are pretty much the same as the facets you have come across in other components, such as the toolbar facet on a Panel Collection component.

In this example, the page template will have three facets: "main," "topAccordion," and "bottomAccordion." The names aren't important other than to give a useful indication of their position or use. In this case, the template will have a main center with the left column containing two accordion panels.

Attributes

When creating a page template, you can also define template attributes. These are like parameters that can be passed into the template by the page using the template. This might be useful if you want to pass page-specific information into the template. For example, within the page template, you might define that the starting position of the panel splitter is controlled by an attribute. Any page that uses the template can customize this starting position by setting the value of the attribute.

In this example, the page template will define three attributes: one to define the panel splitter starting position, and two, which are strings, to use as labels in the panel accordion that appears in the template. This means that every page that uses this template will have the same consistent look and feel but the consumer of the template will be able to customize the starting position of the panel splitter and the labels that appear in the panel accordion.

Facet Definitions	Attributes	Model Parameters			
Name	Type	Default Value		Required	
splitterPos	java.lang.Integer	200		☐	
acc1Label	java.lang.String			☐	
acc2Label	java.lang.String		...	☐	

Template Layout

You can now click OK on the Create JSF Page Template dialog and get on with the job of designing the template. In this template, you want a Panel Accordion component in the left column containing two Show Detail Item components. In the top area of the template, you can add a company logo, and the remaining column in the panel splitter is for the main page content, as shown in Figure 17-2. Creating this layout is just like creating any other ADF Faces page, using layout containers, images, and other UI components. The only difference is when it comes to wiring up the facets and attributes.

Defining the Template Facets   When you created the page template, you defined three different facets. These facets are the areas in which the consumer of the template can add their own content. To define an area in the template as a facet, drag and drop a Facet Ref component

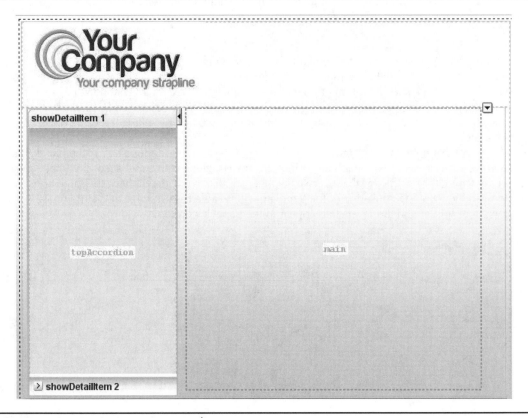

FIGURE 17-2. *Designing a page template*

from the Component Palette onto the appropriate place on the page and define which facet it references. Notice that the list of facets that you defined is shown as you add the Facet Ref.

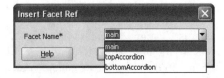

Do the same for the other facets, as shown in Figure 17-2, and finalize the layout of your template.

Referencing Template Attributes   When you created the page template, you also defined three attributes. You now have to reference these template attributes from the appropriate components in the template.

First, you should set the panel splitter starting position to the appropriate attribute. To do this, select the Panel Splitter component and find the *SplitterPosition* property. Using the Expression Builder dialog, set *SplitterPosition* to "#{attrs.splitterPos}." This defines that the value for this property will come from the template attribute *splitterPos*. So, a page designer would supply a value for *splitterPos* when they use this template.

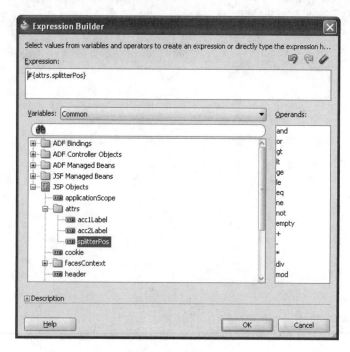

You can also do the same for the *Text* property of each of the Show Detail Item components inside the Panel Accordion component. Again, this means that the text label for each of these panels will come from the template attribute, for which page designers supply a value when they use the template.

Using a Page Template

Now that you have created a page template, the next step is to build pages based on that page template. Typically, you would package the page template into a library to be shared among your development team—and you will find out more about this when looking at declarative components later in the chapter—but for the moment, as long as the page template is in your project, you will be able to use it.

When you create a JSF page, one of the options is to create a page based on a template. Selecting this option will create the page and automatically apply, by reference, the chosen template.

When viewing the page in the visual page editor, you will immediately notice that some areas of the page are grayed out while others are not. The areas that are not grayed out are the facet references that were created in the template. These are the areas on the page where content can be placed.

Defining Values for Template Attributes

You also defined that this page template has three attributes that could be set by the page designer using the template to allow the customization of the starting position of the panel splitter and the labels for the panel accordion. These attributes are presented as properties in the Property Inspector, so you need to select the template and open the Property Inspector.

TIP
It can be difficult to select the reference to the template from within the visual editor, in which case you should use the Structure window.

Customization		
Other	acc1Label:	Order History for #{bindings.CustFirstName.inputValue}
	acc2Label:	Customer Locations
	Id:	pt1
	PartialTriggers:	
	splitterPos:	200
	Value:	
	ViewId:	/corpTemplate.jspx

As shown, you can set these properties to a literal value, such as a *splitterPos* "200," or the property can reference a binding. In this case, *acc1Label* is bound to the customer's first name.

NOTE
Because the template is referenced, if the template changes, then the referencing page will change as well. You can test this by making a change to the template, saving it, and then refreshing the page that uses the template.

Declarative Components

Page templates help you ensure a consistency in page layout; however, that only goes so far in ensuring a consistent application look and feel. Declarative components are another weapon in your armory and allow you to build reusable composite components such as a customer details panel or a toolbar of buttons. These declarative components can then be packaged up and used by the development team on pages just like regular ADF Faces components.

Creating a Reusable Customer Panel

Let's take the first of those examples. Suppose that while designing the application, you find that there are many instances where you display customer information. You might find that the same collection of fields and data is being used on many different pages. Rather than creating this panel of UI components every time, declarative components allow you to build the component once, and deploy it into the Component Palette to be made available along with all the other ADF Faces components.

Let's take a look at the steps for building, deploying, and then using a declarative component.

Creating a Declarative Component

Declarative component development would typically happen in a separate project from the main application development effort, so create a new ADF ViewController project. The next step is to create the declarative component in that project. Select **File | New** and, in the New Gallery dialog, select **JSF** and then **JSF Declarative Component**. This displays the Create JSF Declarative Component dialog in which you define information for the name of the component, the library name in which the component will be packaged, and also facets and attributes. As shown in Figure 17-3, enter "customerPanel" for *Declarative Component Name* and click Add Tag Library to define a name for the library. Create a tag library with *Tag Library Name* set to "ComponentLibrary."

Having done that, you now need to specify the facets and attributes. Just like a page template, a declarative component can have a number of facets, the areas within the component where the consumer of the component can add their own content. If you want to define a facet where the consumer of the component can add their own content, you can do so here.

Attributes, as with page templates, are used as parameters to pass information into the declarative component. Since this declarative component is going to be displaying data, you need a way of passing that data into the component. In this case, define three attributes, one for each of the fields in the declarative component. As shown in Figure 17-3, add the three attributes

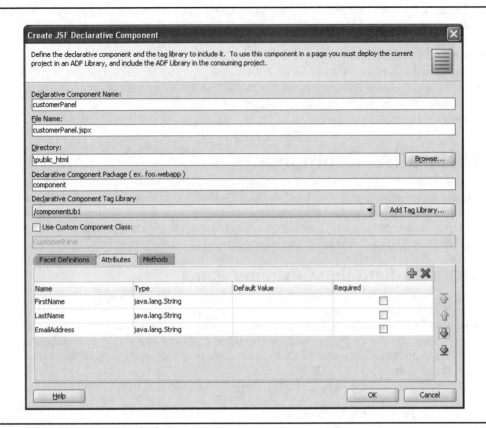

FIGURE 17-3. *Creating a JSF declarative component*

FirstName, *LastName*, and *EmailAddress*. You will use these attributes to pass in the data values for each of the input text fields in the declarative component.

You can now create and lay out your components by dragging and dropping from the Component Palette. Once the layout is complete, you need to assign the declarative component attributes to the appropriate UI component properties. In this case, the *Value* property of each field should be set to the appropriate attribute using EL; for example, "#{attrs.EmailAddress}."

This indicates that the value for this field comes from the *EmailAddress* attribute. You will see how these attributes are populated later.

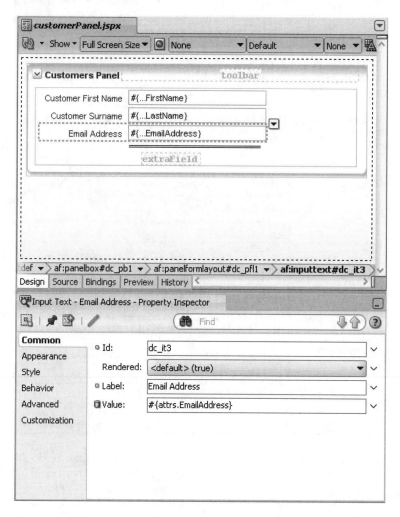

NOTE
For both declarative components and page templates, "attrs" is the default name for the collection of attributes for that component or template. However, you can change this by setting the Var *property of the component or template.*

Packaging and Deploying a Declarative Component

Once you are happy with the layout of the component, the next stage is to package it up into a reusable library. Double-click the project to display the Project Properties dialog, select Deployment, and click New to create a new deployment.

In the Create Deployment Profile dialog, set *Archive Type* to "ADF Library JAR File" and enter a name for the deployment. Here you are defining the information to allow the declarative component to be packaged up into a reusable library. You can accept the other default values by clicking OK.

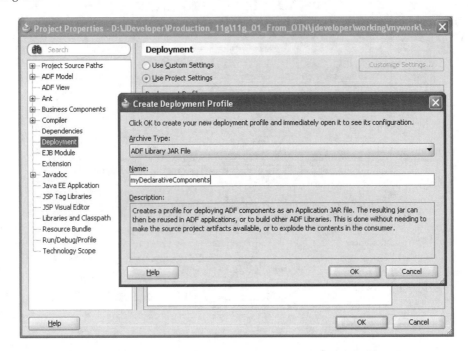

You now need to physically deploy that library to the file system. To do this, right-click the project name and select **Deploy** and then the name of the deployment profile you just created. JDeveloper displays a dialog to indicate where in the file system the library is being deployed. Take note of the directory path to where the library is deployed. You will need this later.

NOTE
Generally speaking, these reusable libraries would be deployed to some shared location where developers who need the components could discover and use them.

Using a Declarative Component

Now that you have created this composite component and published it in a library, the developer who wants to use this new component has to import this library into his or her project.

Importing a Declarative Component

To import the declarative component, ensure that you can view the Resource Palette and then, from the main menu, select **File | New** and, in the New Gallery dialog, select **Connections** and then **File System Connection**. In the Create File System Connection dialog, enter a name for the connection and select the path to the deployment directory that you previously noted.

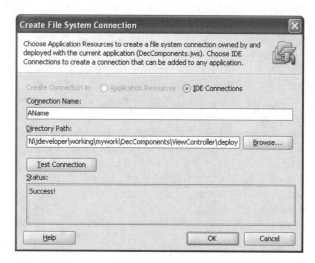

JDeveloper now has a direct connection to the library containing the declarative component, as shown in the Resource Palette. You now have to add that library to the current project. Select the project in which you want to add the declarative component, right-click the library myDeclarativeComponents.jar inside the new file connection, and select **Add to Project**.

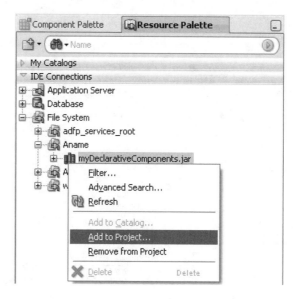

The declarative component has now been added to the project and is available in the Component Palette just like all the other ADF Faces components.

TIP
If you have trouble locating the component, you can use the search feature of the Component Palette or, from the drop-down list, select the tag library in which you placed the component.

Using a Declarative Component on a Page

The declarative component now behaves like any other component, meaning it can be dragged and dropped onto a page and have properties set. Given that you want this component to be bound to some data, you need to set the attribute properties of the declarative component to reference the bindings for the data you want to display. Like a template, each of the attributes defined in the declarative component appears as a property in the Property Inspector.

Select the declarative component in the Structure window and reference the appropriate bindings for *EmailAddress*, *FirstName*, and *LastName*. For example, *EmailAddress* would be set to "#{bindings.CustEmail.inputValue}."

TIP
If you need a reminder of how to create a binding, refer to Chapter 10.

Summary

In this chapter you have learned how to ensure consistency in your pages by using templates and reusable declarative components. Specifically, in this chapter you have discovered that:

- A page template can be based on a predefined quick start layout.

- A page template defines facets, which are areas where the consumers of the template can place their own content.

- Attributes can be defined on a page template to allow the template to be parameterized.

- Declarative components allow reusable composite components to be shared among developers.

- Declarative components can also define facets where the user of the component can add their own UI components.

- Declarative components can define attributes to allow information to be passed into the declarative component.

- Declarative components can be imported into the Component Palette and used like other ADF Faces components.

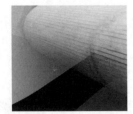

PART
IV

Common Coding Patterns

CHAPTER
18

Common Business Service
Coding Examples

s you have seen throughout the preceding chapters, JDeveloper and Oracle ADF provide a whole raft of features to enable you to build a pretty powerful application with no real need to roll up your sleeves and dive into code. Having said that, not all your development will be drag and drop, and as you get further into developing applications and encounter more-esoteric requirements, you will want to exploit the flexibility you get with code.

As you have already seen, JDeveloper allows you to generate subclasses of framework classes and add your own code to those subclasses. This chapter introduces some common examples that you can use as the foundation of your first ventures into programmatic development of your application.

Coding in the Entity Object

As you have now discovered, the entity object provides the cache for your application data. Therefore, if you need to programmatically manipulate that cache as part of the application processing, then you can generate a subclass of the `EntityImpl` class and add code there.

Generally speaking, operations that involve data validation, augmenting the getting and setting of data values, and overriding the creation and removal of rows and DML operations would be performed in a subclass of `EntityImpl`.

NOTE
Remember, you can generate a subclass of `EntityImpl` from the entity object editor. Select the Java *tab, click the edit pencil icon, and select* Generate Entity Object *Class. You can choose which methods should be exposed in this class.*

Setting an Attribute Value Depending on Another Attribute

A simple example of a situation in which you might add code to control an entity object is where you want to programmatically set the value of one attribute depending on the value of another attribute. For example, in the application built so far, if you change the product ID of an order item to be a different product, then the unit price of that line item is unchanged. It might be better to reset the price when the product ID is changed (to prevent the user from changing the order for a $2 box of pencils to an order for an executive oak desk and still being charged only $2 for it!).

To implement the resetting of the price, generate the `OrderItemsImpl` class from the OrderItems entity object, ensuring that you choose to generate accessors.

In the `OrderItemsImpl` class, you will find a method `setProductId()`. This is the method called whenever the value in the ProductId attribute is changed. To force the unit price of the order item to be reset, add the following code:

```
public void setProductId(Number value) {
    setAttributeInternal(PRODUCTID, value);
    //Now set the unit price to null
    final Number newUnitPrice = null;
    setUnitPrice(newUnitPrice);
}
```

NOTE
*The new unit price is set after the call to `setAttributeInternal()`.
This ensures that the new unit price is only set if the product ID is
successfully changed. Also note that the call to `setUnitPrice()`
takes a parameter of type `oracle.jbo.domain.Number`.*

This is a simple enough example, but the concept of setting an attribute as a result of the change to another attribute is one that you may use over and over again.

Getting an Attribute Value from a Different Entity Object

The solution provided in the preceding section doesn't exactly fit your requirement. Although it forces the unit price to be reset, the line total will now throw an exception since it is a calculation based on the unit price, which is being set to null. A better solution is to extend this example and set the unit price to the recommended list price for the product. But how can you programmatically access the list price, which is part of the ProductInformation entity object?

The answer is by using an association accessor. When you created the business service, JDeveloper created associations between some of the entity objects. You can go back and check the association that links the OrderItems and ProductInformation entity objects, as shown in Figure 18-1. This shows that OrderItems can access ProductInformation via an accessor, which also is called ProductInformation.

FIGURE 18-1. *Defining accessors in an association*

If you look at the `OrderItemsImpl` class, you will see a method `getProductInformation()`. This is the method that allows to you access the ProductInformation entity object. You can now change the code to

```
public void setProductId(Number value) {
    setAttributeInternal(PRODUCTID, value);
    //Now set the unit price to the list price
    ProductInformationImpl prodInfo =
        (ProductInformationImpl)getProductInformation();
    final Number newUnitPrice = prodInfo.getListPrice();
    setUnitPrice(newUnitPrice);
}
```

TIP

By also generating the `ProductInformationImpl` class and choosing to expose accessor methods, you can use the type-safe method `getListPrice()`, rather than calling `getAttribute()` defined on the `EntityImpl` class.

This is a common example of where you need to access an attribute in a different entity object. The code will use the association accessor method, `getProductInformation()`, to access the ProductInformation entity object. You can then call any of the accessor methods on `ProductInformationImpl` to read attribute values.

Overriding the Deletion of an Order

Because the entity object is responsible for updating and deleting application data, you can place in an entity object class any code you require to augment or override that behavior.

A common example of this is where, rather than deleting a row from the database, you want to set a flag to mark that the row is in a deleted state but still physically in the database. For example, suppose you decide that you want to maintain the history of all orders ever placed. That means that if a user attempts to delete an order, the status of the order should be set accordingly and the DML operation to delete the record from the database should be bypassed.

NOTE

Chapter 6 included a similar example but coded in the view object. By coding in the entity object, you are ensuring that this behavior is enforced for all possible view objects based on this entity object.

To implement this use case, generate the `OrdersImpl` class from the Orders entity object and choose to expose accessors, DML operations, and the remove method.

Overriding the remove() Method

This first step is to augment the default behavior when the framework removes a row from the entity object cache by updating the status of the order. To do this, locate the `remove()` method in the `OrdersImpl` class and add the following code to set the order.

```
public void remove() {
    final Number ORDER_CANCELLED = new Number(3);
```

```
setOrderStatus(ORDER_CANCELLED);
super.remove();
}
```

The code simply sets the order status of the order item to indicate it has been cancelled—in the data model, this is represented by the value 3—and then performs the default operation of removing the row from the entity object cache.

NOTE
You would typically define the constant ORDER_CANCELLED outside the method, but it is included here for completeness.

Overriding the DML Operation
So far you have updated the order to show it has been cancelled, but these changes have not yet been committed to the database. If the default DML operation now fires, the rows that have been removed from the entity object cache will be removed from the database, which in this case is not what you want. Instead, you want to override the DML operation for the order to perform an update rather than a delete. This ensures that the rows are updated to show the new status and that they are not removed from the underlying database table.

In the `OrdersImpl` class, locate the `doDML()` method and change the code as follows:

```
protected void doDML(int operation, TransactionEvent e) {
    if (operation == DML_DELETE) {
        operation = DML_UPDATE;
    }
    super.doDML(operation, e);
}
```

This "tricks" the Orders entity object into thinking it should perform an update, so that it will never delete an order.

TIP
You can test this behavior in the ADF Business Components Browser, where you can see the updated order status when you delete an order, commit the change, and then requery the data. However, the fact that you can see the order with the new status might not be exactly what you want, in which case you could change your view object, using a view criteria, to show only orders that have not been cancelled. That way, you still retain archived orders in the database but don't show them to the application user.

Overriding the Check of an Updatable Attribute
Of course, adding a view criteria to filter out these cancelled orders would prevent the application user from seeing, and therefore being able to reopen, an order. A more robust strategy might be to simply make a cancelled order read-only in the entity object cache. That way you can ensure that, regardless of the view object being used, the underlying entity object will never allow a cancelled order to be changed.

To do this, you can override the `isAttributeUpdateable()` method on the entity object. The framework calls this method to check whether an entity object attribute is updateable. In this case you want to indicate that, for any order that has been cancelled, none of the attributes in the order can be updated.

Open the `OrdersImpl` class and, from the main menu, select **Source** | **Override Methods**. This displays the Override Methods dialog, in which you can choose which method you want to override in the `OrdersImpl` class. Locate `isAttributeUpdateable()` and click OK.

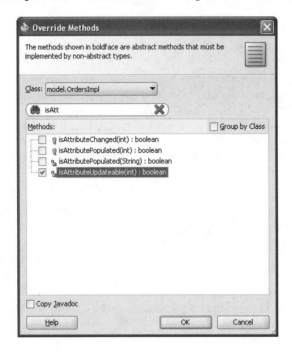

Now you can change the method as follows:

```
public boolean isAttributeUpdateable(int index) {

    final  Number ORDER_CANCELLED = new Number(3);
    if (this.getOrderStatus().equals(ORDER_CANCELLED)) {
        return false;
    }
    return super.isAttributeUpdateable(index);
}
```

NOTE
Remember, Number is `oracle.jbo.domain.Number` *and not*
`java.lang.Number,` *so make sure you use the correct type.*

So, now when the framework checks to see if an attribute of the Orders entity object is updateable, it will return false for any cancelled order. This will ensure that the framework does not allow a cancelled order to be updated.

TIP

For a cancelled order, this code will prevent the update of all order attributes; however, the parameter index *indicates which attribute is being checked, so you have the flexibility to decide which attributes are updateable and which are not.*

Coding in the View Object

While the entity object defines a cache for application data, a view object defines application-specific views of that data. This means that if you want to programmatically manipulate only a specific view of data, either changing the filter applied to that view object or updating a view object attribute, you can do so in a subclass of ViewObjectImpl or ViewRowImpl.

Let's take a look at some common examples of programmatically manipulating the view object.

Dynamically Setting a View Criteria

Consider the example that for the OrdersView view object, you want to either create your own search feature or, depending on some runtime action, filter that view object. In this case, you can add code to the OrdersViewImpl class to dynamically filter the view by applying a view criteria.

The first step is to create a view criteria on OrdersView called OrdersModeViewCriteria that uses a bind variable to filter OrderMode.

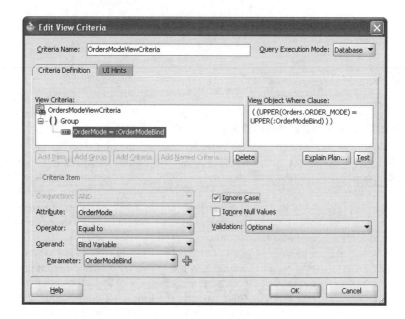

Now generate the `OrdersViewImpl` class, ensuring that you choose to include bind variable accessors. You can then add the following code:

```
public void changeOrderModeFilter(String mode) {
    ViewCriteria vc = getViewCriteria("OrdersModeViewCriteria");
    setOrderModeBind(mode);
    applyViewCriteria(vc);
    executeQuery();
}
```

This will find the view criteria, and then use a generated bind variable accessor to set the value of the bind variable. The code will then apply the view criteria and re-execute the query.

If you choose to expose this method to the UI, you must expose it in the client interface. This feature can be found under the *Java* tab of the OrdersView view object editor. You can then bind to this method and parameter from the UI by dragging and dropping the method from the Data Controls panel onto the page, as shown next, to provide a custom search feature on orders.

| View ▾ | Search Order Mode | online | ⊙ | ⊞ Detach |

OrderId	Order Date	Mode	Order Total
2458	16/08/1999	online	£78,279.60
2355	26/01/1998	online	£94,513.50
2356	26/01/2000	online	£29,473.80
2359	09/01/1998	online	£5,543.10
2360	14/11/1999	online	£990.40
2361	13/11/1999	online	£120,131.30
2362	13/11/1999	online	£92,829.40
2363	24/10/1999	online	£10,082.30

TIP
You may want to set ChangeEventPolicy *to "ppr" on the binding to ensure that the table of orders is refreshed when the button is clicked.*

Changing Values Across a View Object

The code you have just written controls which rows the view object will retrieve; however, suppose you want to write code that operates on a specific row. Let's assume that you want to be able to apply a discount to a customer's orders. This might be a useful feature to expose to the application operators so that if they are speaking to a customer who is considering moving suppliers, the operator can apply a one-time loyalty discount to encourage the customer to remain as a customer. This will require that, for a specific customer, the code iterate through the orders view object and apply the discount on the order total for any open orders.

To do this, generate the `CustomersViewRowImpl` class, which represents a single customer row. Because CustomersView and OrdersView are linked by a view link, and that view link defines an accessor, the `CustomerViewRowImpl` class can access the orders for that customer using `getOrdersView()`. You can therefore add the following code to `CustomersViewRowImpl`:

```
public void applyLoyaltyDiscount() {
    final Number OPEN_ORDER = new Number(1);
    final Number DISCOUNT = new Number(50);
    //Get the orders for this customer
    RowSet orders = (RowSet)getOrdersView();
    if (orders != null) {
```

```
        //loop through all the customer orders
        while (orders.hasNext()) {
            OrdersViewRowImpl currentOrder =
                (OrdersViewRowImpl)orders.next();

            //if the order is open then apply the discount
            if (currentOrder.getOrderStatus().equals(OPEN_ORDER)) {
              //Get the current order total
              Number orderTotal = currentOrder.getOrderTotal();
              //Deduct 50 off the total
              currentOrder.setOrderTotal((Number)orderTotal
    .minus(DISCOUNT));
            }
        }
    }
}
```

TIP
As noted before, by also generating the `OrdersViewRowImpl`
class, which represents an order row, the current row can be cast
to `OrdersViewRowImpl`*, which means you can use the type-safe*
methods such as `getOrderTotal()`.

So, looking at the code, it returns the orders for the specific customer and then iterates through those rows. If the order is currently open, then the discount is applied. You could, of course, extend the method to update the promotion code to reflect that a loyalty bonus has been applied and can only be applied once.

In order to allow the method to be called from a client, you have to expose it by selecting the *Java* tab of the CustomersView view object editor and exposing it as a client row interface.

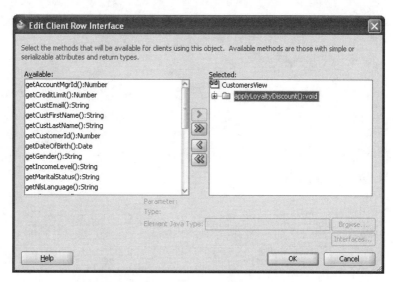

This method could now be called from a UI page by dragging the method from the Data Controls panel onto a page as, for example, a toolbar button.

Summary

This chapter has taken you through your first steps of programmatically accessing the features of ADF Business Components; in particular, you have learned that:

- Using a subclass of `EntityImpl`, you can set attribute values in response to other attribute values changing.
- Association accessors can be used in the `EntityImpl` subclass to programmatically access rows in a different entity object.
- The `EntityImpl` subclass allows you to override operations such as create, remove, and DML operations.
- You can programmatically apply a view criteria to a view object in the `ViewObjectImpl` subclass.
- You can write code against a single view object row using the `ViewRowImpl` subclass.

CHAPTER
19

Common UI
Coding Examples

hroughout this book, the focus has been on using the declarative framework features to build rich Fusion applications. However, in places the book has dipped into areas where you might typically augment the framework behavior with your own code.

This chapter introduces some programmatic concepts and provides common examples of where you might choose to write custom UI code.

TIP
While you are still getting up to speed on the technology, a good mantra to follow would be "only add code to the ViewController by exception." That is not to say you should never write code in managed beans to control UI functionality; however, there are two good reasons for considering this code-by-exception rule. First, chances are that the Oracle ADF framework already implements the feature you want to add, obviating the need for you to code it; the problem might just be finding that feature. Second, when you start to write UI-specific code, you may find yourself beset by the intricacies of JSF. So, before you roll up your sleeves and write code, ensure that the use case you are looking to implement can't already be implemented using declarative features of Oracle ADF.

How to Programmatically Access Page Bindings

As you have progressed through the book, you have built data-bound pages by dragging and dropping from the Data Controls panel, with JDeveloper automatically wiring each UI component to the underlying data control via a binding. As you start to write real-world applications, occasionally you may need to programmatically access these data-bound UI components. For example, you may want to update or read the value in a UI component or programmatically call a method. You can achieve this programmatic access of business service data and methods by accessing the binding layer from within a managed bean.

TIP
If you need a refresher, Chapter 15 explained how to create a managed bean.

As you found out in Chapter 11, the binding context provides the binding to your business service, and each page of the application has a binding container that defines the bindings for the UI components on the page. Oracle ADF provides an API that allows you to programmatically access the binding context and the binding container. These are represented by the objects BindingContext and BindingContainer.

In order to access the binding for the current page, you require the following code in the appropriate managed bean:

```
BindingContainer bindings = BindingContext.getCurrent().getCurrentBindingsEntry();
```

This code finds the binding context and returns the binding container for the current page. Any time you wish to programmatically access the binding, you would use this code, in which case you may choose to encapsulate the code in a method such as

```
public BindingContainer getBindings() {
    return BindingContext.getCurrent().getCurrentBindingsEntry();
}
```

NOTE
On writing this code, you may be prompted to import
`oracle.binding.BindingContainer` *and* `oracle.adf.model`
`.BindingContext.` *Ensure that these are added to the list of imports.*

How to Programmatically Access an Attribute Value

Now that you have an object that represents the binding container for a page, you can access those bindings to read and write values from and to the business service. For example, you could assign the following code to a button to read the value of the CustLastName binding and convert it to lowercase:

```
public void buttonPressBinding(ActionEvent actionEvent) {
    // Add event code here...
    AttributeBinding attr =
        (AttributeBinding)getBindings().getControlBinding("CustLastName");
    String selectedCust = (String)attr.getInputValue();
    attr.setInputValue(selectedCust.toLowerCase());

}
```

As before, JDeveloper will automatically prompt you for any imports. Ensure that you import `oracle.binding.AttributeBinding`.

NOTE
This example assumes you have written the previously described
`getBindings()` *method. Note also that the value passed to*
`getControlBinding()` *must exactly match the name of the binding*
or you will get an exception.

In the preceding code, an object, AttributeBinding, is used to reference an attribute binding to CustLastName. A call to `getInputValue()` and `setInputValue()` can be used to read and write the values referenced by the attribute binding.

How to Programmatically Execute a Method

Now that you know how to access an attribute binding, you might want to take the next step and access a method binding. For example, suppose that when a user clicks a particular button, you want some code to execute that includes a call to a bound method. This is very similar to the code in the previous example:

```
public void buttonPressCallMethod(ActionEvent actionEvent) {
    // Add event code here...
    OperationBinding operationBinding = getBindings().
getOperationBinding("Commit");
    operationBinding.execute();
}
```

NOTE
On writing this code, you may be asked to import oracle.binding
.OperationBinding.

In this example, getOperationBinding() returns the binding for the commit action on which an execute() method can be called. You should, of course, ensure that the binding you are calling exists on the page.

NOTE
You might be thinking, "surely, dragging and dropping the commit operation from the Data Controls panel is doing the same thing?" And that is correct in this simple case; however, this example shows that you have the flexibility to call a bound method, possibly as the result of more complex programmatic logic.

How to Programmatically Access the UI Context

Now that you know you can programmatically access the binding layer through the BindingContext object, you may wonder whether you can access other features of the UI framework in the same way. Yes, you can. Features like error messages and partial page rendering (PPR) are implemented by framework objects called FacesContext and AdfFacesContext, and, just like BindingContext, these objects give you programmatic access to the UI framework features you have been building through drag and drop and the setting of properties.

FacesContext gives access to the information relating to the rendering of the current page, whereas AdfFacesContext provides access to specific ADF Faces features, like PPR.

Let's look at two simple examples where these objects can be programmatically accessed.

Programmatic Display of Messages

Consider the following example: You have written in a managed bean some code that will alert the user when an error occurs. This could be an error handled by the application, such as the user not being authorized to access a specific piece of data, or it could be a programmatic error that should, at the very least, alert the user to an unexpected failure.

Accessing FacesContext

To programmatically display an error or warning message, you need to add your message to the FacesContext object, which will then be displayed when the page-processing cycle completes.

To demonstrate this in a simple example, add a button to a page, and in a managed bean add the following code:

```
public void TestMessageButton(ActionEvent actionEvent) {
    // Add event code here...
    FacesMessage fm = new FacesMessage("A Programmatic Info Message");
    fm.setSeverity(FacesMessage.SEVERITY_INFO);
    FacesContext context = FacesContext.getCurrentInstance();
    context.addMessage(null, fm);
}
```

This code will create a new message, set the message type to an information message, and then add the message to the FacesContext object, where the framework automatically displays it in a pop-up dialog.

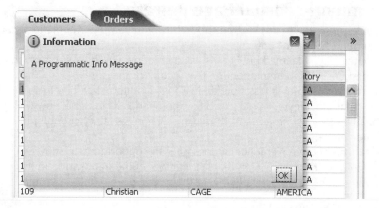

Displaying Messages Inline

Expanding on the preceding example, you can also associate the message with a specific UI component. To do this, you need to expose the UI component in the managed bean using the *Binding* property, as demonstrated in Chapter 15. You can then change the button code as follows:

```
public void TestMessageButton(ActionEvent actionEvent) {
    // Add event code here...
    FacesMessage fm = new FacesMessage("A Programmatic Info Message");
    fm.setSeverity(FacesMessage.SEVERITY_INFO);
    FacesContext context = FacesContext.getCurrentInstance();
    context.addMessage(getCustLastNameField().getClientId(context), fm);
}
```

NOTE
In this example, `getCustLastNameField()` *is the accessor created when setting the* Binding *property for the UI component. This was covered in Chapter 15 if you need a quick reminder.*

So in this code, the call to `addMessage()` specifies a particular UI component with which the message should be associated.

Programmatic Partial Page Refresh

The example presented in this section shows how you can programmatically access ADF Faces features through AdfFacesContext.

In Chapter 13 you learned how to display a task flow as a dialog; however, there was one piece of unfinished business in implementing that feature of the application. The current framework implementation to display a task flow dialog doesn't automatically refresh the data on the calling page. This means that if you create, or edit, customer details in a task flow dialog, when you dismiss the dialog, the table UI components displaying Customers table will not immediately be refreshed to show the change.

While this is an inconvenience, it does offer the opportunity to show you the flexibility that you have to code around any feature, or limitation, of the framework. In this example, you will see how you can programmatically trigger the partial page refresh of a component.

Introducing the Return Listener

The crux of the solution is that when the task flow pop-up dialog is dismissed, you want to programmatically force a refresh of a particular component—in this case, the Customers table. So, what event will fire when control returns from the task flow dialog? The answer is that the button that launches the task flow dialog has a property called *ReturnListener*. This "listens" for the completion of the event that the button launched; when the event completes, the method indicated by *ReturnListener* is called.

For the *ReturnListener* property, create a new method in a managed bean and define a method to be called when control returns from the task flow dialog.

You now have a managed bean in which you can programmatically trigger the refresh of the table. Since you have to be able to reference the table UI component from code, you need to expose that component in the managed bean.

TIP
As previously noted, look for the Binding *property of the table. This can be used to expose this component inside a managed bean.*

You now have all the pieces in place; the last thing is to write some code. In the managed bean, add the following code:

```
public void refreshCustomersTable(ReturnEvent returnEvent) {
    // Add event code here...
    AdfFacesContext adfFacesContext = AdfFacesContext.getCurrentInstance();
    adfFacesContext.addPartialTarget(getT1());
}
```

NOTE
The call to getT1() *references the accessor created through the* Binding *property for accessing the Customers table.*

The code uses the AdfFacesContext object to specify which component should be added to the list of components automatically refreshed. In this case, this will force a refresh of the Customers table.

Summary

You have now taken your first steps into programmatically controlling features of the UI. As noted earlier, many application features can be built without the need to write code in the ViewController project. However, this chapter has demonstrated some common techniques for doing so. Specifically you have learned that:

- You can programmatically access the binding layer through BindingContext and BindingContainer objects.
- Information associated with a page can be accessed through the FacesContext object.
- The AdfFacesContext object allows programmatic access to features such as PPR.

Congratulations! You've taken your first, but considerable, steps in understanding how to build a Fusion application with JDeveloper and Oracle ADF. Throughout this book you have been learning about the essential building blocks and key features. There is, of course, much more to learn, but you should now be in a position to explore these new areas from a solid grounding in Fusion application development.

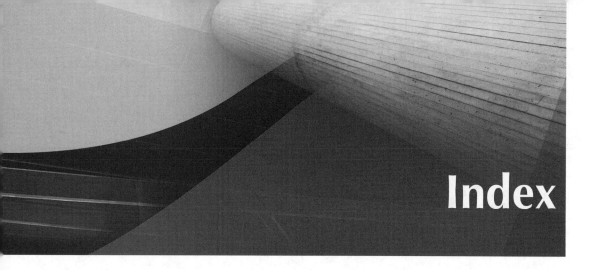

Index

References to figures are in italics.

GET YOUR FREE SUBSCRIPTION
TO *ORACLE MAGAZINE*

Oracle Magazine is essential gear for today's information technology professionals. Stay informed and increase your productivity with every issue of *Oracle Magazine*. Inside each free bimonthly issue you'll get:

- Up-to-date information on Oracle Database, Oracle Application Server, Web development, enterprise grid computing, database technology, and business trends
- Third-party news and announcements
- Technical articles on Oracle and partner products, technologies, and operating environments
- Development and administration tips
- Real-world customer stories

If there are other Oracle users at your location who would like to receive their own subscription to *Oracle Magazine*, please photocopy this form and pass it along.

Three easy ways to subscribe:

① Web
Visit our Web site at **oracle.com/oraclemagazine**
You'll find a subscription form there, plus much more

② Fax
Complete the questionnaire on the back of this card
and fax the questionnaire side only to **+1.847.763.9638**

③ Mail
Complete the questionnaire on the back of this card
and mail it to **P.O. Box 1263, Skokie, IL 60076-8263**

ORACLE®

Want your own FREE subscription?

To receive a free subscription to *Oracle Magazine*, you must fill out the entire card, sign it, and date it (incomplete cards cannot be processed or acknowledged). You can also fax your application to **+1.847.763.9638. Or subscribe at our Web site at oracle.com/oraclemagazine**

O **Yes, please send me a FREE subscription** *Oracle Magazine*.   O No.

O From time to time, Oracle Publishing allows our partners exclusive access to our e-mail addresses for special promotions and announcements. To be included in this program, please check this circle. If you do not wish to be included, you will only receive notices about your subscription via e-mail.

O Oracle Publishing allows sharing of our postal mailing list with selected third parties. If you prefer your mailing address not to be included in this program, please check this circle.

If at any time you would like to be removed from either mailing list, please contact Customer Service at +1.847.763.9635 or send an e-mail to oracle@halldata.com. If you opt in to the sharing of information, Oracle may also provide you with e-mail related to Oracle products, services, and events. If you want to completely unsubscribe from any e-mail communication from Oracle, please send an e-mail to: unsubscribe@oracle-mail.com with the following in the subject line: REMOVE [your e-mail address]. For complete information on Oracle Publishing's privacy practices, please visit oracle.com/html/privacy/html

X

signature (required)   date

name   title

company   e-mail address

street/p.o. box

city/state/zip or postal code   telephone

country   fax

Would you like to receive your free subscription in digital format instead of print if it becomes available? O Yes O No

---

YOU MUST ANSWER ALL 10 QUESTIONS BELOW.

① WHAT IS THE PRIMARY BUSINESS ACTIVITY OF YOUR FIRM AT THIS LOCATION? (check one only)

- ☐ 01 Aerospace and Defense Manufacturing
- ☐ 02 Application Service Provider
- ☐ 03 Automotive Manufacturing
- ☐ 04 Chemicals
- ☐ 05 Media and Entertainment
- ☐ 06 Construction/Engineering
- ☐ 07 Consumer Sector/Consumer Packaged Goods
- ☐ 08 Education
- ☐ 09 Financial Services/Insurance
- ☐ 10 Health Care
- ☐ 11 High Technology Manufacturing, OEM
- ☐ 12 Industrial Manufacturing
- ☐ 13 Independent Software Vendor
- ☐ 14 Life Sciences (biotech, pharmaceuticals)
- ☐ 15 Natural Resources
- ☐ 16 Oil and Gas
- ☐ 17 Professional Services
- ☐ 18 Public Sector (government)
- ☐ 19 Research
- ☐ 20 Retail/Wholesale/Distribution
- ☐ 21 Systems Integrator, VAR/VAD
- ☐ 22 Telecommunications
- ☐ 23 Travel and Transportation
- ☐ 24 Utilities (electric, gas, sanitation, water)
- ☐ 98 Other Business and Services _____

② WHICH OF THE FOLLOWING BEST DESCRIBES YOUR PRIMARY JOB FUNCTION? (check one only)

CORPORATE MANAGEMENT/STAFF
- ☐ 01 Executive Management (President, Chair, CEO, CFO, Owner, Partner, Principal)
- ☐ 02 Finance/Administrative Management (VP/Director/ Manager/Controller, Purchasing, Administration)
- ☐ 03 Sales/Marketing Management (VP/Director/Manager)
- ☐ 04 Computer Systems/Operations Management (CIO/VP/Director/Manager MIS/IS/IT, Ops)

IS/IT STAFF
- ☐ 05 Application Development/Programming Management
- ☐ 06 Application Development/Programming Staff
- ☐ 07 Consulting
- ☐ 08 DBA/Systems Administrator
- ☐ 09 Education/Training
- ☐ 10 Technical Support Director/Manager
- ☐ 11 Other Technical Management/Staff
- ☐ 98 Other

③ WHAT IS YOUR CURRENT PRIMARY OPERATING PLATFORM (check all that apply)

- ☐ 01 Digital Equipment Corp UNIX/VAX/VMS
- ☐ 02 HP UNIX
- ☐ 03 IBM AIX
- ☐ 04 IBM UNIX
- ☐ 05 Linux (Red Hat)
- ☐ 06 Linux (SUSE)
- ☐ 07 Linux (Oracle Enterprise)
- ☐ 08 Linux (other)
- ☐ 09 Macintosh
- ☐ 10 MVS
- ☐ 11 Netware
- ☐ 12 Network Computing
- ☐ 13 SCO UNIX
- ☐ 14 Sun Solaris/SunOS
- ☐ 15 Windows
- ☐ 16 Other UNIX
- ☐ 98 Other
- ☐ 99 None of the Above

④ DO YOU EVALUATE, SPECIFY, RECOMMEND, OR AUTHORIZE THE PURCHASE OF ANY OF THE FOLLOWING? (check all that apply)

- ☐ 01 Hardware
- ☐ 02 Business Applications (ERP, CRM, etc.)
- ☐ 03 Application Development Tools
- ☐ 04 Database Products
- ☐ 05 Internet or Intranet Products
- ☐ 06 Other Software
- ☐ 07 Middleware Products
- ☐ 99 None of the Above

⑤ IN YOUR JOB, DO YOU USE OR PLAN TO PURCHASE ANY OF THE FOLLOWING PRODUCTS? (check all that apply)

SOFTWARE
- ☐ 01 CAD/CAE/CAM
- ☐ 02 Collaboration Software
- ☐ 03 Communications
- ☐ 04 Database Management
- ☐ 05 File Management
- ☐ 06 Finance
- ☐ 07 Java
- ☐ 08 Multimedia Authoring
- ☐ 09 Networking
- ☐ 10 Programming
- ☐ 11 Project Management
- ☐ 12 Scientific and Engineering
- ☐ 13 Systems Management
- ☐ 14 Workflow

HARDWARE
- ☐ 15 Macintosh
- ☐ 16 Mainframe
- ☐ 17 Massively Parallel Processing

- ☐ 18 Minicomputer
- ☐ 19 Intel x86(32)
- ☐ 20 Intel x86(64)
- ☐ 21 Network Computer
- ☐ 22 Symmetric Multiprocessing
- ☐ 23 Workstation Services

SERVICES
- ☐ 24 Consulting
- ☐ 25 Education/Training
- ☐ 26 Maintenance
- ☐ 27 Online Database
- ☐ 28 Support
- ☐ 29 Technology-Based Training
- ☐ 30 Other
- ☐ 99 None of the Above

⑥ WHAT IS YOUR COMPANY'S SIZE? (check one only)

- ☐ 01 More than 25,000 Employees
- ☐ 02 10,001 to 25,000 Employees
- ☐ 03 5,001 to 10,000 Employees
- ☐ 04 1,001 to 5,000 Employees
- ☐ 05 101 to 1,000 Employees
- ☐ 06 Fewer than 100 Employees

⑦ DURING THE NEXT 12 MONTHS, HOW MUCH DO YOU ANTICIPATE YOUR ORGANIZATION WILL SPEND ON COMPUTER HARDWARE, SOFTWARE, PERIPHERALS, AND SERVICES FOR YOUR LOCATION? (check one only)

- ☐ 01 Less than $10,000
- ☐ 02 $10,000 to $49,999
- ☐ 03 $50,000 to $99,999
- ☐ 04 $100,000 to $499,999
- ☐ 05 $500,000 to $999,999
- ☐ 06 $1,000,000 and Over

⑧ WHAT IS YOUR COMPANY'S YEARLY SALES REVENUE? (check one only)

- ☐ 01 $500, 000, 000 and above
- ☐ 02 $100, 000, 000 to $500, 000, 000
- ☐ 03 $50, 000, 000 to $100, 000, 000
- ☐ 04 $5, 000, 000 to $50, 000, 000
- ☐ 05 $1, 000, 000 to $5, 000, 000

⑨ WHAT LANGUAGES AND FRAMEWORKS DO YOU USE? (check all that apply)

- ☐ 01 Ajax
- ☐ 02 C
- ☐ 03 C++
- ☐ 04 C#
- ☐ 13 Python
- ☐ 14 Ruby/Rails
- ☐ 15 Spring
- ☐ 16 Struts
- ☐ 05 Hibernate
- ☐ 06 J++/J#
- ☐ 07 Java
- ☐ 08 JSP
- ☐ 09 .NET
- ☐ 10 Perl
- ☐ 11 PHP
- ☐ 12 PL/SQL
- ☐ 17 SQL
- ☐ 18 Visual Basic
- ☐ 98 Other

⑩ WHAT ORACLE PRODUCTS ARE IN USE AT YOUR SITE? (check all that apply)

ORACLE DATABASE
- ☐ 01 Oracle Database 11*g*
- ☐ 02 Oracle Database 10*g*
- ☐ 03 Oracle9*i* Database
- ☐ 04 Oracle Embedded Database (Oracle Lite, Times Ten, Berkeley DB)
- ☐ 05 Other Oracle Database Release

ORACLE FUSION MIDDLEWARE
- ☐ 06 Oracle Application Server
- ☐ 07 Oracle Portal
- ☐ 08 Oracle Enterprise Manager
- ☐ 09 Oracle BPEL Process Manager
- ☐ 10 Oracle Identity Management
- ☐ 11 Oracle SOA Suite
- ☐ 12 Oracle Data Hubs

ORACLE DEVELOPMENT TOOLS
- ☐ 13 Oracle JDeveloper
- ☐ 14 Oracle Forms
- ☐ 15 Oracle Reports
- ☐ 16 Oracle Designer
- ☐ 17 Oracle Discoverer
- ☐ 18 Oracle BI Beans
- ☐ 19 Oracle Warehouse Builder
- ☐ 20 Oracle WebCenter
- ☐ 21 Oracle Application Express

ORACLE APPLICATIONS
- ☐ 22 Oracle E-Business Suite
- ☐ 23 PeopleSoft Enterprise
- ☐ 24 JD Edwards EnterpriseOne
- ☐ 25 JD Edwards World
- ☐ 26 Oracle Fusion
- ☐ 27 Hyperion
- ☐ 28 Siebel CRM

ORACLE SERVICES
- ☐ 28 Oracle E-Business Suite On Demand
- ☐ 29 Oracle Technology On Demand
- ☐ 30 Siebel CRM On Demand
- ☐ 31 Oracle Consulting
- ☐ 32 Oracle Education
- ☐ 33 Oracle Support
- ☐ 98 Other
- ☐ 99 None of the Above